THE COMMON MIND

André Gushurst-Moore

THE COMMON MIND

Politics, Society & Christian Humanism

From Thomas More to Russell Kirk

Why should a man desire in any way
To vary from the kindly race of men,
Or pass beyond the goal of ordinance
Where all should pause, as is most meet for all?
Alfred Lord Tennyson, "Tithonus"

Quod ubique,
quod semper, quod ab omnibus creditum est
St. Vincent of Lérins

 Angelico Press

First published in the USA
by Angelico Press
© André Gushurst-Moore 2013

For information, address:
Angelico Press, 4619 Slayden Rd. NE
Tacoma, WA 98422
www.angelicopress.com

ISBN 978-1-62138-011-5 (pbk: alk. paper)
ISBN 978-1-62138-013-9 (cloth: alk. paper)

Front cover image: Benozzo Gozzoli, detail of
Procession of the Magi, Palazzo Medici-Riccardi, Florence.

Cover design: Michael Schrauzer

CONTENTS

Foreword

THIS BOOK explores aspects of Christian humanism that are essentially traditionalist and conservative in character. Both those adjectives are of course problematic, but I think they are here unavoidable, given the intention of the book: to consider ways in which the writers elected, in their various ways and in their differing political viewpoints, to conserve the tradition of medieval Christendom, carrying it into the modern period and thus providing an intellectual basis in religion, philosophy, history and literature, for modern Christian conservatism. My hope is that my readers also of differing political views will pursue this book with an open mind, willing to consider broadly what the principles of a Christian politics might be. This book seeks to challenge certain notions on this subject, and to suggest perspectives that can be useful in the political and social challenges of the twenty-first century. Another aim is to challenge the post-Romantic and Byronic image, well established in the Academy, of the writer as rebel, intent on the subversion of all authority. The figures here are pillars of orthodoxy who articulate and enrich a vital tradition, against the disintegrating spirit of their age.

The Common Mind is addressed to common readers, of which group the present writer is one. Each chapter may be read as a separate essay, although I hope that a larger narrative builds and amplifies the central themes as the book proceeds to its end. In the selection of quotations I give ample and memorable examples, in the hope not only of illustrating themes, but of attracting the reader to read further in the originals.

It might be said, briefly, that the book is about writers and readers, books and society, faith and hope—the ongoing struggle for the things that make life worth living.

Stratton-on-the-Fosse
August, 2011

Acknowledgments

PARTS of the following chapters appeared in an earlier form in the following articles:

Chapter 1: "The Common Mind," *Salisbury Review*, Spring 1999; reprinted in *The Chesterton Review*, 2/2001

Chapter 2: "A Man for All Eras: Recent Books on Thomas More," *Political Science Reviewer*, 2003

Chapter 3: "Jonathan Swift versus the Enlightenment," *Salisbury Review*, Autumn 2001

Chapter 4: "'Of Man's First Disobedience': Samuel Johnson and the Whigs," *Salisbury Review*, Winter 2002

Chapter 5: "The Decent Drapery of Life: The Unity of Art and Nature in Edmund Burke," *American Arts Quarterly*, Summer 2002

Chapter 11: "An Integrated Vision," *University Bookman*, Fall 1999

I am especially grateful to the Wilbur and Earhart Foundations for grants that allowed me to pursue some of the research and writing of this book.

I am very grateful, too, for the hospitality, encouragement and support of Annette Kirk and the Russell Kirk Center, where some parts of the book were presented as seminar papers.

In addition, Ian Crowe, Bruce Frohnen, Jeff Nelson, Ben Lockerd, Jim Cooper, Sandra Sanderson, Dale Ahlquist, and Stratford Caldecott also offered enormous encouragement at different times over the protracted period after which this book finally saw the light of day.

I am grateful that, teaching at such a place as Downside, I have been able to pursue the ideas here in the classroom and in conversation with many pupils, colleagues and members of the monastic community of St. Gregory the Great, in particular, Dom Leo Maidlow Davis, O.S.B., Head Master of the School.

Acknowledgments

I am enormously grateful to my editor at Angelico Press, John Riess, and all his team for their superb work.

My wife, Bruna, and children, Alexandra (who helped to type the manuscript), Christian and Josephine, have been inspirational and tolerant beyond measure.

I dedicate this book to my parents, Edwin and Floria, my first and best teachers.

1

Introductory

The Common Mind and Christian Humanism

The Sense of Loss

IF ONE WERE TO JUDGE by the English tradition, a characteristic emotion in modernity is the sense of loss, often expressed in the nostalgia that is consequent upon it, and frequently seen in images that have a medieval form. Shakespeare's line, "Bare ruined choirs, where late the sweet birds sang,"[1] alluding perhaps to the dissolution of the monasteries, is an early modern example of this nostalgia. In Shakespeare's words, the poet's sense of oncoming age and decay is expressed in an image that recalls immense social upheaval and the ruin of a familiar, older and more gentle social order. This understanding of the Middle Ages appears again in English literature in the Romantic period, where it stands as a contrast to the post-Enlightenment rationalism which was giving birth to industrialism, and informs, for example, "The Deserted Village" of Oliver Goldsmith. William Cobbett, another witness to and critic of incipient industrialism was to identify, in his *History of the Reformation in England*, most social ills as coming from the Reformation. In the Victorian period, with the Gothic and Catholic Revivals, Romantic medievalism bore fruit in a wide-scale project of the recovery of medieval forms, even as their opposites in the form of utilitarian materialism, were also gaining in strength. With

---

1. Shakespeare, Sonnet 73, *The Sonnets*, ed. John Dover Wilson (Cambridge: CUP, 1966), p. 39.

the twentieth century, we have a descent into total warfare, "the modern age in arms" as Evelyn Waugh put it, and the sense of loss also involved the turning of many writers to medieval religious forms. The sense of loss that is so characteristic of modernity seems, in England at least, inextricably bound up with the loss of the medieval world, whether it take the form, at one extreme, of the Catholic conversion of early twentieth century *literati*, or at the other, of jigsaw puzzles of dubious aesthetic quality, depicting idyllic English village scenes, where little has changed since the cottages were built. But to what extent, if any, is this connection to the pre-modern, pre-industrial world of the Middle Ages more than just nostalgia— the regret, say, for a youth that is past, the imaginary "land of lost content"?[2]

An examination of Philip Larkin's 1972 poem "Going, Going" might be useful at this point. Shakespeare's early modern "bare ruined choirs" reappear here in late modernity in a poem in which nostalgia undoubtedly informs the social vision, which is one of disintegration:

> I thought it would last my time—
> The sense that, beyond the town,
> There would always be fields and farms,
> Where the village louts could climb
> Such trees as were not cut down;
> I knew there'd be false alarms
>
> In the papers about old streets
> And split level shopping, but some
> Have always been left so far;
> And when the old part retreats
> As the bleak high-risers come
> We can always escape in the car.
>
> Things are tougher than we are, just
> As earth will always respond
> However we mess it about;

2. A.E. Housman, "Into my heart an air that kills," *A Shropshire Lad* (London: The Folio Society, 1986), p. 64.

Introductory

Chuck filth in the sea, if you must:
The tides will be clean beyond.
—But what do I feel now? Doubt?

Or age, simply? The crowd
Is young in the M1 cafe;
Their kids are screaming for more—
More houses, more parking allowed,
More caravan sites, more pay.
On the Business Page, a score

Of spectacled grins approve
Some takeover bid that entails
Five per cent profit (and ten
Per cent more in the estuaries): move
Your works to the unspoilt dales
(Grey area grants)! And when

You try to get near the sea
In summer . . .
    It seems, just now,
To be happening so very fast;
Despite all the land left free
For the first time I feel somehow
That it isn't going to last,

That before I snuff it, the whole
Boiling will be bricked in
Except for the tourist parts—
First slum of Europe: a role
It won't be hard to win,
With a cast of crooks and tarts.

And that will be England gone,
The shadows, the meadows, the lanes,
The guildhalls, the carved choirs.
There'll be books; it will linger on
In galleries; but all that remains
For us will be concrete and tyres.

Most things are never meant.
This won't be, most likely; but greeds
And garbage are too thick-strewn

To be swept up now, or invent
Excuses that make them all needs.
I just think it will happen, soon.[3]

The medieval image of the "carved choirs," expressive of an eva-
nescent, graceful, ethereal beauty and a common (both familiar and
shared) sight in England, expresses so much of what is being lost to
the contemporary ills that Larkin catalogues with cumulative force:
the despoliation of the common; commercial greed; gracelessness in
building, manners, and public life generally; and environmental
pollution, whether of our green spaces, or in the noise of the incon-
tinent young. Is "nature" ("things") tough enough to endure in
man's despite? Can his own nature endure his pollution of himself?
Ultimately, Larkin is doubtful. His poem is not just about the 1970s
but rather about the social reality of contemporary Western life, as
contrasted with a better time, seen dimly and pre-rationally in "The
shadows, the meadows, the lanes,/The guildhalls, the carved
choirs." The feeling of a departure, at some point, from a better
England, is visible all around, and, inevitably, questions occur: How
did we come to live like this? Why does it feel wrong? "Where is the
outrage?" "Why aren't they screaming?" (as Larkin says elsewhere).[4]
Where are the roots of a society of gentleness, order, politeness and
restraint, and how have we lost them? And if it is not just I who
desire these things, and if there is a general human need for them,
why are our desires not met, or our voices heard? Who authorizes
what most of us do not want? And even if we admit that nostalgia
was not invented in modernity, discontent with the present appears,
the more we examine it, to be more than just perennial nostalgia.
The discarded image, as C.S. Lewis put it, of the medieval world,
continues to haunt us in modernity, even as "medieval" persists,
with infinite irony, as a synonym for "barbaric." *Pace* Larkin, and as
we shall see, the medieval proves astonishingly enduring, not just in
the religious buildings of a thousand years, or in institutions of law

---

3. Philip Larkin, "Going, Going," in *Collected Poems*, ed. A. Thwaite (London:
Faber, 2003), p. 133.
4. "The Old Fools," ibid., p. 131.

and government, or in places of learning, but in its peculiar vision. Not only the "carved choirs" remain. This book seeks to show that the vision that made them is recoverable, having been reiterated continually into modernity.

Disintegration

Larkin's late twentieth century vision is a muted reiteration of what has possessed our culture most fully since the end of the Great War. In "MCMXIV," written in 1960, Larkin says retrospectively, imagining the men joining up, "Never such innocence again."[5] In 1919, William Butler Yeats wrote prophetically, in "The Second Coming," and in lines that have echoed down the twentieth century:

> Turning and turning in the widening gyre
> The falcon cannot hear the falconer;
> Things fall apart; the centre cannot hold;
> Mere anarchy is loosed upon the world,
> The blood-dimmed tide is loosed, and everywhere
> The ceremony of innocence is drowned;
> The best lack all conviction, while the worst
> Are full of passionate intensity.

So many, and not only the religiously or conservatively inclined, have been conscious that in late modernity, and then post-modernity, this poem sums up their fears for the future, when

> Surely some revelation is at hand;
> Surely the Second Coming is at hand.
> The Second Coming! Hardly are those words out
> When a vast image out of Spiritus Mundi
> Troubles my sight: somewhere in sands of the desert
> A shape with lion body and the head of a man,
> A gaze blank and pitiless as the sun,
> Is moving its slow thighs, while all about it
> Reel shadows of the indignant desert birds.
> The darkness drops again; but now I know
> That twenty centuries of stony sleep

5. "MCMXIV," ibid., p. 99.

Were vexed to nightmare by a rocking cradle,
And what rough beast, its hour come round at last,
Slouches towards Bethlehem to be born?[6]

Certainly, from a religious and conservative viewpoint, in the twentieth century, and into the twenty-first, we feel an increasing sense of disintegration and separation—from the past, within individuals and within communities, which increasingly seem to hold little in common except the will to be as different as they please from any sense of the normal. (This, paradoxically, leads to a dull uniformity of the lowest common denominator.) There is separation from religious practice as church attendance falls; there is separation from the family, as more people live alone; there is the sense that schools no longer pass on inherited learning and approved standards, but rather exist for the purposes of social engineering. We see the decline of civility and manners, and the screen celebration of the violent, the cruel and the *outré*. In art and literature there are the constant themes of trespass, crime, transgression, and the denial of beauty and decorum. Yeats's image of the "rough beast," the embodiment of some new revelation, haunts us too, along with the ghost of Christendom, and the century that followed Yeats's poem provided again and again evidence of the bestial in human life, as war succeeded war, ideology upon ideology.

"The time is out of joint," the religious mind concludes, with Hamlet. In the early years of the twenty-first century, it is not we who are mad, we are convinced, but some collective disintegration is going on around us, celebrated by many for its freedom, vitality and novelty, such that we become convinced, in our sanguine moments, of a collective insanity in which we do not share. We are aware of fragmentation, atomization, and the paradox of the "privatization" of truth, and the disappearance of privacy. We see the disappearance of respect for public authority and the increase of public power wielded by the state. We are aware of alienation from our neighbors and our neighborhoods, and the expansion of virtual communities of single-interest similarity, and electronic friendship

6. W.B. Yeats, "The Second Coming," *Collected Poems* (London: Macmillan, 1982), p. 210.

groups. We see a fragmentation in culture, and a fragmentation in languages, a babble of tongues where an argot or cant replaces a common language of thought, feeling and understanding. Most people, we might argue, who desire the normal see it as indispensable to their flourishing, and the flourishing of their families. The normal person, who seeks a stable relationship, particularly in marriage, and children, sees the essential part that institutions play in this development. Schools, churches, neighborhoods, are seen as part of the order of society that gives support for the ideas of home. Yet we are aware of things within ourselves that threaten this flourishing, and we see powerful forces at work in society, which threaten to pull them apart. Strangely, these forces are part of the very political establishment itself. But through which avenues did we arrive in New Sodom? The attempt to trace back to the point at which things went wrong can be to embark on a long trail: to the Sixties, the Second World War, the First World War, Darwin, the French Revolution, Rousseau, Francis Bacon, the Reformation. Perhaps we can agree that the loss of Eden was a definitive moment, although even the Fall of the Angels preceded the Fall of Man.

The Common Mind

A broad and reasonably dispassionate historical analysis, therefore, would suggest that the forces of disintegration have always been with us, as have the forces of integration. G.K. Chesterton articulated a sense of the integrating tendency in human tradition, calling it "the common mind," in a passage that occurs in his 1906 biography of Charles Dickens:

> [Dickens'] power, then, lay in the fact that he expressed with an energy and brilliancy quite uncommon the things close to the common mind. But with this mere phrase, the common mind, we collide with a current error. Commonness and the common mind are now generally spoken of as meaning in some manner inferiority and the inferior mind, the mind of the mere mob. But the common mind means the mind of all the artists and heroes; or else it would not be common. Plato had the common mind; Dante had the common mind; or that mind was not common. Commonness means the quality common to the saint and the sinner, to

7

the philosopher and the fool; and it was this that Dickens grasped and developed. In everybody there is a thing that loves babies, that fears death, that likes sunlight: that thing enjoys Dickens. And everybody does not mean uneducated crowds; everybody means everybody.[7]

What Chesterton is referring to here is a principle of integration, and integrity, in the nature of the human person, and in the nature of human society. It is cognate with natural law in the Aristotelian and Thomist sense, and an idea that human nature is perennial and has an objective reality. Dickens, insofar as he was, in Chesterton's words, not so much a novelist as a mythologist, tapped into this subterranean mine of archetypes.

This reality of human nature is one that transcends periods, classes, circumstances, and individuals—while simultaneously always and only existing in them. This is evidenced by the continuity and similarities in great literature (or humane letters), just as in its enormous variety. The great writer, to borrow Alexander Pope's words, articulates, "What oft was thought, but ne'er so well expressed."[8] He does not so much speak to us as speak for us, of the common and enduring realities of human life. We recognize life in, for example, the stories of Dickens, rather than learn of it, because we too possess something of the mind of the author. Great art (as in Dante) or true philosophy (as in Plato) show us what we already subconsciously feel and desire to know consciously, to have "imaged forth," or brought into the light of common day. This is true of all great art and philosophy (including political philosophy) that understand the existence of an objective natural order, and an eternal spirit at the heart of it. The notion that human nature does not essentially change (however much manners, customs, and even laws, may vary in time and place) is an essential premise of this view of the world, and is proved by the continuing relevance of the great philosophers and artists, perhaps quintessentially by Shakespeare.

This, then, is the first way in which we might speak of a "common

---

7. G. K. Chesterton, *Charles Dickens* (London: House of Stratus, 2001), pp. 46–47.
8. Alexander Pope, "An Essay on Criticism," *Pope: Poetical Works*, ed. H. Davis (Oxford: OUP, 1978), p. 72.

mind": the mind that at various levels of thought, feeling and understanding, embracing the ordinary person, and the man of genius in whom the human may be seen to an unusually rich or developed degree, recognizes a common human nature subsisting in all the vagaries of time and place. This sense of the common mind brings us to what we call "common sense." This is an idea that many thinkers and writers return to, but it does not find broad acceptance in post-modernity, where ideas of disintegration (the original, the novel, the transgressive) sit ill with it. One might argue that common sense has been in decline since the Middle Ages, and Chesterton expresses its vulnerability to the vicissitudes of historical change when he describes it as "a fairy thread, thin and faint, and as easily lost as gossamer."[9] But it is difficult to see how any of the great medieval cultural achievements, and those upon which have been built and still depend, such as "commonwealth" and "common law," can endure without some belief in common sense. The medieval *sensus communis* is integral to the authority of both orthodoxy, and of parliaments. Even radicalism can often appeal to norms which errant authority had abandoned. Chesterton saw the French Revolution in these terms, and also William Cobbett, who "did not feel exactly that he was 'in revolt,' he felt if anything that a number of idiotic institutions had revolted against reason and against him."[10] Common sense is sanity, and in a healthy society, stable yet possessing the means of change in the light of experience and circumstances, it is the common mind that rules. By contrast, when a society departs from sane norms, a heavy reckoning will have to be made before it is returned to them.

For Chesterton, the common mind achieved its highest philosophical expression in the work of St. Thomas Aquinas, the great philosopher of common sense:

> Since the modern world began in the nineteenth century, nobody's system of philosophy has really corresponded to everybody's sense of reality; to what, if left to themselves, common men would call common sense. Each started with a paradox; a peculiar

9. Chesterton, op. cit., p. 56.
10. Ibid., p. 101.

point of view demanding the sacrifice of what they would call a sane point of view. That is the one thing common to Hobbes and Hegel, to Kant and Bergson, to Berkeley and William James. A man had to believe something that no normal man would believe, if it were suddenly propounded to his simplicity; as that law is above right, or right is outside reason, or things are only as we think them, or everything is relative to a reality that is not there. The modern philosopher claims, like a sort of confidence man, that once we will grant him this, the rest will be easy; he will straighten out the world if once he is allowed to give one twist to the mind.[11]

Just as a heresy, as a part of the truth that becomes detached from all the other truths, grows so large in the eyes of its adherents that it blocks out the sun of balanced and integrated Truth, so in a time (such as ours) when orthodoxy is the only heresy, disintegration of belief is the cause and consequence of a fragmented society. The common mind, however, is accessible to everyone, and belongs to all, being in no sense a private quality, even though it is expressed in substantial terms only by a few men of genius. Thomism is the fullest and most profound expression of the common mind. It is, as Chesterton reminds us, the philosophy of sanity, being as it is integrative, universal, sensible and reiterative of the common understanding of experience rooted in the sense and refined by reason. To quote from Chesterton's biography again, in a passage of consummate brilliance:

> Against all this [modern thought] the philosophy of St. Thomas stands founded on the universal common conviction that eggs are eggs. The Hegelian may say that an egg is really a hen, because it is part of an endless process of Becoming; the Berkelian may hold that poached eggs only exist as a dream exists, since it is quite as easy to call the dream the cause of the eggs as the eggs the cause of the dream; the Pragmatist may believe that we get the best out of scrambled eggs by forgetting that they ever were eggs, and only remembering the scramble. But no pupil of St. Thomas needs to addle his brains in order to adequately addle his eggs; to put his

11. G.K. Chesterton, *St. Thomas Aquinas* (Teddington, Middx: Echo Library, 2007), p. 70.

head at any particular angle in looking at eggs, or squinting at eggs, or winking the other eye to see a new simplification of eggs. The Thomist stands in the broad daylight of the brotherhood of men, in their common consciousness that eggs are not hens or dreams or mere practical assumptions; but things attested by the Authority of the Senses, which is from God.[12]

For Chesterton, as for Aquinas, an objective reality does not merely exist as a remote dogma, but may be apprehended by all sane human beings, via the senses and reason, which provide the basis of common sense. Sanity thus appears as a vast wholeness, connecting man and God, matter and mind, heart and soul. The difference between St. Thomas and Hegel is, for Chesterton, simple: "St. Thomas was sane and Hegel was mad," and "the Thomist philosophy is nearer than most philosophies to the mind of the man in the street."[13] It seems that this view was not peculiar to Chesterton, writing some seven hundred years in retrospect; a figure contemporary with Aquinas, Bartholomew of Capua, concurred with Chesterton's views. Simon Tugwell, in an introductory survey of the life of Aquinas, quotes Bartholomew, adding that it is "the comment that would have probably pleased Thomas most of all." Bartholomew says of Aquinas that "people of all sorts can easily benefit from his writings according to whatever little intellectual capacity they have, and that is why even the laity and people who are not very bright look for his writings and desire to have them."[14] Thomism epitomizes the whole of the mediaeval culture from which we directly inherit the common mind.

Christian Humanism

The chapters that follow are essentially concerned to trace, through studies of aspects of the works of twelve literary figures, the continuity of the integrating, common mind into modernity. It is argued here that this cohesive tradition helps to keep the West from anar-

12. Ibid., p. 71.
13. Ibid.
14. Simon Tugwell, O.P., ed., *Albert and Thomas: Selected Writings* (New York, NY: Paulist Press, 1988), p. 236.

chy. Insofar as the common mind determines by its presence or absence the kind of society that obtains at any given point in time, all these studies have a political view, recognizing that the *polis* rests on shared cultural norms, whether secure or not. In modernity, from the Reformation onwards, we see a continuing drama of disintegration, in which the forces of integration continue a work of conservation, defense, restoration and recovery. The common mind, which in its largest sense is the mind of Europe, the settled mind of the West, constitutes a continuing tradition from the Reformation to the present day, always at work in redeeming the time, usually in opposition to the spirit of the age. And as the continuity of the common mind involves the continuity of a medieval understanding of man, built on a classical past, we can call it, usefully, Christian humanism: it is the work of Christian humanists to preserve, and pass on, the common mind. We see this process, first, in Thomas More's defense of the medieval consensus, against the forces of disintegration in his time. It is there in Swift's attack on Enlightenment notions of a separation between mind and matter, and the disintegrating claims of "pure" reason. We see it in Samuel Johnson's hostility to Whiggery, something that Yeats defines for us:

> Whether they knew or not,
> Goldsmith and Burke, Swift and the Bishop of Cloyne
> All hated Whiggery; but what is Whiggery?
> A levelling, rancorous, rational sort of mind
> That never looked out of the eye of a saint
> Or out of drunkard's eye.[15]

("All's whiggery now," replies the seventh sage.) In Burke's titanic literary barricade against the French Revolution, the most disintegrating event since the Reformation, we see a defense of the common mind, and its incarnation as the most important strand of Anglo-American conservatism. In the poetry and political philosophy of Samuel Taylor Coleridge, we see a Romantic articulation of the unity of life, and the interrelated and mutually necessary insti-

---

15. W.B. Yeats, "The Seven Sages," *Collected Poems* (London: Macmillan, 1982), p. 271.

tutions of Church and State. In the Victorian John Henry Newman, we see a rediscovery of medieval faith, and the spiritual revivifying of a nation struggling with the aridities of Benthamite utilitarianism. In Orestes Brownson, "America's Newman," we see a rediscovery of the theological principles of human society. Benjamin Disraeli's Romantic medievalism was an imaginative counterweight to Victorian materialism, and G. K. Chesterton's Catholic medievalism was a similar force in the context of what John Coates has called "the Edwardian cultural crisis."[16] In T. S. Eliot's work, we see a philosophical and modern healing of the Cartesian split between mind and matter, and in C. S. Lewis we see a restatement of the traditional nature of man, against the view of scientific materialism. In Russell Kirk we see an imaginative defense of human norms in an age of boredom. It is a representative, but by no means exhaustive, company of twelve Christian humanists.

Certain themes will be seen to appear and reappear in these studies; all proceed from the traditional, Judaeo-Christian common sense of what it means to be human, and concern its preservation in the individual person and in society. These are all important themes in the Christian humanist tradition in modernity. The integrating force of Christian humanism might be considered as the Christian impulse to build up the kingdom of God on earth, in the various levels of society in which people actually live. This impulse also provides a means of rediscovery of the integrating principle in the republic of letters. It will also be seen that the writers here have the effect of commenting on each other, across the barriers of time. Not only do dead writers influence those who come after them, but the writings of those who follow them, in the tradition of thought we call Christian humanism, frequently show insights, out of their shared, common mind, that illuminate the writers of the past in ways that less sympathetic commentators do not.

16. See John Coates, *Chesterton and the Edwardian Cultural Crisis* (Hull: Hull University Press, 1984).

1. The Inheritance of the Humane

For the Christian humanists of the Renaissance, including Thomas More, the inheritance of the classical past, especially in the form of its humane letters (as opposed to divinity), was fundamental. In a sense, humanism is itself the study of what it means to be human, via the medium of humane letters. Cicero's *De Officiis* (*On Duty*) was a central text for the humanists of the northern Renaissance. It expresses the values of the Roman *humanitas*: understanding, benevolence, compassion, mercy, fortitude, judgment, prudence, eloquence and honor. The study of classical humane letters was also a study of language, and especially rhetoric. The essential Renaissance literary form is the dialogue. Activity in controversy, and a public virtue, were products of the concern for rhetoric, and we see in much of the work of the figures in this book a similar concern for the public good. The study of humane letters by Christians better enables them to pass on the Gospel. Just as this Christian humanism may be distinguished from classical humanism, which includes a good deal of the stoicism of, especially, Marcus Aurelius, so also it can be distinguished from the secular humanism that developed from the Renaissance onwards. In many respects, secular humanism may involve a return to aspects of classical humanism, with its idea of a different, pagan kind of virtue than that involved in Christian humanism. But secular humanism is also frequently an aspect of Enlightenment rationalism, in which the Christian virtue of charity becomes a humanitarianism devoid of Christian faith. Although in time secular humanism follows Christian humanism, which follows classical humanism, they also represent three different philosophical positions, and may be held as such.

2. Law

Another theme that recurs in these writers is a sense of the law of human nature, the *ius rationale* seen in medieval developments of the classical idea. In modernity we see an ongoing tension between, on the one hand, "top-down" ideas of law, as in Justinian's Roman law, and the Napoleonic code: "What pleases the prince has the force of law." Against this is the sense of a law that overarches the prince, too, and exists especially in medieval understandings of

14

English law, as in Bracton's "The King must not be under man but under God and under the law, because the law makes the king."[17] For Christian humanists in the English and American political tradition, the English common law tradition expresses the idea of a sovereignty of the natural law working through the conscience of every person. The political consequences for such an understanding of law are rule by consent, limited government, constitutional balance, a separation of powers, rights and duties, not to mention the Anglo-American tradition of liberty, which may be the greatest gift that England has made to the world, growing directly out of a medieval, Christian polity that implies freedom under a human law that is itself subject to the law of God. As the secular power has grown further away from the Christian tradition, and so acknowledges no laws of God (since His existence has become doubtful where not obviously harmful), the balance in law has shifted, apparently in favor of liberty. But the Christian humanist critique of society in modernity questions whether freedom to do things once illegal has made us less free from the power of the State that grants these new liberties. The old freedom was a freedom for self-government, as a people and as a person; to what extent does an increasingly secular world threaten this?

3. Common Sense, Reason and Language

Renaissance humanism, as we have noted, was very closely concerned with language, and this is also a continuing theme in the writers with whom we are concerned. It is recognized that the common good depends, to a large extent, on the state of the language. In the Christian tradition, the Word (the *Logos*) is capitalized, and seen as Christ himself. In contrast, the devil is the father of lies, the antithesis of reason and meaning. The Christian humanist asks, to what extent is public discourse, in life and letters, informed by the Christian understanding of the proper identification of language, truth and reality? Does public language, especially political language, exist to reveal or conceal? Christian humanism recognizes that language may be corrupt and corrupting, and may be, at differ-

---

17. L. L. Blake, *The Royal Law* (London: Shepheard-Walwyn, 2000), p. 41.

ent times, and among different persons, a more or less fruitful means of revealing the common mind. Public language may be reduced to a kind of cant, as in Dr. Johnson's definition of the word:

A corrupt dialect used by beggars and vagabonds.
A particular form of speaking peculiar to some certain class or body of men.
A whining pretension to goodness, in formal and affected terms.
Barbarous jargon.
Auction.[18]

To what extent is the language of public life cant, rather than a higher and more humane language? Language must be protected, re-stored and nourished if it is not to decline, and our common life decline with it. The humanism of George Orwell's "Politics and the English Language" will be echoed by the Christian humanist; except that Orwell eschewed the religious dimension to reality, and of language, there is nothing significant with which a Christian could disagree, on religious grounds, with what he says in that crucial essay. Good prose, said Orwell, should be like a windowpane, and surely this applies to political discourse, too. Yet too often the contemporary politician takes refuge in the uncertainties in postmodern conceptions of language, which do not see that the *logos* should correspond to an objective reality.

4. Literature

Increasingly, in the modern period, a value is seen not only in the study of pre-Christian humane writers, but also in the writing of a new literature, especially in the vernacular, and in which the imagination plays a central role. The reading and writing of imaginative literature is a private act with public consequences, sometimes a public purpose. From More's *Utopia*, through Swift's *Gulliver's Travels*; through the moral prose and poetry of Samuel Johnson; the writing of Burke, especially the *Reflections*; the poetry and creative criticism of Coleridge; the spiritual prose of Newman that is also a classic of our literature; the novels of Disraeli; the stories of Chesterton, Lewis, and Kirk; and the poetry of Eliot: all this constitutes a

---

18. E.L. McAdam and G. Milne, eds., *Johnson's Dictionary: A Modern Selection,* (London: Macmillan, 1982), p. 113.

Christian humanist strand in English literature that has a religious, philosophical, political and social dimension—in other words, a public function. Until very recently indeed, one could say that the vast majority of literary works in English were explicitly or implicitly Christian, but in the main, the works that concern us in the following chapters have a particularly moral, religious or political character. They reveal aspects of their authors, their societies and the Christian humanist tradition, depending on our viewpoint. Imaginative literature may be seen thus, not as an escape from the public sphere, but as an essential means of engagement with it, and it is difficult to imagine a political class that can represent the common mind if it has no appreciation of the republic of letters. The Christian humanist bears witness that so much of what it is to be human is intrinsic to language and to literature, and the state of both has enormous capacity for good or ill in the public sphere. Christian humanism is in a radical tension with the spirit of post-modernist literary theory, which in deconstructing texts finds an abyss at the heart of them. In the sense in which post-modernism does the work of the devil, it is at the farthest remove from the creative function of literature.

5. Education

Another recurring theme in the following chapters is that of education, particularly in terms of what is taught and studied, and to what ends. In Christian humanism, the use of literature, widely interpreted, is part of the broad (liberal) education of the well-rounded person, that is, the ideal of Newman's "gentleman." Such persons are capable of self-rule, and therefore of influencing the public towards responsible freedom and limited government by the state. We might describe Newman's "gentleman" as the integrated person, in whom the head, heart and spirit, the rational, affective and spiritual, are educated and developed. The medieval university, in which knowledge was conceived of as a whole, remains the model of a liberal education, in times when the utilitarian and instrumentalist view of knowledge seems to prevail, and the young are trained for work rather than for living. Even Francis Bacon, in many respects an early Renaissance example of the disintegrative tradition, can remind us

17

"*abeunt studia in mores*: studies pass into the character."[19] Without a moral basis to education, the common mind may be lost to atrophy and decay, in a communal forgetting, and a culture that is dead to its well-springs in the past.

6. Politics and Religion

In Christian humanism, then, politics is a moral and essentially theological problem. This is in contrast to the spirit of Machiavelli, who has been a powerful force in modernity, and who effected a split between humanistic method and humanistic morality. In Machiavelli, the ends of the state necessitate the means to be employed, and it is the right of the prince to determine these in an unfettered way. In the period since Machiavelli we can see the progress of tyranny on the one hand, and the progress, on the other, of countries possessing a balanced constitution, which have developed to protect freedom, and the conscience of individual subjects and citizens. We see particularly the success of those countries which have to some extent inherited the English common law tradition, and the political institutions that have grown from it. These countries have not only stability and freedom, but have been markedly more favorable to Christianity and to religion in general. In modernity, from the Reformation onwards, we have seen the universal tendency of tyranny, at least, to control religion tightly, but more often to crush it. In liberal secularism, religion may not fare much better. In considering the question, "what is the role of the Church in relation to the State?" Christian humanism suggests a degree of separation and a degree of integration. More generally, religion, the cult, is at the basis of our whole culture, including the political dimension. Without a healthy religious dimension, a nation's political life is likely to decline into the contest for, and exercise of, mere power, unrestrained by reason, natural law, or the educated mind, heart and spirit, by humanity in the fullest sense: in short, politics becomes separated from the common mind.

The twelve writers who follow provide us with insights into the common mind, and show us the Christian humanist in tension

19. Francis Bacon, *The Essays*, ed. J. Pitcher (London: Penguin, 1985), p. 210.

with the modern spirit. In many respects, with the passage of time, the authors become conscious of writing in a tradition of those who have gone before. They provide a commentary on each other in a way that works outside of time; Thomas More can illuminate Swift as much as vice versa. There is a breadth to the definition of the literary in most of these figures, and letters are an integrated part of the life of each; both the letters and lives of these figures had a political, or at least public dimension, in the higher sense of "public." They all exemplify an effort at integration in times of disintegration—which to some extent is any time, although some times are more disturbed than others. They show, moreover, an aspect of the common mind, potentially uniting all people, in that it subsists in those who possess genius, a superb excess of the human, rather than in something different in nature. They are potent witnesses to what is in all of us. In other words:

> . . . what there is to conquer
> By strength and submission, has already been discovered
> Once or twice, or several times, by men whom one cannot hope
> To emulate—but there is no competition—
> There is only the fight to recover what has been lost
> And found and lost again and again; and now, under conditions
> That seem unpropitious. But perhaps neither gain nor loss.
> For us, there is only the trying. The rest is not our business.[20]

20. T. S. Eliot, "East Coker," *The Complete Poems and Plays of T. S. Eliot* (London: Faber, 1969), p. 182.

2

Thomas More

And the Christian Context of Temporal Authority

MORE: Imagine...

> ...that you sit as kings in your desires,
> Authority quite silenc'd by your brawl,
> And you in ruff of your opinions clothed,
> What had you got? I'll tell you. You had taught
> How insolence and strong hand should prevail,
> How order should be quell'd—and by this pattern
> Not one of you should live an aged man;
> For other ruffians, as their fancies wrought,
> With selfsame hand, self reasons and self right
> Would shark on you, and men like ravenous fishes
> Would feed on one another.

SHAKESPEARE, et al., *Sir Thomas More*

"That's just what I have been saying," he said. "There is no place for philosophers among kings."

"Yes, there is," I answered, "but not for that academic philosophy which fits everything neatly into place. There is, however, another, more sophisticated philosophy which accommodates itself to the scene at hand and acts its part with polish and finesse. It is this philosophy that you should use."

SIR THOMAS MORE, *Utopia*, Book I, 1516

Thomas More ranks with William Langland before him, and Edmund Burke after him, among the greatest of our Reforming Conservatives.... [They] place almost first among the order of things which has come down to them, and which they feel it their duty to preserve, such a measure of unity, small or great, as the Christendom of their age has been able to inherit.

R. W. CHAMBERS, *Thomas More*, 1935

THE WORDS ASCRIBED to Shakespeare in the play *Sir Thomas More* might be taken as a metaphor for the great saint and statesman speaking to the modern world, from the turbulence of his own sixteenth century. Shakespeare, with the characteristic uncanny insight of this greatest poet of human nature, points us to a central feature of More's mind: the connection between the self, our desires, our private opinions, and civil disorder. The promise of modernity is that we should all, free individuals, sit "as kings in [our] desires" and in our views; and we could be forgiven for visualizing that image in the lineaments of the first modern English monarch, Henry VIII. The dramatic context of Shakespeare's lines is, of course, Evil May Day, 1517, when More, as under-sheriff of London, attempted to reason with rioting apprentices, who were intent on hurting foreigners. Despite some initial success, More failed to avert the riot, just as he failed, in life, to avert the onset of a modern politics. However, what we see in the works of Thomas More, and a message that endures, is the character of the common mind as an image of society, and of a Christian *polis*, that includes the elements of conscience, reason, law, tradition and the restraint of political power by its constitutional dispersal.

On January 14, 1999, Congressman Henry Hyde, on the floor of the United States' Senate, spoke thus:

> Sir Thomas More, the most brilliant lawyer of his generation, a scholar with an international reputation, the center of a warm and affectionate family life which he cherished, went to his death rather than take an oath in vain.[1]

---

1. John Guy, *Thomas More* (New York, NY: Oxford University Press, 2000), p. 1.

The speaker was Chairman of the House Judiciary Committee, and the occasion was the opening of the impeachment trial of President William Jefferson Clinton. For Robert Bolt, in the introduction to his play *A Man for All Seasons* (1960), More was "a man with an adamantine sense of his own self." In Volume 2 of his *History of the English-Speaking Peoples* (1956), Winston Churchill wrote that

> More stood forth as the defender of all that was finest in the medieval outlook. He represents to history its universality, its belief in spiritual values, and its instinctive sense of other-worldliness.[2]

G. K. Chesterton considered that

> He may be counted the greatest Englishman, or at least the greatest historical character in English history. For he was above all things historic; he represented at once a type, a turning point and an ultimate destiny.[3]

More was also a hero of the old Soviet Union. Seen as a proto-communist, his name appeared on an obelisk unveiled in Moscow's Alexandrovsky Gardens in 1918. And not only in the last century was More seen as highly significant. Jonathan Swift wrote in his *Concerning the Universal Hatred Which Prevails Against the Clergy* that More was "a person of the greatest virtue this Kingdom ever produced." A man for all seasons indeed, and for all kinds of people, appealing here to a conservative American Republican, an agnostic British liberal, a Whiggish Conservative British Prime Minister, an English Catholic apologist, atheistic Russian Communists, and a Tory Anglican priest with anti-Catholic views. Moreover, Thomas More has probably never been read, or read about, so widely as he is today, fascinating scholars and general public alike. He has become the patron of innumerable schools and colleges, and by act of Pope John Paul II became the patron of politicians and statesmen. The contours of his life are inscribed on the consciousness of diverse and widely separated peoples, such that his iconic and dramatic status,

2. Winston Churchill, *A History of the English-Speaking Peoples,* Vol. 2 (London: Cassell, 1974), p. 50.
3. In *Essential Articles for the Study of Thomas More*, Richard S. Sylvester and Germain P. Marc'hadour, eds. (Hamden, CT: Archon, 1977), p. 567.

invaluable to us though it is, can easily obscure what is just as important for us—his writings.

Whether historical, philosophical, scholarly or controversial, Thomas More's works show a concern for "the best state of the commonwealth," that which was to be conserved, extended, defended or improved in European society. Despite the passage of time since More's death, and the vicissitudes of Western civilization in that time, his concerns may still be recognized as ones for all seasons: the problem of innovation versus traditional order; the distribution of authority in a balanced constitution set against the pressure of centralizing and absolutist power; the demands of community and the rights of private property; the use of positive law for coercive purposes at variance with common law and natural law; the subversion of the established rights of popular assemblies and their misuse by the will to power; the limits of free speech and the responsibilities of conscience; the respectful use of our common language as opposed to the sophistical subversion of meaning. These were Thomas More's concerns, and they should be ours. More's mind was both medieval and modern, both scholastic and classical. We see the influence of Aquinas (of course) and Aristotle, Augustine and Plato, Cicero, Thucydides, Lucian and Sallust. But he was, we should remember, primarily a common lawyer, and from his legal training in the Inns of Court, he would have been familiar with the world described by Sir John Fortescue in *De laudibus legum anglie* (c. 1470), and was probably familiar with the work itself. At the Inns of Court, More would have received an abiding sense of the importance of natural law in English common law. He was, we can admit, strongly drawn to detachment from the world. However, he chose the road of engagement rather than withdrawal, the practice of law rather than the contemplation of the divine. The reason given that he chose "to marry rather than burn" is not so persuasive as is seeing his decision in the context of the reason for which he disagrees with Hythloday in Book I of *Utopia*: the Ciceronian ideal of an engaged, practical virtue.

Fortescue will have given More a high idea of the common law, as a source of English liberty, and a means for the diffusion of justice and equity through the commonwealth. Common law gave customary "determinations" of the natural law, the belief that all men are endowed with moral reason, and the ability to perceive what is just. It underpins the jury system, although Thomas More did not believe that juries could be trusted without judges. However, he did not trust simply to individuals either, no matter how elevated and honorable their position in the realm. Neither popes without councils, nor kings without parliaments, nor judges without courts, could be depended upon to determine rightly either spiritual or temporal law. More believed in the free play of rational discourse within properly constituted assemblies, as for instance in *Utopia*, but such discourse needed to have parameters set and terms informed by authority, that is, judges spiritual or temporal. Authority, as the context of order, and order as the context of happiness, depended on this careful balance of individual and community, neither of which can properly exist without the other. Another principle that More will have taken from Fortescue was that kings were bound by the law, and indeed did not make law themselves, but rather existed to uphold and defend it. The limits of kingship (or central executive power, as we might call it) and the claims of reason, or natural law, provide an important thread in More's life and works, and in his time we see the claims of absolutism growing.

Unlike Luther, More did not put his faith in princes. According to William Roper, he advised Henry VIII not to overstate the power of the Papacy when he was compiling his book asserting, against Luther, the seven sacraments of the Church:

> I must put your Highness in remembrance of one thing, and that is this. The Pope, as Your Grace knoweth, is a Prince as you are, and in league with all the other Christian Princes. It may hereafter so fall out that Your Grace and he may vary upon some points of the league, whereupon may grow breach of amity and war between you both. I think it best, therefore, that that place be amended, and his authority more slenderly touched.[4]

More sensed early on the danger of arbitrary power, particularly to

---

4. William Roper, *The Life of Sir Thomas More* (London: C. Whittingham, 1822), pp. 65–66.

himself, saying that his head was not worth as much to Henry VIII as a field of France. His own father, Judge John More, had been imprisoned by Henry's father on a trumped-up charge, until he paid a fine of hundreds of pounds. Thomas More's first action as a member of Parliament had been to oppose levels of taxation proposed by Henry VII, and he wrote lines critical of the dead king on the accession of his son. More's greatest work, apart from *Utopia*, was written against another king, Richard III, and creates substantially the picture of the tyrant that Shakespeare was to inherit and pass on so memorably. *The History of King Richard III* has been seen as propaganda intended to curry favor with the Tudor establishment, but the work was not written until after Henry VII died, and was not published at all in More's lifetime. The *History* is a vituperative portrait in the manner of Thucydides, an exercise in the moral imagination. Richard is a Machiavellian prince who will use any means to secure his ends, and his means are to dissemble, to cultivate a separation within himself of appearance and reality. More was a lover of irony, and used it in its sense of play throughout his works, to reveal rather than conceal. In Richard, however, irony in its more pernicious sense of dissimulation is seen as an attack on meaning itself. Richard enacts, in the dramatic scheme of the *History*, a pretended virtue, while at the same time performing vicious actions. His treatment of Shore's adulterous wife, for instance, draws More's revealing irony:

> ... in conclusion when no color could fasten upon these matters, then he laid heinously to her charge that thing which herself could not deny, that all the world wist was true, and that nonetheless every man laughed at to hear it then so suddenly, so highly, taken: that she was nought of her body. And for this (as a goodly continent prince, clean and faultless of himself, sent out of heaven into this vicious world for the amendment of men's manners) he caused the Bishop of London to put her to open penance, going before the cross in procession upon a Sunday with a taper in her hand.[5]

---

5. Thomas More, *The History of King Richard III*, in *Utopia and Other Writings*, James J. Greene and John P. Dolan, eds. (New York, NY: Meridian Books, 1984), p. 184ff.

To cultivate, as the Machiavellian does, a separation of meaning between appearance and reality, is to embrace the disintegrated life, and in a prince it is particularly dangerous for the commonwealth: *corruptio optimi pessima*. More was to be concerned with the integration of appearance and reality throughout his life, forced as he was in the end to conform himself to the role of martyr on the scaffold, a stage that was at once a place of execution and of play. In a sense, Richard, like Luther, was all that More did not want to be.

The meaning of More's *History of King Richard III* is quite unambiguous, and may be considered an attack on those who attack meaning itself by playing roles that, apparently virtuous, fracture the connection between common sense (widely understood) and language, or between appearance and reality. In this sense, the *History* anticipates the attacks on Luther and Tyndale. The meaning of *Utopia*, in contrast, has been debated since its publication at Louvain in 1516. However, we would be wrong to conclude that its meaning is too subtle to be discerned. A duality of appearance and reality is at play in *Utopia*, as well as other dualities inherent in the dialogue form: Book I and Book II; reality and ideal; More and Hythloday; Europe and Utopia. There is an apparent duality within the main character himself: Hythloday means "talker of nonsense" and Raphael means "God has healed"—the name of the archangel who brings healing to blind Tobit. Hythloday appears to talk nonsense to some, particularly the lawyer and the friar in Book I, but the character of More, in contrast, welcomes much of what he has to say at the end of Book II. *Utopia* is a contribution to the Renaissance debate about the *optimus status reipublicae*, rather than a blueprint for society or, indeed, a self-contained political philosophy. It posits the value of common human reason in the ordering of society, as opposed to the oppressive rule of arbitrary absolutism, the dangers of which are seen in Book I. More's *Utopia* stands for reason and natural law against the craft and guile of Machiavelli's *The Prince*. Rather than put his faith in the necessary evil of an unscrupulous prince, More shows what might be achieved by discourse in properly constituted assemblies, and by open-minded, reasonable men—men like Cardinal Morton in Book I.

In its discussion of the best state of the commonwealth, its acceptance of a Christian imperative towards social reform, its enactment of reasoned debate upon public matters, and its attitude of judicious inquiry, Book I of *Utopia* shows us the humanist project at work. It also points us towards an answer to what we might call the riddle of the Charterhouse: why did More choose the active rather than the contemplative life, and then apparently create a hypothetical society that bears many characteristics of a monastery? The answer seems to involve the question of balance. In its ideal, medieval society involved a careful balance of public and private things such that the two were not so discrete, or even antithetical, as they have become since the birth of modernity. As Book I outlines, the balance of the mixed form of ownership represented by the community of property in the monasteries, and the private (or familial) holdings outside them, was becoming upset under the pressure of the economic upheavals of More's time. The privatization of property, in the enclosure of common land by the powerful, would lead to the destruction of the common ideal, both in the monasteries and in the class who depended on the common land for the maintenance of themselves and their families. This economic fact reflected the intellectual bases of Catholic Europe. More knew that on every level of the Christendom that was his world, a subtle and complementary interchange of the private and the common was at work to keep the individual person and the community in fruitful balance. Conscience is the faculty that negotiates this balance in moral action. Thus, the examination of the condition of England and Europe in Book I focuses on the moral consequences of the pride and greed of dynastic wars and imperial ambitions: dislocation from society after military service, unemployment, robbery, and the potent symbolic inversion of the sheep eating up the people. Hythloday's analysis seems largely accepted in Book I, but his remedy of the abolition of private property is opposed by the character of More in the story, and there is no reason to suppose that the view of More the author was any different.

Hythloday embodies two extremes without being able to integrate them, or bring them into balance. He advocates the holding of all property in common, but he has privatized himself completely. One of the first things we learn about him is that he has given away all his property, dividing it among his brothers, in order that he might travel the world. "Now I live exactly as I please,"[6] he boasts, and he does not intend to give up his happy state by entering the service of kings. He thus resembles a peculiarly modern type of man, one who would be at home in the fictitious world of the modern liberal utopia, where one may do exactly as he pleases, having yielded up all control over matters of importance to the all-powerful, benevolent state (a paradox with which we currently grapple). In the real world of More, meaning comes from common consent, rather than from private illumination, as in the case of Hythloday's version of the Platonic philosopher king, Utopus, the founder of Utopia. Whatever is good in Utopia remains nowhere so long as Hythloday maintains his separation from the political world, where the exercise of many private consciences work to bring about the common good. Custom and tradition, representing the accumulated wisdom of conscience, is an important aspect of this process, since as Peter Giles says to Hythloday, "Long usage has provided us with much that makes for pleasant living, and we have discovered certain things by experience which no amount of mental effort could have produced."[7] Hythloday's retreat into his own private authority (the character of More reminds us at the end of Book II that Hythloday would not like to be contradicted) should be disquieting to us as we hear his description of Utopia, just as the claim of a private authority by Henry VIII or Martin Luther disquieted Thomas More.

Thus, although the most obvious classical influence on *Utopia* is Plato, the work does not endorse the Platonic tradition of government being in the hands of a specialist who has the leisure (*otium*) and expertise to rule. Over against this is the Ciceronian tradition of civic humanism, in which the commonwealth is served by the duty of all to their fellow men in their common business (*negotium*) of life. Hythloday is a type of the Platonic traveler whose ideal is located outside of Europe, which seems to his mind utterly mired in corrupt laws designed for the rich to rob the poor. In Book I, for

6. Ibid., p. 32.
7. Ibid., p. 51.

28

instance, he makes some strong criticisms, with which More appears to sympathize, of enclosures. But Hythloday resembles the Western intellectuals of the first half of the twentieth century who went to the Soviet Union and saw a shining vision of the good society. His idealism is his strength, but also his weakness. In contrast to Hythloday, the character of More adopts a Ciceronian view of the value of philosophy in political life which does not depend on the virtuous, all-powerful prince—something of which Hythloday, admittedly, despairs of ever seeing:

> "There is no place for philosophers among kings," [said Hythloday].
>
> "Yes there is," [More] answered, "but not for that academic philosophy which fits everything neatly into place. There is however, another, more sophisticated philosophy which accommodates itself to the scene at hand and acts its part with polish and finesse. It is this philosophy that you should use. Otherwise, it would be as if, while a comedy by Plautus were being acted . . . you were suddenly to appear in a philosopher's garb and recite the passage from the Octavia where Seneca debates with Nero."[8]

Seneca of course, like More, tried to influence a tyrant for good, and was to lose his life for his pains; it was not a role that More wanted to play. The dramatic metaphor is striking, and reveals More's sense of life both as play and as a play, but the main point here is that he resists the kind of abstract, speculative philosophy in politics that Edmund Burke was also to reject some two hundred years later. The ending of *Utopia* suggests a desire, however, that the Ciceronian and Platonic positions might achieve some kind of synthesis, as the character of More welcomes, under qualification, what Hythloday tells him of Utopia.

The description of Utopia that we (and the character of More) receive from Hythloday in Book II is neither ridiculous nor repulsive, as are, for instance, some of the lands that Gulliver comes across in his travels. More's purpose is not satirical, although there is a certain ambiguity in his approach towards both England and Utopia in

8. Ibid., p. 48.

the book as a whole. A central puzzle has been how a Catholic martyr can appear to approve of a Utopian society that bears many of the marks of our modern, liberal, secularized democracy in that it countenances euthanasia, divorce, married priests, and women priests, but not private property, corporal mortification, or hunting and even dislikes the unfortunate necessity of killing animals for food. The totalism of Utopia we find discomforting; it reminds us of communism or national socialism, or of modern dystopian fiction such as Orwell's *Nineteen Eighty-Four*, despite the lack in Utopia of the brutality on which those regimes were founded. We have to conclude that there is much of which More does not approve in Utopia, a heathen country which is nonetheless on the verge of conversion to Christianity, partly because it is peculiarly receptive to it. What More does approve, however, is the place of reason among the Utopians, the felicity that it promotes, and the common life that it makes possible. There is freedom of conscience, although freedom of speech is confined to certain situations and contexts, something which More approved. Licit pleasure, the highest being virtue, is regarded as a proper end of human life, and should be noted against any impression we might receive of a drab uniformity—of dress, for example.

What attracts More in Hythloday's description of Utopia is the unfettered fruitfulness there of natural law. Hythloday devotes more attention to religion than to any other aspect of Utopia, and like the pre-Christian ideal republics of classical (humane) letters, Utopia shows what might be achieved, despite the lack of the Christian Revelation. The Utopians fall into error—fallen nature cannot help that—and, as we have noted, they sanction such things as euthanasia and divorce on "reasonable" grounds. But even here their philosophy does not wholly err: there are all sorts of restrictions on euthanasia and divorce that would not be recognized in our society. The essential way in which Utopia differs from either the modern liberal, secular democracy or the modern totalitarian state is that it is founded on religion, one that arises from a natural religious sense. More follows Cicero in assuming an innate religious sense,[9]

9. Cf. Edmund Burke, *Reflections on the Revolution in France*: "Man is by his constitution a religious animal."

in addition to the five physical ones, which allows the Utopians to achieve a largely common monotheism, and to have intimations of a greater revelation. The natural religion of Utopia is in accord with the principles of natural law as understood by the Church, following Aristotle. They were, moreover, principles that the Protestant reformers were to call into question:

> The virtuous life is consonant with nature, as ordained by God himself. He follows the path of nature who allows reason to master his passions. Reason first enkindles in us mortals love and adoration of the Divine Majesty to whom we owe what we are and what we ever will be. Secondly, reason shows us the possibility of and excites in us the desire for leading a life that allows the least anxiety and the greatest happiness for ourselves, a life dedicated to mutual help.[10]

Happiness and pleasure are the ends of human life for the Utopians, but it should be noted that virtue is for them the highest pleasure. It is this which allows them freedom from tyranny, and freedom from religious enthusiasm. A Christian convert among them who begins to preach the cult of Christ with more zeal than prudence, and who condemns all other religions in Utopia, is ultimately exiled for sedition rather than for his contempt of those other religions. Denial of the immortality of the soul or of the existence of Providence are the only religious opinions that are forbidden freedom of expression, but it should be remembered that the norms of Utopia are quite different from the norms of Christendom, which possesses Revelation. It is to this point that the character of More alludes at the end of Book II, though he does not mean that Christendom is released from the norms of natural law; rather, his whole purpose is to direct attention to these norms as part of the humanist project of reform.

This project included the improvement of the condition of the academy, and the extension there of liberal learning. It is difficult to overestimate the importance for Thomas More both of established traditions of meaning, and of human reason as an indispensable means by which meaning is discovered or articulated. Language is

10. Greene and Dolan, op. cit., p. 69.

the incarnation of meaning, and just as reason is possessed by every man, so is language, to a greater or lesser degree. Since meaning arises from discourse, rather than from the individual mind, language must be capable of being commonly understood, if reason is to exist at all. In writing to Martin Dorp, about the time that he was writing *Utopia*, More attacked the grammarian sophists of his day who threatened "the destruction of the liberal arts":

> ... a new kind of nonsense, worse than that of the sophists, has gradually replaced dialectics. With its mask of brilliant wit, this nonsense has great appeal for its hearers.[11]

After examining the contorted, insane "logic" of some of their examples, whereby meaning is enforced by strict grammatical rules at variance with plain reason, More asserts that

> words do not belong to a particular profession. They are not private property, to be borrowed by anyone who wants them for his own private use. Speech is, to be sure, a common possession, but they spoil some of the words that they have gotten from cobblers. They have taken them from the common people, and they misuse what is common. But it is their objection that their rule of logic demands a certain interpretation. Will this damned rule, designed in some corner by men who hardly know how to speak, impose new laws of speech on the world? Grammar teaches correct speech. It does not devise extraordinary rules of language but advises those who are unskilled in the ways of speech how to observe the world's ordinary customs of speech.[12]

Except that today we are faced with a perverse kind of anti-grammar rather than grammar-gone-mad, More could be writing about post-modernist thinkers:

> The precepts of dialecticians are not so demanding as they are persuading, for it is their duty to follow our custom in the use of language and to force us to move in any direction, with reasons that are true. On the other hand, sophists lead us to a spot where we are surprised to find ourselves. They accomplish this through their

11. Ibid., p. 143.
12. Ibid., p. 144.

deceptive use of words. The cleverness by which men show that they are victorious in an argument and the ingenuity by which they decide in their own favor is both stupid and a foolish use of cleverness and ingenuity; for we do not understand their way of using words, which is contrary to universal acceptance.[13]

Like the Catholic Faith and reason, language is for More a common possession, all three serving the purpose of communication, in the various levels of meaning of that word. That More is writing about Latin in the letter above merely intensifies his anti-élitist point; the universal language should be seen as truly universal and made accessible, not hidden. Writing in English, More's own style is accessible, fluent, supple, engagingly humorous and full of commonplace and homely illustration, and it is worth noting that in his "History of the English Language," prepended to his great dictionary, Samuel Johnson devoted more space to More than to Chaucer.

The threat that More perceived from the Protestant reformers, then, was a threat to commonly understood meaning, accessible to all people of whatever degree, and established by long tradition. The point where More clearly sees Luther's direction for the first time is in reading *On the Babylonish Captivity*. In this work, Luther attacked the whole sacramental system of Catholic Christianity, and especially the doctrine of transubstantiation. The Mass was the centre of More's spirituality and, indeed, the centre of the whole of Christendom. The doctrine of transubstantiation points to a continuing incarnation of spirit and matter, spreading out into the whole of medieval civilization. The fury of More's response to Luther is explained by what he perceived to be at stake: the whole structure of meaning upon which his world depended. Luther is depicted as the spreader of "insane calumnies," and like the sophistical, pedantic grammarians in the letter to Dorp, and the incipient forces of princely absolutism against which *Utopia* stands, Luther's attack on the doctrine of the Eucharist is one against common sense, innate reason, itself. Heresy, for More, threatened the basic order of the medieval mind, and More's hatred of it is similar to the hatred of racism in our time. It would not be an overstatement to

13. Ibid., p. 145.

say that he considered it a crime against humanity, in the particular sense that the medieval humanist and classical idea of man as a rational creature whose nature enabled him to reach Godwards was threatened. Instead of reason, Luther posited the will. God himself did not work according to reason, but according to his own inscrutable purpose. He allows, for instance, the existence of tyrants who must not be opposed because

> The world is far too wicked to be worthy of good and pious lords. It must have ... tyrants. This and other chastisement are rather what it has deserved, and to resist them is nothing else than to resist God's chastisement. As humbly as I conduct myself when God sends me a sickness, so humbly should I conduct myself towards the evil government which the same God also sends me.[14]

The reformers gave over all earthly authority to the prince and his laws, continental Roman unlike English law seeing the prince as lawgiver rather than its protector. The prince should keep to the divine law as revealed in Scripture, but the idea that the laws of the land arising from natural law had some authority over the king was being increasingly brought into question. The English follower of Luther, William Tyndale, wrote:

> He that judgeth the king judgeth God. ... If the king sin he must be reserved unto the judgement and vengeance of God ... the king is in this world without law, and may at his lust do right and wrong and shall give accounts but to God only.[15]

However much the Protestant emphasis on the exclusive temporal authority of the prince was a reaction against the revolt of the German peasantry, inspired by Luther's earlier cry of Christian liberty, it was no doubt fed by growing political ideas of absolutism, and by the view that man was entirely mired in corruption, entirely at the mercy of God's will, damned unless justified by faith alone. The whole of the temporal sphere, previously seen in the Catholic scheme as having been brought into a sacramental order, was seen

---

14. Martin Luther, quoted in C. Morris, *Political Thought in England: Tyndale to Hooker* (London: OUP, 1953), p. 42.

15. William Tyndale, quoted in ibid., p. 37.

as essentially lawless except for the force of will of a (possibly, but not necessarily) Christian prince. The order to which Thomas More looked was written in the heart of man, and protected and restrained both king and subject, and however much he inclined temperamentally towards judges than juries in the practice of the law, he always believed the group to be more authoritative than the individual.

The two means through which More argued against the heretics were the law and letters, means whereby reason could reveal truth. He was asked to write in English against the Protestants by Cuthbert Tunstall, Bishop of London, who permitted him to read and own the heretical writings. In the *Dialogue Concerning Heresies* (1528), More emphasizes that reason as well as faith is needed for the interpretation of Scripture, and his emphasis includes also the importance of humane letters:

> I deny not but that grace and God's especial help is the great thing therein, yet useth he for an instrument man's reason thereto. God helpeth us to eat also but yet not without our mouth.... [R]eason is by study, labor, and exercise of logic, philosophy and other liberal arts corroborate and quickened, and that judgement both in them and also in orators, laws and stories, much ripened. And albeit poets be with many men taken but for painted words, yet do they much help the judgement and make a man among other things well furnished of one special thing [wit] without which all learning is half lame ... And, therefore, are in mine opinion these Lutherans in a mad mind that would now have all learning save Scripture only, clean cast away.[16]

In the same work, More defends the translation of Scripture into the vernacular, under authority; when later accused by Tyndale of double standards, More pointed out the mischievous intent of Tyndale's choice of words. *The Confutation of Tyndale's Answer* (1532–33) is lengthy and vituperative, but it is worth noting a revealing fictional exchange between Barnes, a heretic friar, and a simple housewife. Barnes fails to satisfy the housewife on his interpretation of Scripture; she points out that the reformers disagree among themselves:

16. Greene and Dolan, op. cit., p. 200.

All this considered, I were a but a fool to leave the known Catholic Church, whom I have hitherto taken for my very mother, and come from her to yours, of the truth of which you are after all in doubt. For if I leave this mother Church, where am I to seek another?[17]

More's point that a simple housewife can see more clearly than the heretics is ironical but indirectly it is a defense of common sense, that a housewife may judge of these matters at all. This view is in keeping with More's not opposing in principle the translation of Scripture into the vernacular, but he does believe that common people must receive the Scripture from authorized preachers so that private judgment does not lead to error; juries need judges, and vice versa.

More's "Tower Works" and especially his letters, are particularly revealing of his thoughts and feelings on human society, and on how this connected with his own self. Alvaro de Silva, in the introduction to his edition of More's last letters, entitled "Good Company," places More in his historical and literary context. We are given a few biographical details leading up to his imprisonment and fourteen-month captivity, and comparisons are suggested with the prison literature of the twentieth century, such as that of Solzhenitsyn and Bonhoeffer. In literary terms (as, we might suppose, in spiritual) this was More's most fruitful period. As De Silva says,

> More's "Tower Works" are not only a splendid example of the genre but also represent the height of his literary accomplishments. In spite of the physical and psychological conditions he endured, More did not abandon the craft he had cultivated for many years. Like most Renaissance writers, he wanted to be useful, and so, as helpless prisoner of his conscience, he wrote to strengthen himself, and then others.[18]

Not only these letters (those which survive of what must have been many more) but also the *Dialogue of Comfort* and the *De Tristitia*

---

17. Thomas More, in *The Confutation of Tyndale's Answer*, quoted in C. Hollis, *St. Thomas More* (London: Burns and Oates, 1961), p. 160ff.

18. Alvaro de Silva, ed., *The Last Letters of Thomas More* (Grand Rapids, MI: Eerdmans, 2000), p. 8.

Christi attest favorably to De Silva's judgment, and serve to emphasize Gerard Wegemer's point, in *Thomas More on Statesmanship*,[19] about the importance of literature to More the Christian humanist. If the use of humane letters is to teach man through a knowledge of man, then this is as true for the self as for others. In these letters, we see Thomas More "making his soul" in a literary form that integrates the public and the private. This is a different form than the polemic used against the Protestant reformers, but there is a similar underlying humanist purpose, in the use of literature to incarnate truth in the language of men. More is a Christian humanist, somewhere between Luther and Erasmus, in a balance that enabled him to criticize, in *Utopia*, the humanist project—a project, however, he never rejected. As De Silva says:

> More is, from beginning to end, from the Island of Utopia to the Tower of London, ever the dedicated humanist. Not to see this, is, I think, to misunderstand him and to make him a fanatic, a reactionary, and a humanist writer who completely lost his emotional control and whose voluminous polemical writings should be dismissed not only as boring but insane. Nothing can be further from the truth.[20]

In support of this statement, De Silva cites Brendan Bradshaw who "argues for the coherence of Thomas More in this war of words: one million words in defense of his faith against new Protestant doctrines. More became a controversialist because he was a Christian humanist."[21]

We have seen, too, how a number of other oppositions converge in Thomas More, and are, in a way that can certainly be debated, either resolved or held in tension. He was medieval and modern, European and English, a stylist in Latin and in the vernacular, both contemplative and active. No doubt this was due in part to his peculiar position in history, straddling the medieval and the modern divide, but more so to his integrating mind and personality. Perhaps the most impor-

---

19. Gerard B. Wegemer, *Thomas More on Statesmanship* (Washington, DC: CUA Press, 1998).

20. De Silva, op. cit., p. 7.

21. Ibid., p. 7.

tant resolution for us is that of the duality of the individual and the community, and the resolution centers upon More's understanding of the word *conscience*. As De Silva makes clear, More's understanding is something quite different to, and more sophisticated than that which the word generally means in modernity:

> The word conscience is conspicuous throughout the last letters, appearing a total of more than one hundred times, and more than forty times in a single letter (Letter 12 in this volume). Indeed, More's prison epistolary can be read as a lasting monument in praise of conscience. The spirit of modernity has always prided itself on being precisely such a monument, claiming, above all else, the freedom of the individual and his or her conscience, the so-called autonomy of the "I". But More knew of the possibility of a "fabrication of conscience," or what he refers to in another letter as "framing a conscience."[22]

De Silva alludes to Kierkegaard and Newman to show that conscience implies being alone with God, and therefore it finds a freedom not in autonomy, but in relationship:

> Conscience (from Latin *con-scire, scire cum*) denotes a "certain knowledge that we have with another." The particle cum denotes "a being together, an accompanying"—"it signifies in union, in relation to, in common, together with."[23]

Although De Silva, in the context of More's Tower works, rightly places his emphasis on conscience as "the knowledge of Christ, the wisdom of Christ, the knowledge of oneself with Christ and in Christ,"[24] this understanding of conscience goes also to the heart of More's understanding of the Church as a company in Christ. But as De Silva says,

> [t]he Latin particle is also the key to fully understanding two other words intentionally and insistently present in his last writings in the Tower, comfort (*cum + fortitudo*) and company (*cum + panis*).[25]

22. Ibid., p. 10.
23. Ibid.
24. Ibid.
25. Ibid.

In his period of captivity, More was very aware of finding strength and sustenance from being together with the saints who had suffered before him. As De Silva puts it:

> Modernity may have little use for the sense of eternity, or for what Chesterton called "the democracy of the dead," but for More it was undoubtedly a great source of moral strength, consolation, and joy. His Utopians believed that "the dead move about among the living and are witnesses of their words and deeds," and therefore the living "go about their business with more confidence because of reliance on such protection."[26]

It is an illustration that quite pointedly reminds us that Utopia was not entirely removed from More's idea of the good society, however much it falls short.

De Silva's edition of More's last letters allows him to contrast More with Machiavelli, a contrast brought out by two telling quotations from the Italian:

> "I love my city more than my own soul," wrote Machiavelli to Francesco Vettori. In this brutal assertion, transcendence has been blotted out, and the tragic consequences are better known to us than to Machiavelli.[27]

> Niccolo Machiavelli had a very different view of things when he wrote, "And of conscience we should not take account because where there is, as in us, the fear of hunger and prison, that of hell neither can nor should find room."[28]

The civic humanism of More was of course quite different from that of Machiavelli, who has hitherto found a more useful place in modernity. However, De Silva emphasizes the point that More has as much a claim to be considered a political thinker, and one in whom there is matter with which to counter Machiavelli's limitations. For More can also speak to us in modern accents, as these letters show; there is all the modern concern with self, in a literary art of self-fashioning. More in prison, however, is not confined in

26. Ibid., p. 15.
27. Ibid., p. 19.
28. Ibid., p. 14.

solipsism, but rather embodied that quality which resolved Cicero's paradox: *numquam se minus otiosum esse quam cum otiosus, nec minus solum quam cum solus esset.*[29]

Despite a certain homage to the inescapable pattern of heroic virtue that More's final months present, the revisionists would have us see him as having painted himself into a corner, in a kind of political failure that had fortuitously released him from others and given him the monkish cell he had always wanted. As Richard Marius puts it:

> It is perhaps not too much to speculate that once he had refused the oath and been confined to the Tower, More became locked in an inner world of his own, a world where he atoned for his early decision to marry and to forsake priesthood, a world where he endured on earth part of the purgatory that a secular man like himself must expect after death, a world where private struggle so filled his being that he had no room for the struggle and fate of others who, now, he thought, in the intense psychic freedom from care given him by his captivity, could be left to God.[30]

But as John Guy has shown, this "paradigm of sin and atonement" for marriage does not hold water, and close attention to the last letters suggests that, far from retreating into himself, More was moving into another company, or communion, that did not exclude anyone, not friends, family or (ultimately, he prayed) even foes.

In the final analysis, it was for this principle at the heart of Christendom that Thomas More was willing to undergo imprisonment and execution. To Thomas Cromwell, he wrote:

> And, therefore, since all Christendom is one corps [body], I cannot perceive how any member thereof may without the common assent of the body depart from the common head. And then if we may not lawfully leave it ourselves, I cannot perceive (but if the thing were a treating [under discussion] in a general council) what the question could avail whether the primacy were instituted by God or by the Church. As for the general councils assembled law-

---

29. "Never less idle than when wholly idle, nor less alone than when wholly alone." Cicero, *De Officiis*, III, i, p. l. Cf. J. H. Newman, *Apologia Pro Vita Sua* (London, UK: Sheed and Ward, 1979), p. 10.

30. Richard Marius, *Thomas More* (London: Arnold, 2000), p. 471.

fully, I never could perceive but that in the declaration of truths to be believed and to be standen to [followed], the authority thereof ought to be taken for undoubtable, or else were there in nothing no certainty, but through Christendom upon every man's affectionate reason, all things might be brought from day to day to continual ruffle and confusion, from which by the general councils, the spirit of God assisting, every such council well assembled keepeth and ever shall keep the corps of his Catholic Church.[31]

In More's view, neither a prince, nor any other person could consider himself free of either natural law, or positive law made on the basis of natural law, or divine law. Conscience has come to mean little more nowadays than a right to private judgment, but for More, conscience, like positive law, had to be conformed to a higher law. One is obliged to act on what one believes to be true, but what one believes to be true has to be informed by reason and Revelation. Conscience, therefore, comes to mean not simply what I believe but what we believe, that which is known together. In this respect, when Robert Bolt spoke of More in the preface to his play *A Man For All Seasons* as "a hero of selfhood," the phrase is potentially misleading. More died not believing in the autonomy of the self, but in the self as integrated with, and sustained by, the communion of saints in the whole Church—militant, suffering and triumphant. His own integrity was but the reflection and personalizing of the integrity of the Church and of Christendom. His paradoxical position of being a lone conformist reminds us that consensus cannot be reduced to the majority opinion at a particular moment in time. Rather, consensus must be seen in the context of history. History has proved that the death of Thomas More, although marking the end of the medieval consensus he embodied, did not see the death of the perennial principles which underpinned it, and for which Thomas More died.

The historical More may evade us, but his importance endures in the moral imagination. Why is it that, as John Guy, says, we all think we know More? Perhaps we know him as the integrated man, another sense of the Renaissance ideal of *hominum omnium horarum*: as Richard Marius wrote, "somehow very much an indis-

---

31. Greene and Dolan, op. cit., p. 259.

pensable ideal we cherish for ourselves."[32] He is the imagined mirror of our best selves, a personality in which the common humanity he affirmed is transfigured and seen as heroic. He endures as a part of the common mind because he did not, unlike some of his contemporary opponents, loathe the human nature given him, despite his awareness of its limitations. The peculiar force of Robert Bolt's drama (doubtless, as Guy says, "appalling history") derives from the inherently dramatic qualities of Thomas More's personality and life, and it is perhaps through the moral imagination that Thomas More can be best known today. A knowledge, however, of his writings will not only deepen this picture, but also provide us with his even more valuable philosophy, one "which accommodates itself to the scene at hand and acts its part with polish and finesse."

32. Marius, op. cit., p. 519.

3

Good Company

Jonathan Swift versus the Enlightenment

God hath given the bulk of mankind a capacity to understand reason when it is freely offered; and by reason they would easily be governed, if it were left to their choice.

SWIFT, *Some Free Thoughts upon the Present State of Affairs*, 1714

[T]o study Newton is a chore, though to keep company with Swift is a delight.   RUSSELL KIRK, *The Intemperate Professor and Other Cultural Splenetics*, 1965

THE NINETEENTH-CENTURY caricature, owing much to Thackeray, of Jonathan Swift as a monstrous, obscene, filth-besotted, irreligious and finally insane genius, has been much modified in the twentieth century, although suspicions and doubts remain. The real Swift was more human, more complex and more attractive than Thackeray's distortion, although the works, especially *Gulliver's Travels*, are still apt to elude sensible reading. Thackeray's picture has metamorphosed into a congeries of modern rather than Victorian distortions. Typically, the twentieth century mind is ill-equipped to read Swift; a simplistic political outlook, and a stupefied incomprehension of transcendent religion, have meant that modern readers have recoiled from the savage indignation of this Anglican priest, and the apparently reactionary tendencies of a disappointed Toryism that Swift at first sight presents.

A look below the surface is hardly more attractive to the liberal mind: a profound distrust of intellectualism, rationalism, and "enthusiasm" opens up. Many of these misunderstandings and unsympathetic feelings are present in George Orwell's stimulating but misleading essay, "Politics vs. Literature: An Examination of *Gulliver's Travels*,"[1] and taken together with Thackeray, one might conclude from both that Swift was not only unhealthy, but wrong. Orwell likes Swift, even if he disagrees with what he understands to be his meaning, and his inheritance of the Swiftian plain style, and adept use of political satire, seem to make him an eminently suitable commentator. He also makes many percipient political observations, particularly concerning totalitarianism. The clarity of Orwell's prose is always stimulating, and in this as in his characteristic liberal assumptions, he may serve as a useful touchstone for a reading of Swift from the conservative viewpoint.

Insofar as Swift is read at all today, it is highly selectively, and with little understanding of the political and (even more important) religious context. *Gulliver's Travels*, which is still read, continues to be seen as a desperate indictment of human nature. Attention is focused on the negatives, on that in which Swift did not believe: meliorative political, social and scientific progress that would free the essential goodness of man. What he did believe in, although inaccessible to the liberal mind, needs to be asserted in our time as it was in his: a religious view of human nature, and religion based on faith rather than reason; a discriminating clarity of moral judgment; and the abiding authority of common sense in secular things, based on unchanging human nature. As a conservative, and as a Tory, Swift challenges many of the preconceptions that those vexed words present.

Religion is the basis of the positive values with which Swift satirized his times. Evelyn Waugh, who closely resembled Swift as man and writer, once resisted the title of satire[2] for his own art, observing that satire was only possible in an age of shared values, a situa-

---

1. George Orwell, *Collected Essays, Journalism and Letters*, Vol. 4, Sonia Orwell and Ian Angus, eds. (London: Penguin, 1970), p. 241.
2. See Evelyn Waugh, *Essays, Articles and Reviews of Evelyn Waugh*, ed. Donat Gallagher (London: Methuen, 1988), p. 304.

tion that no longer obtained in the twentieth century. There is some disingenuousness here; in Swift's time a shared consensus concerning the nature of truth no longer obtained either. After the upheavals of the Reformation, and especially the English Civil War, truth was no longer patent, but often hidden. Swift was a man of the Restoration of 1660, not only of the monarchy, but also of the Church of England—established, episcopal and "catholick." He also adhered to the terms of the Glorious Revolution of 1688, which settled the struggle between an absolutism of the monarchy and an absolutism of democracy, in favor of a constitutional monarchy. His position was characteristically Anglican; the settlement resisted the dangers of what was considered Roman Catholic superstition on the one hand, and Puritan enthusiasm on the other, dangers both to the soul and the commonwealth. All reasonable people could be united in the established Church, a spiritual counterpart to the political constitution that also preserved the whole people against excesses:

> Where security of person and property are preserved by laws which none but the whole can repeal, the great ends of government are provided for whether the administration be in the hands of the One, or of Many. Where any one person or body of men, who do not represent the Whole, seize into their hands the power in the last resort, there is properly no longer a government but what Aristotle and his followers call the abuse and corruption of one. This distinction excludes arbitrary power in whatever numbers; which notwithstanding all that Hobbes, Filmer and others have said to its advantage, I look upon as a greater evil than anarchy itself; as much as a savage is in a happier state of life than a slave at the oar.[3]

Swift rejected the absolutism of kings and Puritan commonwealths, and in his own time he was more concerned with the threat of the latter. His crucial shifting of support from the Whigs to the Tories was in reaction to the proposal to remove penalties against Dissenters in Ireland. The Tories, in contrast, supported the Church of

---

3. Swift, "The Sentiments of a Church of England Man," in *Works of the Rev. Jonathan Swift*, arr. T. Sheridan (New York, NY: W. Durrell and Co., 1812), pp. 312–313.

England against measures to extend political rights for merely occasional conformity to the established religion. Dissent and enthusiasm always threatened a return of the Puritan tyranny, and the Church Established was a great bulwark against tyranny from any political direction.

It is also in Swift's underlying religious assumptions that we find his distrust of intellectualism, rationalism and enthusiasm, all three of which are seen as similarly disintegrative and at odds with common sense:

> I believe thousands of men would be orthodox enough in certain points, if divines had not been too curious, or too narrow, in reducing orthodoxy within the compass of subtleties, niceties, and distinctions, with little warrant from Scripture and less from reason or good policy.[4]

Swift's appeal is frequently to reason, which is of course always something greater than mere logical progression in argument. Moreover, faith guides reason but does not contradict it. Even though he considered the Church of Rome to have added invented mysteries to those clearly affirmed by Scripture, mystery is at the heart of Swift's religion:

> Therefore I shall again repeat the doctrine of the Trinity, as it is positively affirmed in Scripture: that God is there expressed in three different names, as Father, as Son, and as Holy Ghost; that each of these is God, and that there is but one God. But this union and distinction are a mystery utterly unknown to mankind.
>
> This is enough for any good Christian to believe on this great article, without ever inquiring any further. And this can be contrary to no man's reason, although the knowledge of it is hid from him.[5]

Man's reason operates within the sphere of the readily apparent, and errs when it trespasses further than that which can be commonly understood. Mystery is accessible only to faith, which leads

4. Swift, "Thoughts on Religion," *The Prose Works of Jonathan Swift*, D. D., Vol. III, ed. T. Scott (London: G. Bell and Sons, 1898), p. 308.

5. Swift, "On the Trinity," in ibid., Vol. III, p. 131.

the reason. Similarly, reason controls the passions, which yet have their function and providential purpose:

> Although reason were intended by providence to govern our passions, yet it seems that, in two points of the greatest moment of the being and continuance of the world, God hath intended our passions to prevail over our reason. The first is, the propagation of our species. . . . The other is, the love of life, which, from the dictates of reason, every man would despise, and wish it at an end, or that it never had a beginning.[6]

It is in the sphere of the passions that Swift's satire is most savage, his reason most indignant, but it is to other symptoms of the disintegrated mind that he also directs his lash. Rationalism is the refusal to accept the proper claims of faith; enthusiasm the refusal to accept the proper claims of common sense; intellectualism the refusal to accept the proper claims of mystery. They are all manifestations of pride, which is seen under the satiric eye as madness.

Furthermore, it is in the context of religion, particularly the social position and function of the Anglican priest, that Swift's literary purpose and strictures on style are to be understood. Truth is inevitably bound up with questions of language. It is as a clergyman and as a gentleman that he writes to a younger clerical gentleman on what to avoid in preaching:

> I defy the greatest divine, to produce any law either of God or man, which obliges me to comprehend the meaning of omniscience, omnipresence, ubiquity, attribute, beatifick vision, with a thousand others so frequent in pulpits.[7]

It is essential that the preacher, by definition more learned than his audience, take into account their condition:

> . . . it is not very reasonable for them to expect, that common men should understand expressions, which are never made use of in common life. No gentleman thinks it safe or prudent to send a servant with a message, without repeating it more than once, and

---

6. Swift, "Thoughts on Religion," op. cit., p. 309.
7. Swift, "A Letter to a Young Gentleman," in *The Writings of Jonathan Swift*, R. A. Greenberg and W. B. Piper, eds. (New York, NY: Norton, 1973), p. 474.

endeavouring to put it into terms brought down to the capacity of the bearer.[8]

Also to be avoided is "letting the pathetick part swallow up the rational":[9]

> A plain convincing reason may possibly operate upon the mind both of a learned and an ignorant hearer, as long as they live; and will edify a thousand times more than the art of wetting the handkerchiefs of a whole congregation, if you were sure to attain it.[10]

Swift shared the neoclassical view of the uniformity of human nature, but he clearly divides people into the learned and the ignorant; the former have an obligation of duty, the latter an obligation of obedience. Society depends on a class of gentlemen, men of learning, and (as important) taste: the lack of these qualities continually threatens civilization:

> I would engage to furnish you with a catalogue of English books published within the compass of seven years past, which at the first hand would cost you an hundred pounds; wherein you shall not be able to find ten lines together of common grammar, or common sense.
>
> These two evils, ignorance, and want of taste, have produced a third; I mean the continual corruption of our English tongue.[11]

Thus, we should distinguish learning (of which Swift is clearly in favor, and like Thomas More, advocated it for women) and intellectualism. The one is broad and leads to wisdom; the other is narrow and leads to folly. The one is associated with a class, such as the clergy, the other with an élite, such as the Royal Society. It is always Swift's concern to reach a wide audience. One reason that *Gulliver's Travels* has always appealed to children as well as adults is that Swift himself followed the advice he gave to a young gentleman. As Dr. Johnson wrote:

> [Swift's] style was well suited to his thoughts, which are never subtilised by nice disquisitions, decorated by sparkling conceits, elevated by ambitious sentences, or variegated by far-sought

8. Ibid., p. 477.
9. Ibid., p. 475.
10. Ibid., p. 477.
11. Ibid., p. 449.

learning. He pays no court to the passions; he excites neither surprise nor admiration; he always understands himself, and his
readers always understand him: the peruser of Swift wants little
previous knowledge; it will be sufficient that he is acquainted with
common words and common things. . . .[12]

In Swift's view, élites such as the Puritans are always in danger of
becoming persecutors. The widest diffusion of discourse within the
whole commonwealth is the best protection against tyranny. However, this is to be distinguished from freethinking, which Swift continually mocked. Again, the problem is a disintegration from
context, and the threat of the tyranny of the minority, which in the
case of the freethinker is a minority of one. As Swift put it in one
masterly satire:

> It is the indispensable duty of a freethinker, to endeavour forcing
> all the world to think as he does, and by that means make them
> freethinkers too. You are also to understand, that I [i.e., a Mr. Col-
> lins] allow no man to be a freethinker, any further than as he dif-
> fers from the received doctrines of religion. Where a man falls in,
> though by perfect chance, with what is generally believed, he is in
> that point a confined and limited thinker.[13]

In the "Letter to a Young Gentleman," Swift makes clear his belief
that, in any case, freethinking is not based on "liberal education," or
on reason, but on vice, and will only be found among those

> oppressing their tenants, tyrannizing over the neighbourhood,
> cheating the vicar, talking nonsense, and getting drunk at the
> sessions. . . . It is from such seminaries as these, that the world is
> provided with the several tribes and denominations of free-think-
> ers; who, in my judgement are not to be reformed by arguments
> offered to prove the truth of the Christian religion; because, rea-
> soning will never make a man correct an ill opinion, which by rea-
> soning he never acquired.[14]

---

12. Samuel Johnson, *Lives of the English Poets*, Vol. II (London: Dent), p. 267.
13. Swift, "Mr. Collins's Discourse of Freethinking," Scott, ed., Vol. III, op. cit.,
p. 179.
14. Swift, "A Letter to a Young Gentleman," in Greenberg and Piper, eds., op.
cit., p. 484.

If a man says he is a freethinker, Swift seems to say, then pity his family, his friends and his neighbors (here consider, for instance, Percy Shelley, Tom Paine, and Bertrand Russell). Freethinking was never far from factionalism in Swift's mind; both were essentially manifestations of unprincipled self-interest. He thus shared Dr. Johnson's, rather than Edmund Burke's, view of party, as being a movement away from the whole rather than a movement towards it. Orwell's comment that "Swift was one of those people who are driven into a sort of perverse Toryism by the follies of the progressive party of the moment,"[15] apart from being anachronistic, fails to take into account much of the cast of Swift's mind already discussed here. Orwell also says that Swift is "a Tory anarchist, despising authority while disbelieving in liberty,"[16] and this seems even more wide of the mark. Orwell fails to take into account Swift's religion, a thing Orwell simply did not understand, and he also fails to take into account Swift and Ireland.

It is in Ireland, a country for whose religion and people he felt detestation and contempt, that Swift is remembered best, and most accurately. While Dean of St. Patrick's cathedral in Dublin, he opposed Walpole's Whig policies that restricted Irish commerce to the point of non-existence. In Swift's opinion, unable to improve their lot, the people had become morally degraded, so that both the people and their circumstances became blameworthy. He never descended to sentimentality or partiality, but there can be no doubt of his moral outrage:

> Whoever travels this country, and observes the face of nature, or the faces, and habits, and dwellings of the natives, will hardly think himself in a land where either law, religion, or common humanity is professed.[17]

The excoriating Swiftian vision is best expressed in Irish circumstances, particularly in the *Modest Proposal*, where with terrifying logic, he proposes measures that could serve as a satire on Malthu-

15. Orwell, op. cit., p. 243.
16. Ibid., p. 253.
17. Swift, "A Proposal for the Universal Use of Irish Manufacture," in Scott, ed., Vol. III, p. 26.

sian ideas of population control, sixty-nine years before the essay *On Population* was first published. Swift's starting point is that common humanity is lost, and he makes it follow logically from this that it would be a good idea for the poor to sell, and the rich to buy, their children for food:

> I grant this food will be somewhat dear, and therefore proper for landlords; who, as they have already devoured most of the parents, seem to have the best title to the children.[18]

The diabolic vision of dehumanization has fore-echoes of a Nazi death camp:

> Those who are more thrifty (as I must confess the times require) may flay the carcase; the skin of which, artificially dressed, will make admirable gloves for ladies, and summer boots for fine gentlemen.[19]

The dehumanization is reflected in the use of numbers, calculation and the presentation of human beings as commodities. There is also a sense of how economic circumstances demoralize the poor and make them complicit in their own degradation:

> Sixthly, This would be a great inducement to marriage, which all wise nations have either encouraged by rewards, or enforced by laws and penalties. It would increase the care and tenderness of mothers towards their children, when they were sure of a settlement for life, to the poor babes, provided in some sort by the publick, to their annual profit instead of expence. We should soon see an honest emulation among the married women, which of them could bring the fattest child to the market. Men would become as fond of their wives, during the time of their pregnancy, as they are now of their mares in foal, their cows in calf, or sows when they are ready to farrow; nor offer to beat or kick them, (as it is too frequent a practise) for fear of a miscarriage.[20]

Were Swift to believe what he says, he would of course be mad. He reminds us of the truth of Chesterton's observation that "The

---

18. Swift, "A Modest Proposal," in Greenberg and Piper, eds., op. cit., p. 504.
19. Ibid., p. 505.
20. Ibid., p. 507.

madman is not the man who has lost his reason. The madman is the man who has lost everything except his reason."[21] But Swift is not mad: he is portraying madness. Similarly, in Book IV of *Gulliver's Travels*, the madness of Gulliver is not the madness of Swift. The sleep of reason brings forth monsters, but so does the sleep of everything except reason, in the form of policy that takes no account of morality. In Ireland, Swift was well placed to see and imagine this.

It is from the background of Swift's religious, philosophical and political assumptions that we should approach *Gulliver's Travels*, which of his major works is the one that has lasted best. It is a time-less satire on human folly. Swift is a Christian humanist, and a moral realist; he believes in revealed and objective truth; he is with the ancients and against the moderns; he is skeptical of melioration and sees change as decay. In this sense, *Gulliver's Travels* is Swift's most thoroughgoing critique of the assumptions of the Enlighten-ment. Man is not inherently good, but inclines always to folly and wickedness. As a species, he is unlovable, and has only the capacity for reason:

> I hate and detest that animal called man, although I hartily love John, Peter, Thomas and so forth. [T]his is the system upon which I have governed my self for many years (but do not tell) and so I shall go on till I have done with them. I have got materials towards a treatis proving the falsity of that definition *animal rationale*; and to show it should be only *rationis capax*.[22]

One can here contrast Swift the Christian humanist with the free-thinking humanitarian. (Consider, again, Shelley, Paine, Russell.) Swift's hero, Gulliver, displays a capacity for reason, which some-times leaves him altogether when he is in the grip of pride and mad-ness. He is untrustworthy as a narrator, and we can no more be sure that his traveler's tales are any more truthful than the host of others proverbially untrustworthy. Gulliver is even more ambiguous as an authority than Hythloday in More's *Utopia*, and to identify his

21. Chesterton, *Orthodoxy* (New York, NY: Doubleday, 1990), p. 19.
22. Swift to Alexander Pope, Sept. 29, 1725, in Greenberg and Piper, op. cit., p. 585.

views with those of the author is unwise. Gulliver displays the characteristics of the madman that Swift outlines elsewhere:

> But when a man's fancy gets astride his reason, when imagination is at cuffs with the senses, and common understanding, as well as common sense, is kickt out of doors; the first proselyte he makes, is himself, and when that is once compass'd, the difficulty is not so great in bringing over others; [a] strong delusion always operating from without, as vigorously as from within. For, cant and vision are to the ear and the eye, the same that tickling is to the touch.[23]

In neoclassical fashion, Swift distrusted the imagination (paradoxically writing one of the greatest works of the moral and political imagination), and is able to distance himself from the tale by putting it into the mouth of Gulliver. Being imaginative, Gulliver is untrustworthy, but nonetheless the forms that inhabit his tale are instructive.

The four voyages of *Gulliver's Travels* work as a series of reversals. In the voyage to Lilliput, a satire on England under the Whigs, we see madness on the political level. Lilliput is contrasted with the good sense of Brobdingnag, which is then contrasted with the madness of Laputa, which is in turn contrasted with the good sense of Houyhnhnmland. Gulliver is a giant, then a pigmy; wise, then foolish; admirable, then contemptible. It is not, however, in the climactic final voyage that we should look for a positive expression of Swift's views, which (if they are anywhere) should be identified with those of the king of Brobdingnag. This agrarian kingdom most closely resembles an improved England, whereas Houyhnhnmland is, as we shall see, utterly removed from what people really are, or could be; the first two books are closer to either reality than are the third and fourth books. In contrast to the petty machinations and ludicrous follies of Lilliput, the problem in Brobdingnag is Gulliver himself. He offers to introduce gunpowder to the king, who is horrified at the uses to which it is put in Europe, and forbids Gulliver, on pain of death, to speak of it again. "A strange effect of narrow

---

23. Swift, *A Tale of a Tub*, in ibid., pp. 350–351.

principles and short views!"[24] exclaims Gulliver to the reader. The king of Brobdingnag

> ...confined the knowledge of governing within very narrow bounds; to common sense and reason, to justice and lenity, to the speedy determination of civil and criminal causes; with some other obvious topicks which are not worth considering [says Gulliver]. And, he gave it for his opinion; that whoever could make two ears of corn, or two blades of grass to grow upon a spot of ground where only one grew before; would deserve better of mankind, and do more essential service to his country, than the whole race of politicians put together.[25]

Gulliver's view of narrowness is not unlike that of some political intellectuals nowadays, that to conceive of limited government is to betray a limited mind.

The artistic weakness of Book III, the journey to Laputa and other places, was first noted by Johnson; more recently, Quintana concurred. Swift apparently abandoned unity of place, but rather as in T.S. Eliot's *The Waste Land*, the chaotic form mirrors the content: Book III of the *Travels* is a journey into madness. The theme of the whole book is intellectual folly, and what we would call nowadays, scientism. The Royal Society is memorably satirized in the Academy of Lagado, and the flying island of Laputa, which can move over an enemy and wreak terrible havoc, is an astonishingly prescient piece of science fiction. In the image of the flying island we have a picture of detachment—of science separated from humanity. The scientists of the flying island embody Swift's satire against Descartes, a mixture of solipsism and abstraction:

> Their heads were all inclined to the right, or the left; one of their eyes turned inward, and the other directly up to the zenith.[26]

They are so absorbed in abstract speculation that they do not attend to the speech of others unless they are flapped on the head by a servant holding an inflated bladder. The philosophy of disintegration

---

24. Swift, *Gulliver's Travels*, in ibid., p. 110.
25. Ibid., p. 111.
26. Ibid., p. 132.

from the practical realities of life creates a political disconnection, too. The flying island also represents centralized authority and / power entirely removed from the people, who are completely at its mercy. It is not tied to the people, but floats above them, arbitrary and ruthless. Swift's prescience includes the dehumanizing effects of total war and saturation bombing from the air:

> If any town should engage in rebellion or mutiny, fall into violent factions, or refuse to pay the usual tribute; the king hath two methods of reducing them to obedience. The first and the mildest course is by keeping the island hovering over such a town, and the lands about it; whereby he can deprive them of the benefit of the sun and rain, and consequently afflict the inhabitants with dearth and diseases. And if the crime deserve it, they are at the same time pelted from above with great stones, against which they have no defence, but by creeping into cellars and caves, while the roofs of their houses are beaten to pieces.[27]

Further on in the satire, Swift allegorically describes the campaign he led in the *Drapier Letters* of 1724 against the introduction of a debased currency. The floating island is also England, hovering over the Irish. The effects and processes of the Protestant ascendancy and Whiggery in Ireland, taught Swift, as they were to teach Burke, the name and nature of tyranny.

Swift sees the rationalism of science as partial and transitory. In Glubbdubdrib, Gulliver has Aristotle magically returned to the present, where he converses with Descartes:

> He [Aristotle] said, that new systems of nature were but new fashions, which would vary in every age; and even those who demonstrate them from mathematical principles, would flourish but a short period of time, and be out of vogue when that was determined.[28]

Compared with the permanent truths of Aristotle, the work of both Newton and Descartes seems circumscribed, even parochial, being so much a feature of their age. Orwell accuses Swift of "a lack of

27. Ibid., p. 144.
28. Ibid., p. 169.

curiosity," and if by "curiosity" is meant an abstract love of discovery and invention which has no connection with the other humane areas of life, then we can repeat that Swift has no love of intellectualism. Pure reason is closely allied in his mind with tyranny. However, broad learning, possessed by a "gentleman of liberal education,"[29] will make for a developed moral personality. Orwell himself quotes Swift's ideal of learning, as that which Gulliver found so unsatisfactory among the Brobdingnagians:

> The learning of this people is very defective; consisting only in morality, history, poetry and mathematicks; wherein they must be allowed to excel. But, the last of these is wholly applied to what may be useful in life, to the improvement of agriculture and all mechanical arts; so that among us it would be little esteemed. And as to ideas, entities, abstractions and transcendentals, I could never drive the least conception into their heads.[30]

But what Orwell does not seem to see is that the humane and practical arts here mentioned are not superior by reason of their utility alone. The distinction between science applied to agriculture, and science applied to warfare (as in Laputa) is a moral one; the former improves the human condition, the latter worsens it. Swift implies that science in the context of humane learning is safe, whereas science in the context of abstraction (which is hardly a context at all) is dangerous; it tends, like freethinking, to tyranny. In Glubbdubdrib, where Gulliver sees Aristotle conjured up, he also

> had the honour to have much conversation with Brutus; and was told that his ancestor Junius, Socrates, Epaminondas, Cato the Younger, Sir Thomas More and himself, were perpetually together: A sextumvirate to which all the ages of the world cannot add a seventh.[31]

The voyage to Glubbdubdrib is concerned with the truth of history, and how truth must be seen in the context of history. The sextumvirate above are distinguished by their common opposition to

---

29. Swift, "A Letter to a Young Gentleman," in ibid., p. 484.
30. Swift, *Gulliver's Travels*, in ibid., p. 111.
31. Ibid., p. 167.

tyranny, and it is notable that given Swift's views on Roman Cathol-icism, Thomas More is the only modern in the group.

It is the final book of *Gulliver's Travels* that, in its climactic power, makes Swift most often remembered for a befouled misanthropy (the Yahoos) and a complacent, odious rationalism (the Houyh-nhnms). "The dreary world of the Houyhnhnms was about as good a Utopia as Swift could construct,"[32] wrote Orwell, and others have taken at face value that Swift thinks human beings should live like rational horses. This is not, however, his point. Swift is no more attracted to the society of the Houyhnhnms as a model for human-ity than are countless readers of *Gulliver's Travels*. The book is a sat-ire against the Deists, on the one hand, and the Hobbesians on the other. For Swift, man is neither an animal of pure reason, nor is he a human beast. Gulliver's final response to the Houyhnhnms and the Yahoos, of emulation on the one hand and repulsion on the other, are both signs of one kind of madness: the misanthropy that Swift did not share. That Swift himself was incapable of reason by the time of his death is indirectly assumed to be a further identification with Gulliver. But, *pace* Orwell, Swift did not "go mad." We now assume that he succumbed to a paralytic stroke, senility, and the Menière's Disease from which he suffered for much of his life. But Orwell's grasp of the totalitarian nature of Houyhnhnmland is accurate, even if he misses Swift's satirical point. The society of the Houyhnhnms has a ruling class and an underclass, much like the Party and the Proles in *Nineteen Eighty-Four*, or other scientific dys-topias of the twentieth century, like those of Huxley and Wells. Deism and Hobbesianism are both symptoms of disintegration, the emphasizing of the part in place of the whole. Swift, as opposed to Gulliver, saw the providential dimension of the passions, and could see the limitations of reason without faith. Reason is all the Houyh-nhnms have, and consequently they come short of what man should be as an individual and as a society. For Gulliver to worship reason is to fall into pride, the root of all human misery.

Gulliver's Travels as a whole illustrates, beyond any topical satire,

32. Orwell, op. cit., p. 256.

what F. P. Lock has called Swift's "politics of common sense,"[33] something that implies, in Swift, a balanced view of reason itself. Just as he opposes a disintegrated intellectual specialization in learning, so also he opposes the idea of a special expertise in the political sphere. As Lock puts it:

> In a pamphlet written in 1715, although not published until 1765, Swift returned to the theme of the politics of common sense: "God intending the Government of a Nation in the severall Branches and Subordinations of Power, hath made the Science of Governing sufficiently obvious to common capacities; otherwise the world would be left in a desolate Condition, if great Affairs did always require a great Genius, whereof the most fruitfull Age will hardly produce above three or four in a Nation" (P.W.viii.138). This conviction was to find its way into the original constitution of Lilliput, where "they believe that the common Size of human Understandings, is fitted to make the Management of publick Affairs a Mystery, to be comprehended only by a few Persons of sublime Genius, of which there seldom are three born in an Age" (I.vi.59).[34]

Although Swift believed that those who occupy offices of state should be qualified for what they do, he is clearly opposed to the idea of an élite political class disconnected from the reality of common humanity: this is the political counterpart to the scientism of the Academy of Lagado, and makes for the politics of the flying island. Common sense, on the other hand, makes for limited government in accord with the reality of human nature, and the fallen human condition.

To see Swift as a Christian humanist, it is not necessary to see him as a medievalist, which he clearly was not. (He did, however, disapprove of the plundering of the Church at the Reformation.) As a Tory, especially one close to Robert Harley (the Earl of Oxford) and Henry St. John (Viscount Bolingbroke) there were always suspicions of Jacobitism; after all, the Tories were originally those in the reign of Charles II who defended the royal prerogatives and the

---

33. F. P. Lock, *The Politics of Gulliver's Travels* (Oxford: The Clarendon Press, 1980) p. 123.
34. Ibid., p. 134.

status of the Church of England, and insofar as the Stuart cause was bound up with a defense of the monarchy against the great Whig lords, then Swift could be suspected of Jacobite leanings, as was Johnson after him. But Swift's acceptance of the terms of the 1688 revolution is consistent with his politics of common sense. He was no principled extremist, and always put what really made for better lives of the people—peace, religion, moderation, stability and order—above any abstract idealism. Public debate of religious principles always threatened public order, and Swift avoided it, but his Christian humanism is apparent in his devotion to the social role of the Church of England, and the only government that ever commanded Swift's wholehearted loyalty in his lifetime was the Tory administration of 1710 to 1714, which tried to begin the reversal of post-1688 secularizing trends and establish the closer High Church sympathetic and symbiotic relationship between Church and State. Swift believed in the idea of a constitution of Church and State—an idea that Coleridge, as we shall see in a later chapter, was to revive and elaborate.

Like Johnson, Swift had the neoclassical pessimism (or, should one say, Christian realism) about human life, but Orwell's sense of Swift's "inability to believe that life . . . could be made worth living"[35] is groundless. In a condition where "much is to be endured, and little to be enjoyed," Swift's moral realism is invariably mixed with irony. It is laughter and liberty—that which can only be possessed by a reasonable man, and not by a rationalist—that are to be treasured in this sublunary world. Allan Bloom wrote:

> I do not know about Gulliver, but Swift is surely one of the funniest men who ever lived. His misanthropy is a joke; it is the greatest folly in the world to attempt to improve humanity. That is what it means to understand man. . . . To understand is to accept; *Gulliver's Travels* makes misanthropy ridiculous by showing us the complexity of our nature and thereby teaching us what we must accept.[36]

35. Orwell, op. cit., p. 256.
36. Alan Bloom, "An Outline of *Gulliver's Travels*," in Greenberg and Piper, eds., op. cit., p. 661.

W. B. Yeats, in his poem "The Seven Sages," and in his free version of the epitaph Swift composed for himself, points to the other great theme of Swift's life and works:

> Swift has sailed into his rest;
> Savage indignation there
> Cannot lacerate his breast.
> Imitate him if you dare,
> World-besotted traveller; he
> Served human liberty.[37]

It is of this last word on Swift that we should remind ourselves, as it goes to the heart of what Swift meant, and continues to mean for us. He anticipates Burke in asserting that if liberty is anything to be valued at all, it exists as a consequence of authority rather than in spite of it.

---

37. W. B. Yeats, "Swift's Epitaph," in ibid., p. 277.

4

"Of Man's First Disobedience"
Samuel Johnson and the Whigs

Tory: One who adheres to the antient constitution of the state, and the apostolical hierarchy of the church of England, opposed to a whig.
Whig: The name of a faction.

SAMUEL JOHNSON, Dictionary, 1755

One of the ironies of literary history is that its most compelling and authoritative symbol of common sense—of the strong, imaginative grasp of concrete reality—should have begun his adult life, at the age of twenty, in a state of such intense anxiety and bewildered despair that, at least from his own point of view, it seemed the onset of insanity.

WALTER JACKSON BATE, The Achievement of Samuel Johnson, 1955

DR. JOHNSON WOULD SEEM to many to be the embodiment—large, bullish, and sturdily independent—of traditional, English common sense. In Boswell, we read about the secure confidence of personal judgment with which, for instance, he dismissed Bishop Berkeley's theory of the insubstantiality of matter, by kicking a stone and saying, "I refute it, thus,"[1] and the vignette seems to sum up much of the Johnsonian *oeuvre*: the indication of the four-square reality of human life, upon which only are we able to erect a sound humane discourse in philosophy, politics or letters. It amused the whiggish

---

1. James Boswell, *Life of Johnson*, Vol. I (London: Heron Books, 1960), p. 292.

Macaulay to see this aspect of Johnson in terms of Fielding's caricature of the Tory squire: Johnson's "rants . . . in everything but the
diction, resembled those of Squire Western."[2] Macaulay sees in
Johnson the kind of clever stupidity, the kind that Orwell saw in
Swift and in "Conservatives of our own day—people like Sir Alan
Herbert, Professor G.M. Young, Lord Elton, the Tory Reform Committee or the long line of Catholic apologists from W.H. Mallock
onwards."[3] What Orwell should have seen in Swift, and what
Macaulay refuses to see in Johnson, is the attempt to integrate the
intellect with the whole personality, and in doing so oppose intellectualism.

But there is more than the merely anti-sophistical in Johnson's
kicking the stone. As Chester Chapin has shown, Johnson was sympathetically aware of, later in his life, the Scottish Common Sense
School of philosophy, that of Thomas Reid and James Beattie. In
opposition to Berkeley and Hume, in whom Lockean empiricism
had led to the doubt of everything (matter in Berkeley's case, and
truth in Hume's), Johnson affirmed the existence of matter, or
truth, external to the mind's perception of it. Beattie had been led to
examine the whole of philosophy back to Descartes, and came to
believe that the whole tradition

> contains within it a fatal flaw—the mistaken assumption that
> "ideas" are "the only objects of thought," which leads finally to the
> culminating skepticism of Hume in which we have a situation
> where "body and spirit, cause and effect, time and space, to which
> we were wont to ascribe an existence independent of our thought,
> are all turned out of existence."[4]

The "Reid-Beattie critique," says Chapin, to which Johnson adhered,
asserted

---

2. Thomas Babington Macaulay, *Critical and Historical Essays*, Vol. II (London:
Dent, 1907), p. 553.
3. George Orwell, "Politics v. Literature: An Examination of *Gulliver's Travels*,"
in *Collected Essays, Journalism and Letters*, Vol. 4 (London: Penguin, 1968), p. 245.
4. C. Chapin, "Samuel Johnson and the Scottish Common Sense School," *The
Eighteenth Century*, vol. 20, no. 1, 1979, p. 53ff.

that all men, or at least the great majority, perceive certain truths which, according to Beattie, "are known by their own evidence" and that unless these truths or "first principles be taken for granted, there can be neither reason nor reasoning."[5]

Reid and Beattie also distinguish reason from common sense. Reason, Beattie says, is

that faculty which enables us, from relations or ideas that are known, to investigate such as are unknown; and without which we never could proceed in the discovery of truth a single step beyond first principles or intuitive axioms.[6]

Common sense, on the other hand, is that

power of mind which perceives truth, or commands belief, not by progressive argumentation, but by an instantaneous, instinctive, and irresistible impulse; derived neither from education nor from habit, but from nature; acting independently on our will, whenever its object is presented, according to an established law, and therefore properly called Sense; and acting in a similar manner upon all, or at least, upon a great majority of mankind, and therefore properly called Common Sense.[7]

That which is self-evident can be neither proved nor disproved by reason or logic, so despite the impregnable rational argument of Berkeley that matter does not exist, the argument is irrelevant.

On the other hand, although Johnson believed in the existence of matter, he was opposed to the philosophic determinism of Joseph Priestley,[8] who attempted to show that everything is matter; as Chapin says, "Johnson adheres to the traditional view in which mind, soul, and spirit are sharply distinguished from matter or body."[9] Materialism tends to fatalistic determinism, and Johnson affirmed the freedom of the will, as did Beattie and Reid. Just as the

5. Ibid., pp. 55–56.
6. Ibid., p. 56.
7. Ibid., p. 56.
8. Priestley's is an early example of scientistic thought. Johnson gave Priestley credit for his scientific experiments, but objected to his extension of the scientific method into the sphere of mind.
9. Ibid., p. 51.

existence of matter is evident to common sense, so is our free will. As Reid put it,

> we have, by our constitution a natural conviction or belief that we act freely—a conviction so early, so universal, and so necessary in most of our rational operations, that it must be the result of our constitution, and the work of Him that made us.[10]

A belief in the freedom of the will, a belief to which Johnson adhered in the face of all philosophical attempts to disprove or qualify it, was central to his Christian humanism. Chapin quotes Johnson in his *Sermon V*:

> If God should, by a particular exertion of omnipotence, hinder murder or oppression, no man could then be a murderer or an oppressor, because he would be withheld from it by a superior power; but then that power which prevented crimes would destroy virtue; for virtue is the consequence of choice. Men would be no longer rational, or would be rational to no purpose, because their actions would not be the result of free-will, determined by moral motives; but the settled and predestined motions of a machine impelled by necessity.[11]

The use of the word "machine" makes Johnson's comment particularly resonant in our age. To what extent is our sense of our moral freedom qualified the more we inhabit a world dominated by machines? To what extent do we in fact become less free to act according to our created human nature? These are questions at the heart of Christian humanist responses to modernity, and especially evident in the twentieth century, but as Johnson's words suggest, they are also implicit in the materialist and deterministic thought, and Christian responses to it, of the eighteenth century.

The mind of Johnson, so penetrating and unencumbered by the merely sentimental or the subjective, is as substantial as was his physical frame. But his substantiality and compass obscure the extraordinary vicissitudes, both mental and physical, of Johnson's life, against which his firmly orthodox and authoritative outlook

10. Ibid., p. 58.
11. Ibid., pp. 59–60.

should be measured. The tensions within Johnson: between powerful activity and guilty sloth; between external authority and personal responsibility; between imagined perfection and ugly reality, all made him aware of the need for order, patterns and rules, all which Walter Jackson Bate has shown. The formality of the Johnsonian persona, the lapidary firmness of his speech and writing, the submission to the order of Church and State even when their legitimacy was highly compromised, provide a necessary bulwark for him against the inherent tendency of both individual and society towards decay. Within the structures of human life, whether they be personal habits, religious observance or (by analogy) the edifice of state and government, the free human being may, by God's grace, constantly remake himself. As Johnson put it in *The Rambler* (No.7):

> The great art ... of piety, and the end for which all the rites of religion seem to be instituted, is the perpetual renovation of the motives to virtue.[12]

Johnson is profoundly skeptical of any forms of determinism that would compromise the freedom of the individual will to overcome, mainly through religious observance, the affliction of a human state wherein there is "much to be endured and little to be enjoyed."[13] His conclusive conviction that, "we know our will is free, and there's an end on it"[14] underpins all his religious and political principles.

The essentials of Johnson's outlook, what has been called his pessimism but should be rather termed his realism, are present, most clearly perhaps, in his poetry. In "London," he gives a Juvenalian picture of the state of Walpole's England, devoid as it was of literary patronage, the scene of Johnson's struggle to earn money on Grub Street, a place where

> This mournful truth is everywhere confessed
> SLOW RISES WORTH, BY POVERTY DEPRESSED.[15]

12. Samuel Johnson, *The Works of Samuel Johnson, LLD,* ed. A. Murphy (London, 1792), p. 45.

13. Samuel Johnson, *Rasselas,* in *The Oxford Authors: Samuel Johnson,* ed. D. Greene (Oxford: OUP, 1984), p. 355.

14. Boswell, Vol. I. op. cit., p. 363.

15. Johnson, "London," Greene, op. cit., p. 6.

"The Vanity of Human Wishes," too, is a Juvenalian satire on the state of British political life, but is, moreover, a consideration of the problems inherent in ambition, and the evanescence of security. Human life is unstable, fluid, and we are unable to resist the debilitation of age or the oppressions of disease:

> From Marlborough's eyes the streams of dotage flow,
> And Swift expires a driveller and a show.[16]

Surveying mankind in its uniform entirety, "from China to Peru," the poet sees man in all his pride and pomp, his ability and scope, and shows how failure and dissolution are as inherent in the exponents of public glory as they are in all men. But this is not the last word, for Johnson sees human misery in Christian terms:

> Pour forth thy fervours for a healthful mind,
> Obedient passions, and a will resigned;
> For love, which scarce collective man can fill;
> For patience sovereign o'er transmuted ill;
> For faith, that panting for a happier seat
> Counts death kind Nature's signal of retreat:
> These goods for man the laws of heaven ordain,
> These goods he grants, who grants the power to gain;
> With these celestial wisdom calms the mind,
> And makes the happiness she does not find.[17]

These final lines of the poem echo similar petitions in the Prayers and Meditations, some of the finest religious English outside the Prayer Book, and summarize Johnson's settled, and practically life-long, response to what the Anglican Prayer Book beautifully calls the "changes and chances of this fleeting world."

These moral virtues are also present in what is perhaps Johnson's most remarkable poem, all the more moving in eschewing any sentimentality towards his dead friend, one of the curious group of outcasts to whom Johnson extended his hospitality. In the "Lines on the Death of Dr. Robert Levet," hope is seen in terms of an imprisoning mine of toil and darkness:

16. Ibid., p. 20.
17. Ibid., p. 21.

> Condemned to Hope's delusive mine,
> As on we toil from day to day,
> By sudden blasts, or slow decline,
> Our social comforts drop away.[18]

Within the real slums of London, and the poverty with which Johnson himself was so intimately acquainted, the "unqualified" Dr. Levet, "Obscurely wise and coarsely kind,"[19] ministered to the poor, becoming, "Of every friendless name the friend."[20] It is again in Christian terms that the value of Levet's life is affirmed: "sure the Eternal Master found / The single talent well employed."[21] Especially, Levet lacked the marks of pride to which Johnson was very sensitive:

> No summons mocked by chill delay
> No petty gain disdained by pride.[22]

Under the discriminating eye of Johnson's keen moral judgment, we are brought back to the Christian virtues of faith, hope (in God) and charity, as the only recourse for fallen human nature, and through which we conform ourselves to what Johnson calls in *The Adventurer*, No. 74,

> the everlasting and invariable principles of moral and religious truth, from which no change of external circumstances can justify any deviation.[23]

It is Johnson's own grasp of the principles of human nature that makes him, *pace* Macaulay, still among the most perspicacious of the critics of Shakespeare, and it is in the Preface to Johnson's edition of the plays that he makes some of his most important statements on art and nature. For example,

---

18. Ibid., p. 35.
19. Ibid.
20. Ibid.
21. Ibid., p. 36.
22. Ibid.
23. Johnson, *The Works of Samuel Johnson, LLD*, Vol. 4 (Oxford: Talboys and Wheeler, 1825), p. 52.

Shakespeare is above all writers, at least above all modern writers, the poet of nature; the poet that holds up to his readers a faithful mirror of manners and of life.[24]

The mirror image, though hardly original, is significant: it implies an objective human nature against which art must be judged as successful or not. Shakespeare's characters are

the genuine progeny of common humanity, such as the world will always supply, and observation will always find.[25]

Thus, perhaps, we may understand how Shakespeare appeals, more than any other author, to different times and places. The permanence that Johnson sees in moral and religious truth, he sees also in the truth to nature of Shakespeare:

Nothing can please many, and please long, but just representations of general nature. Particular manners can be known to few, and therefore few only can judge how nearly they are copied. The irregular combinations of fanciful invention may delight a while, by that novelty of which the common satiety of life sends us all in quest; but the pleasures of sudden wonder are soon exhausted, and the mind can only repose on the stability of truth.[26]

The Johnsonian realism always consists in a desire to "see things as they are" as a secure basis for sanity, good sense and possible consolation. Further, it is in perception rather than in vision, of the apprehension of the object as preceding the formation of an idea, that makes up Johnson's good sense. As Boswell reports, of a visit to the Pantheon on Johnson's Scottish tour:

Sir Adam [Ferguson] suggested, that luxury corrupts a people, and destroys the spirit of liberty. JOHNSON: "Sir, that is all visionary."[27]

"Visionary" is pejorative for Johnson, and he does not share Ferguson's suspicion for the harmless public amusements of which the Scotsman speaks here, a puritanical suspicion that leads him into the

24. Johnson, ed. Greene, op. cit., p. 421.
25. Ibid.
26. Ibid., p. 420.
27. Boswell, *Life of Johnson* (Boston, MA: Carter, Hendee and Co., 1832), p. 290.

whiggish ideas that Johnson criticizes later in their conversation, to which we shall return.

Johnson is always skeptical of attempts to make rules against the usage of nature. We see this in his criticism of Shakespeare and in the guiding ideas of his *Dictionary*, outlined in the Preface. Although Shakespeare ignores the classical rules of dramatic composition, Johnson excuses him readily: "there is always an appeal open from criticism to nature,"[28] which is the ultimate authority in judging of the success of poetry: the Sabbath is made for man, not man for the Sabbath. Thoroughly familiar with the rules of classical criticism, Johnson is aware of their limitations as canons of judgment; there is a freedom in Johnson's mind that arises out of his knowledge and experience, a freedom schooled and earned. His rejection of an absolutism in man-made rules of criticism reflects his rejection of all determinism; human life involves a constant exercise of free will in the face of certain facts of existence: change and decay, the exigencies of chance, the contumely of power. Johnson's actions, *vis à vis* the language in the compilation of his *Dictionary*, also illustrate the character of his conservatism: it arises from a creative relationship between authority on the one hand, and nature on the other, to be contrasted with the absolutism of the Academies, such as that of the French:

> If an academy should be established for the cultivation of our stile, which I, who can never wish to see dependence multiplied, hope the spirit of English liberty will hinder or destroy.... If the changes that we fear be thus irresistible, what remains but to acquiesce with silence, as in the other surmountable distresses of humanity? It remains that we retard what we cannot repel, that we palliate what we cannot cure. Life may be lengthened by care, though death cannot be ultimately defeated: tongues, like governments, have a natural tendency to degeneration; we have long preserved our constitution, let us make some struggles for our language. In hope of giving longevity to that which its own nature forbids to be immortal, I have devoted this book, the labour of years, to the honour of my country....[29]

28. Johnson, ed. Greene, op. cit., p. 424.
29. Ibid., p. 326.

A dictionary exists as a counterweight to the natural and necessary movements of language, which Johnson in typical neoclassical fashion sees as a process of decay. He is doubtful about any kind of change:

> Change, says Hooker, is not made without inconvenience, even from worse to better. There is in constancy and stability a general and lasting advantage, which will always overbalance the slow improvements of gradual correction.[30]

Thus, although it is Johnson's aim to give some stability to the relationship between language and the fixed objective ideas that words denote, he is under no illusions about the extent of authority over the shifting movements of nature.

Against the background of his essentially religious cast of mind, it is mainly as poet, critic, and lexicographer that Johnson's conservatism is, perhaps, best evinced. However, it would be a mistake to think that Johnson was little interested in politics, even if he was primarily a religious thinker, and his guiding philosophy moral rather than political. His political writings are not inconsiderable either in quantity or quality, and Johnson frequently makes allusions to politics even when is writing primarily of letters. Certainly, Johnson was skeptical of general schemes and visions of political amelioration:

> BOSWELL: "So Sir, you laugh at schemes of political improvement."
>
> JOHNSON: "Why, Sir, most schemes of political improvement are very laughable things."[31]

This and other like observations arise from prudence rather than cynicism, and quite possibly concealed what had necessarily to be hidden in Johnson's positive political beliefs, although in this we can only speculate. His Jacobite sympathies, however deep they may have been at different times in his life, could have been at no point openly discussed, either in conversation or in print. The terms of his political discourse had to be the settled and established diver-

30. Ibid., p. 310.
31. Boswell, op. cit., p. 266.

gences of opinion set between the poles of government or opposition, Whig or Tory. But Johnson's Toryism, as expressed for instance in the *Dictionary* definition, is broad and inclusive, resting on the inherited constitution of Church and State, and the "apostolical" authority of the Church of England, rather than any narrow adherence to party, which is his definition of a Whig. Within this broad outline, however, may be discerned a sympathy for Catholicism (broadly defined so as to include the Anglican branch), an abhorrence of licentious or ignorant criticism of established authorities (including the Church of Rome), and personalism. This last entails a respect for the principle of authority acting within the personal freedom and responsibility of, for example, kings and bishops, an authority of persons rather than ideas.[32] Johnson's skepticism for the "visionary" is connected with his consistent opposition to cant—in the *Dictionary* definition, a species of chatter. His deflation of the cant of "patriotism" anticipates Burke's later and more developed antagonism to "the rights of man," and proceeds from a similar grasp of a "good" made specious by its deracination from nature.

Johnson's vigorous adherence to the principle of monarchy has been taken as evidence of an absolutist view of kingship, but he denied the divine right of kings as another abstraction. Nonetheless, for Johnson the principle of subordination persisted. When he conversed privately with George III, he said, memorably, "it was not for me to bandy civilities with my sovereign."[33] The questionable legitimacy of the Hanoverians did not dissolve the claims of authority; the reasons, apart from the moral, were constitutional. As a Tory, according to Johnson's own definition, the authoritative claims on him were historical rather than abstract, proceeding from, firstly, the constitution and, secondly, the Established Church. He could no more give his allegiance to a speculative theory of the divine right of kings than he could to any other abstract scheme of government. James II was "a very good king,"[34] and King William,

---

32. Cf. J. H. Newman: "Toryism is loyalty to persons," whereas liberalism is loyalty to abstract ideas. (Letter to the Duke of Norfolk)

33. Boswell, Heron Books, Vol. I, p. 336.

34. Ibid., p. 543.

"one of the most worthless scoundrels that ever existed,"[35] but James went "too far"[36]—presumably farther than the constitution allowed him, and the claims of the Church of England had to be accommodated within the constitution that also housed the monarchy. Johnson found much satisfactory in the reign of Charles II, principally in ecclesiastical matters.

The other part of Johnson's definition of "Tory" is "opposed to a Whig." Whiggery, or "whiggism" in Johnson's usage, involves fracturing the constitutional framework, and departing from the authority of revealed religious doctrine. Johnson once paid, according to Boswell, the "great compliment" of calling a young lady, in her Tory uncle's hearing, a Jacobite—much to the uncle's offence. Johnson, we might suppose with harmless if rather mischievous humor, explained himself thus:

> A Jacobite, Sir, believes in the divine right of Kings. He that believes in the divine right of Kings believes in a Divinity. A Jacobite believes in the divine right of Bishops. He that believes in the divine right of Bishops believes in the divine authority of the Christian religion. Therefore, Sir, a Jacobite is neither an Atheist nor a Deist. That cannot be said of a Whig; for *Whiggism is a negation of all principle.* [Johnson's emphasis][37]

On another more considered occasion, Johnson observed, however, that

> A wise Tory and a wise Whig, I believe, will agree. Their principles are the same, though their modes of thinking are different. A high Tory makes government unintelligible: it is lost in the clouds. A violent Whig makes it impracticable: he is for allowing so much liberty to every man that there is not power enough to govern any man. The prejudice of the Tory is for establishment; the prejudice of the Whig is for innovation. A Tory does not wish to give more real power to Government; but that Government should have more reverence. Then they differ as to the church. The Tory is not for giving more legal power to the Clergy, but wishes they should

35. Ibid.
36. Ibid., p. 267.
37. Ibid.

have a more considerable influence, founded on the opinion of mankind: the Whig is for limiting and watching them with a narrow jealousy.[38]

Johnson's own views may be distinguished from the "high Tory," but should be identified with the rest of the description above. But in what "principles" are a wise Tory and a wise Whig identical? If we take, as examples, a wise Tory and a wise Whig to be Johnson and Burke respectively, we would say that they both see the constitution as according with nature, and providing the framework within which political life continues from age to age. Their modes of thinking might be different; they might differ on particular issues; they might disagree over matters of fact; they might emphasize one thing more than another. But within the bounds of their similar principles, they remain sane. Johnson and Burke did not agree over the scope of Crown influence, or on the rights of the American colonists; there is more emphasis on expediency and prudence in Burke the practical politician, more on skepticism and authority in Johnson the critic. But when we compare them with any of their contemporaries who advocated disintegration within the Empire or within Europe, we can see that they are more alike than different. It is intriguing to think what Johnson, who died in 1784, would have made of the French Revolution, and Burke's *Reflections* upon it, but it cannot be reasonably imagined that Johnson would have dissented from any of Burke's essential conclusions.

To return to Johnson's conversation, in 1772, with Sir Adam Ferguson, as reported by Boswell:

SIR ADAM: "But, Sir, in the British constitution it is surely of importance to keep up a spirit in the people, so as to preserve a balance against the crown."

JOHNSON: "Sir, I perceive you are a vile Whig.—Why all this childish jealousy of the power of the crown? The crown has not power enough. When I say that all governments are alike, I consider that in no government power can be abused long. Mankind will not bear it. If a sovereign oppresses his people to a great

38. Ibid., Vol. II, p. 396.

√ degree, they will rise and cut off his head. There is a remedy in
human nature against tyranny, that will keep us safe under every
form of government."[39]

The appeal to nature here is the last resort through which the balanced constitution corrects itself, and shows that Johnson presumes
the existence of some capacity for a general and settled communal
judgment, which would act in rare, extreme situations as the final
authority in the state. "The opinion of mankind" as we have seen,
also has its place in the religious establishment. But these are not
circumstances that Johnson expects to see. Normally, authority acts
through established means, through personal agents. In Johnson's
judgment of the state of the balance of powers, the crown is too
weak, presumably because it was locked into the Whig oligarchy
concerned only for its own power, hiding its self-interest beneath a
fog of cant.

It is principally against cant that the best of Johnson's political
writings are directed, whether it is the cry of "liberty" by the supporters of Wilkes; of "patriotism" by every disgruntled group of
political opposition; of "no taxation without representation" by the
American colonists; of "national honour" by the opposition to Lord
North's government in the matter of the Falkland Islands in 1770.
The prevailing tone is polemical, and the common underlying
theme is of the pretense of principled motives acting for the good of
the whole country, which Johnson seeks to reveal as narrowly parti-
san efforts to set different parts of the political whole at one
another's throats. In "The Patriot" (1774), Johnson attacks the disconnection between words and actions, of "patriotic" rhetoric used
to help opposition politicians to a place, and then forgotten. Allusions to Milton are significant. The epigraph to "The Patriot," from
a sonnet Milton wrote against his detractors, and a not uncommon
text in eighteenth century pamphlets, is particularly appropriate,
however, to Johnson's outlook:

> They bawl for freedom in their senseless mood
> Yet still revolt when truth would set them free

39. Ibid., Vol. I, p. 424.

> License they mean, when they cry liberty,
> For who loves that must first be wise and good.[40]

The resonance of the concluding paragraph of the piece is also capped with a return to Milton, this time to *Paradise Lost*, and a comparison of the "patriots" to the anti-hero of the poem. They are, like Satan, "'raised by merit to this bad eminence,' [and] arrogate to themselves the name of Patriots."[41] Milton's great epic picture of how pride distorts language and politics, particularly in Books I and II of *Paradise Lost*, evidently resonates deeply in Johnson's mind. The lines to which he alludes come at the beginning of Book II:

> High on a throne of royal state that far
> Outshone the wealth of Ormus and of Ind,
> Or where the gorgeous East with richest hand
> Show'rs on her kings barbaric pearl and gold,
> Satan exalted sat, by merit raised
> To that bad eminence.[42]

This parody of monarchy opens the debate in Pandemonium, the infernal city, to consider what action the fallen angels should take, like idealistic revolutionaries, against the "throne and monarchy of God," after their expulsion from heaven. The conclusion is decided already by Satan, the debate merely a show of discussion, and the reasoning of the speakers partial, as it is bound to be in those who have separated themselves from the Reason (*Logos*) of the created order. The mock-debate, like Satan's temptation of Eve later in the poem, provides a classical example of political and moral cant.

Johnson could make use of such allusions because he would not have disagreed with the Christian premises of Milton's poem, a fact that makes a reading of Johnson's later *Life of Milton* particularly interesting. Johnson abhorred all that Milton defended in the Parliamentarian cause, and yet, like the wise Tory and the wise Whig, they could agree about first principles: the chain of meaning proceeding

---

40. Samuel Johnson: *Political Writings*, ed. D.J. Greene (Indianapolis, IN: Liberty Fund, 1977), p. 389.

41. Ibid., p. 400.

42. Milton, *Paradise Lost*, Book II, I. 1–6.

from God, through reason and nature, to angels and men. Johnson could also agree with Milton on the fatal consequences for the individual and society when meaning is vitiated by pride—the first sin, both in history and in theology, the primeval fault from which all evil proceeds. Johnson's understanding of nature and reason may be closely identified with Milton's, even though the political conclusions they drew from that understanding were so widely divergent. The idea of nature in Hobbes and Locke failed to make any impression on Johnson's traditional, Christian conception derived from the Scholastics and Aristotle.

For Johnson, the devil was the first Whig. Faction is, at bottom, a refusal to occupy a creative, positive role in the social order that conforms to nature, and involves humility and obedience. The appeal to nature had become highly problematical once the idea had become confused by Hobbes and Locke, and all sides could make easy appeals to an increasingly nebulous idea, but Johnson does not eschew the word altogether. He refers to nature at the beginning of *Taxation No Tyranny*:

> In all the parts of human knowledge, whether terminating in science merely speculative, or operating upon life private or civil, are admitted some fundamental principles or common axioms, which being generally received are little doubted, and being little doubted have been rarely proved. Of these gratuitous and acknowledged truths it is often the fate to become less evident by endeavours to explain them, however necessary such endeavours may be made by the misapprehensions of absurdity or the sophistries of interest.[43]

Here also is the problem of specifying principles, and why we more often remember Johnson for his conclusions: common sense begins in some preverbal norms of the human mind that the reason (understood narrowly as the ratiocinative faculty) does not entirely illuminate. It is easier to agree or disagree than say why we do so. It has always been believed that love of country is a good thing, says Johnson, and here he concurs in the feeling of patriotism if not in

---

43. Greene, op. cit., p. 411.

76

the cant. But there are many who believe that Britain has no right to tax the colonies against their will, colonies that are a part of one political community. Again, Johnson argues from nature:

> These antipatriotic prejudices [of those who support the colonists] are the abortion of Folly impregnated by Faction, which being produced against the standing order of Nature, have not strength sufficient for long life.[44]

He takes up an idea from a speech by Chatham, and looks at all the American colonists as Whigs:

> ... the continent of North America contains three millions, not of men merely, but of Whigs, of Whigs fierce for liberty, and disdainful of dominion; that they multiply with the fecundity of their own rattle-snakes, so that every quarter of a century doubles their numbers.[45]

The comparison with snakes dimly echoes the metamorphosis of the fallen angels in Book X of *Paradise Lost*. In breaking from the mother country, Johnson sees the rebel colonists as rupturing the whole to which they belong by nature, for the sake of pride, greed and selfishness. When the colonists and their supporters appeal to "The laws of Nature, the rights of humanity, the faith of charters, the encroachments of usurpation,"[46] they are abusing reason, lost in "The madness of independence."[47]

Johnson's real antipathy towards the Americans turns on this cardinal point: his moral objection to the hypocrisy of their cries for liberty. Not all laws are well made; sometimes they must be revised, and their revision does not depend on the consent of every individual subject, or group. When legal "rights" support unnatural liberties, they have no meaning, no justice, and no unalterable character—all which depend on conformity to natural law. Johnson doubted whether the Americans were in a position to warn Englishmen that their rights were threatened by the encroachments of the crown:

44. Ibid., p. 412.
45. Ibid., p. 414.
46. Ibid., p. 418.
47. Ibid., p. 438.

We are told, that the subjection of Americans may tend to the diminution of our own liberties: an event which none but the most perspicacious politicians are able to foresee. If slavery be thus fatally contagious, how is it that we hear the loudest yelps for liberty among the drivers of negroes?[48]

Johnson detested slavery, and saw it as being against the natural law: he "doubted whether [it] can ever be supposed the natural condition of man."[49] Boswell relates that

When in company with some very grave men at Oxford, his toast was, "Here's to the next insurrection of the negroes in the West Indies."[50]

Thus, the "rights" of slave owners are as meaningless as is the "right" to abortion for many of us nowadays. Laws cannot be legitimate when they violate the foundation of law itself. Johnson was skeptical, cynical and contemptuous of those who used the language of rights and liberties, secured by power against authority, for their own selfish and inordinate gain.

Johnson understood, partly from the hard school of personal tribulation, that the health of the individual person and the whole community required the vigorous exercise of free powers within an order sanctioned by God and nature. The immense authority that Johnson himself personifies illustrates the creative tension that comes from a free act of obedience to an authority conformed to the natural order. Johnson's own authority is highly personal, and occasionally idiosyncratic, despite his constant attempts to avoid it. His sense of free will and personal responsibility, extending from himself to others, was derived from a profound sense of a sovereign order outside himself, and under which true freedom abides. In a similar way, and for similar reasons, personal experience taught Johnson what G.K. Chesterton also learned and conveyed: that orthodoxy is the last best hope for the free man, and sanity, as well as freedom, is the consequence of orthodoxy.

48. Ibid., p. 454.
49. Boswell, *The Life of Samuel Johnson, LL.D.*, Vol. III (Oxford: Talboys and Wheeler, 1826), p. 181.
50. Ibid.

5

"The Decent Drapery of Life"

The Unity of Nature and Art
in Edmund Burke

Polixenes:	Wherefore gentle maiden Do you neglect them?
Perdita:	For I have heard it said There is an art which in their piedness shares With great creating nature.
Polixenes:	Say there be; Yet nature is made better by no mean But nature makes that mean: so, over that art, Which you say adds to nature, is an art That nature makes.............. The art itself is nature.

The Winter's Tale, IV, iv

Art is man's nature.
BURKE, *An Appeal from the New to the Old Whigs*, 1791

IN HER REJECTION OF gillyflowers and carnations, because their bold streaks look artificial, as if painted onto the petals, Shakespeare emphasizes Perdita's innocence, in the context of his rehearsal of the Renaissance debate on the relationship between art and nature. Perdita's chastity, however, verges on the puritanical, and she is corrected by Polixenes, who also refers in this scene to the art of horticulture, particularly in the grafting of "gentler scions" onto "wilder stock" (*The Winter's Tale*, IV, iv). Shakespeare makes Perdita submit to Polixenes' argument, but the Puritan suspicion of art to which she gives voice was later to emerge in the form of Rousseau and his school. They believed that, if left to itself, and unpolluted by the arts of civilization, nature would produce in the society of man the natural paradise. As the English Puritans emphasized, art is all lies, and leads, especially in the theatre, to moral corruption. Shakespeare had his revenge on them in Malvolio, and we know on which side Edmund Burke fought. For Burke, Rousseau was "the insane Socrates of the National Assembly"[1] who inspired the attempt of the French revolutionaries to return to Year Zero—the "state of nature," or the mythical country in which the state has withered away, and the approach to which has been littered ever since with corpses, in France, in Russia, in China, in Cambodia. At its heart is the false, and ultimately homicidal, separation of art and nature.

Burke's first major publication was *A Vindication of Natural Society* (1756), a satire on the "state of nature" school of Bolingbroke, in whom the ideas of John Locke were changing into the naturalism that was to inspire the English late eighteenth century radicals associated with William Godwin, Percy Bysshe Shelley, Mary Wollstonecraft, and Thomas Paine. Burke's articulation of the argument was almost too well done. Many of the first readers missed the satire, and Godwin remarked painfully, "the evils of the existing political institutions are displayed with incomparable force of reasoning and luster of eloquence, while the intention was to show that these evils were to be considered as trivial."[2] Godwin's misunderstanding of Burke's purpose is at bottom a misunderstanding of Burke's traditional, classical-Christian idea of nature, which Godwin, and the other radicals, replaced with a much straitened paradigm that failed to reflect the real complexity of human life. Their simplification of "Nature," and its guiding spirit of "Reason," is very well articulated by the persona that Burke adopts in his *Vindication*:

1. Burke, *The Writings and Speeches of Edmund Burke*, Vol. IV (New York, NY: Cosimo, Inc., 2008), p. 26.
2. See F.P. Lock, *Edmund Burke: Vol. I: 1730–1784* (Oxford: Clarendon Press, 1998), pp. 85–86.

But unhappily for us, in proportion as we have deviated from the plain Rule of our Nature, and turned our Reason against itself, in that Proportion have we increased the Follies and Miseries of Mankind. The more deeply we penetrate into the Labyrinth of Art, the further we find ourselves from those Ends for which we entered it. This has happened in almost every Species of Artificial Society, and in all times.[3]

In a later preface, Burke had to make clear that far from actually believing this, he considered it the "fairy-land of philosophy," a phrase that points us to the true origin of "natural society" in myth and art, rather than in history. The irony that their ruling idea was a product of art rather than nature seems to have been lost on the naturalistic school, but is in a sense the spring of Burke's satire. The notion of an "artificial society," constituted by a body of positive law, ceremonial religion and complex political constitutions, that was intrinsically rather than contingently corrupt, was not an idea that Burke ever held, even as a large portion of his public life was engaged in fighting real corruption. Burke knew, however, that the corruption was of man's original nature, not his art *per se*, even if that art could become corrupt.

Burke's knowledge and understanding of law was profound. In 1750, not long before the *Vindication* appeared, Burke had arrived in London from Ireland, and began to study law at the Middle Temple. Although he decided to discontinue his formal study of the law, in favor of a literary and political career, his writings and speeches show it is fundamental to his outlook. As Peter J. Stanlis has shown, Burke's conception of law was rooted in the natural law tradition, and as with Thomas More, English common law informed Burke's prudential understanding of natural law. As Stanlis puts it:

Burke's understanding of English common law is pertinent in determining his conception of the Natural Law, because unlike many writers on jurisprudence during the eighteenth century, Burke never treated the Natural Law merely as an abstract code of ethics perceived directly by the naked reason. To Burke the spirit

3. Edmund Burke, *A Vindication of Natural Society*, ed. F. Pagano (Indianapolis, IN: Liberty Fund, 1982), p. 72.

of the Natural Law was embodied in the rules of equity which governed English common law, and was transmitted through legal precedents and prescription. Although Burke by no means identified English common law and the Natural Law, he used his knowledge of both to illuminate their close reciprocal relationship.[4]

The *Vindication*, as a satire on a false understanding of how and why civilization involves corruption, should be seen against the background of Burke's traditional Christian humanism, in which the natural law governs the conception of man in society, rather than in a later, and secular, conception of nature.

An early example of Burke's sense of the arts of civilization gone awry is the later *Tract on the Popery Laws* (1765). As with Swift, it is in Ireland that Burke's sense of injustice is fostered. In the case of the Penal Laws passed in Ireland after the victory of William of Orange over the Jacobite cause, the arts of government and law-making, both so necessary to the promotion of the just and happy society, have become a perverse mechanism of oppression. Legislation calculated to exclude the majority of the community from civil and political rights is, Burke tells us, a misuse of law, which exists to declare rights that subsist in our God-given created nature. Burke's argument from nature is so explicit here that we can almost understand why so many of his contemporaries, not to say subsequent readers, mistakenly see in the later works a reversal of his principles, a movement from a "liberal" concern for the oppressed, to a "conservative" defense of authority. However, Burke's defense of rights is grounded in a "nature" different from the chimera of Rousseau and his school, who mistook the handiwork for the Maker. It is a nature of order and beauty, consonant with the art of a personal God:

> [The people] have no right to make a law prejudicial to the whole community, even though the delinquents in making such an act should be themselves the chief sufferers by it; because it would be made against the principle of a superior law, which is not in the power of any community, or of the whole race of man, to alter—I mean the will of Him who gave us our nature, and in giving

4. Peter J. Stanlis, *Edmund Burke and the Natural Law* (Ann Arbor: University of Michigan Press, 1965), p. 38.

impressed an invariable law upon it. It would be hard to point out any error more truly subversive of all the order and beauty, of all the peace and happiness of human society, than the position, that any body of men have a right to make what laws they please—or that laws can derive any authority from their institution merely, and independent of the quality of the subject matter.[5]

Burke is here writing in the context of the Penal Laws, but it could be in the context of the French Revolution; both are at variance with his insights into the workings of natural law, which in turn is at variance with the pantheistic "Nature" of the radicals.

The hostility to art, a characteristic not only of the radicals of the eighteenth century, but of fundamentalists and extremists of all stripes before and since, habitually goes hand in hand with political despotism, even as it uses the clichés of freedom and liberty. The Burkean political philosophy, however, is interpenetrated by art, and is one of the few examples of political thought that rises to the level of great literature, most notably in the *Reflections on the Revolution in France* (1790). Indeed, as F. P. Lock reminds us, "Burke's earliest ambitions were literary,"[6] he wanted to become a poet; and his *Philosophical Enquiry into the Origin of our Ideas of the Sublime and Beautiful* (1757) had an enormous influence on the late eighteenth- and early nineteenth-century understanding, and artistic treatment, of the sublime. The *Philosophical Enquiry* is characterized by the author's tentative essay into something that he recognizes as essentially mysterious and resistant of systematic theory—that is, the workings of the human mind. Examples are drawn from both art (especially the poetry of Milton) and life in a method that is empirical rather than abstract, as were the "rules" of neoclassical criticism. Burke's conclusions signal a departure from the neoclassical schema, that Samuel Johnson had also found wanting as a critical method. What Burke does have in common with the neoclassicals, however, is an assumption of the universality and uniformity of human nature.

5. Edmund Burke, *Tract on the Popery Laws*, in *The Best of Burke: Selected Writings and Speeches of Edmund Burke*, ed. Peter J. Stanlis (Washington, DC: Regnery, 1963), p. 257.

6. Lock, op. cit., p. 91.

This is announced at the very beginning of the *Enquiry*, in the "Introduction on Taste":

> On a superficial view, we may seem to differ very widely from each other in our reasonings, and no less in our pleasures: but notwithstanding this difference, which I think to be rather apparent than real, it is probable that the standard of both reason and Taste is the same in all human creatures.[7]

A good deal of Burke's analysis of the workings of taste, or how we respond in feelings to natural or artistic objects, is physiological. He discusses, for instance, how the eyes and other sense organs react to sensory phenomena, such as light and darkness, causing variations in our sensations of pain or pleasure. From the outset, Burke is keen to avoid over-simplifications, to move towards definitions on the basis of empirical knowledge, rather than to begin with limiting definitions, and the interplay between what he calls the sublime and what he calls the beautiful is ultimately mysterious. None the less, we can resolve under the heading of the sublime those things which tend to cause painful sensations, especially terror, such as obscurity, power, privation, vastness, infinity, loudness, and bitterness. Beauty on the other hand, is not so much a question of good proportion, as in neoclassical criticism, but that which creates feelings of love. Thus it is clear that in his *Enquiry* Burke is considering the mysterious workings not only of the mind, but of the universe, such that his many examples of the sublime drawn from Milton's *Paradise Lost* are especially appropriate and revealing. Moreover, it is his insights into the nature of the sublime and the beautiful that give him his special authority on the upheavals of the French Revolution, an authority that is even visionary and prophetic when we consider how early in its process he wrote.

There is an instructive contrast to be made between Burke's approach to the Revolution, on the basis of a traditional and subtle understanding of human nature, and the response of the naturalistic radicals such as Thomas Paine and Mary Wollstonecraft, both of

---

7. Edmund Burke, *A Philosophical Enquiry into the Origin of Our Ideas of the Sublime and Beautiful*, ed. Adam Phillips (Oxford: OUP, 1990), p. 11.

whom rapidly produced ferocious replies to Burke's *Reflections*. The burden of their criticism, some of it of a literary kind, is that Burke has substituted verbal theatrics for an honest appraisal of human injustice, a criticism that persists today in the work of a number of scholarly readers who attempt to see Burke as a mere "rhetorician." A distrust of literary art, as something that obscures rather than reveals, is implied. From the outset of *A Vindication of the Rights of Men* (1790), Wollstonecraft rejects the falsities of art. Addressing Burke, she affirms that "It is not necessary, with courtly insincerity, to apologize to you for thus intruding on your precious time," and rejects "the equivocal idiom of politeness, to disguise my sentiments."[8] (Whereas Burke in many places reminds us of the importance of manners[9] in softening and gracing human intercourse, Wollstonecraft sees them as a dishonest impediment to the virtues of plain-speaking.) Burke's art "is only employed to varnish over the faults which ought to have been corrected"; his *Reflections* is compared to a redundant piece of architectural frippery, "an airy edifice—a folly."[10] In contrast, Wollstonecraft has a "simple, unsophisticated sense" of liberty, and rejects the "unnatural customs" that have only served to turn man into an "artificial monster," the rich especially, whose "minds, in fact, instead of being cultivated, have been so warped by education."[11]

Wollstonecraft argues for the simplicity of plain reason over against Burke's notions of common sense, which she mocks here as "sentimental jargon" (and this from someone who defended "sentiment"—natural, untutored feelings—as a trustworthy guide):

> A kind of mysterious instinct is supposed to reside in the soul, that instantaneously discerns truth, without the tedious labor of ratiocination. This instinct, for I know not what other name to give it, has been termed common sense, and more frequently sensibility;

8. Mary Wollstonecraft, *A Vindication of the Rights of Men* (New York, NY: Prometheus Books, 1996), p. 13.

9. Cf. Ian Crowe, "Edmund Burke on Manners," *Modern Age*, Fall 1997, Vol. 39, No. 4, p. 389ff.

10. Wollstonecraft, op. cit., p. 16.

11. Ibid., pp. 14–19.

and, by a kind of indefeasible right, it has been supposed, for
rights of this kind are not easily proved, to reign paramount over
the other faculties of the mind, and to be an authority from which
there is no appeal.[12]

In Wollstonecraft's thinking, feeling and reason do not work in this
integrated way, but nevertheless she chooses to explain them in the
figure of marriage, such that feeling "impregnates" reason to produce "her only legitimate offspring—virtue," in contrast to which
"instinct" is a "bastard vice." (The "rhetoric" here is noteworthy.)
Wollstonecraft understands enough of Burke's purpose to provide
this parody of it, and to reiterate the primacy of pure reason, for
"Who will venture to assert that virtue would not be promoted by
the more extensive cultivation of reason?"[13] and "I know not of any
common nature or common relation amongst men but what results
from reason."[14] Thus, she will not criticize the French National
Assembly "for applying to their understanding rather than to their
imagination,"[15] unlike Burke. The implication is that given the
mental gulf fixed between the two faculties, reason must be the
more trustworthy basis for political progress.

Tom Paine's *Rights of Man* (1791) similarly attempts a critique of
Burke's language, and early on signals its philosophical divergence
from Burke in an approving quotation from Lafayette:

> "Call to mind the sentiments which Nature has engraved in the
> heart of every citizen, and which take a new force when they are sol-
> emnly recognized by all: For a nation to love liberty, it is sufficient
> that she knows it; and to be free, it is sufficient that she wills it."[16]

It is interesting to see how, in this figure of an engraving on the
heart that echoes St. Paul, "sentiments" has replaced "law," and
"Nature" has replaced "God": the difference between naturalism on
the one hand, and natural law on the other, could hardly be more
clearly encapsulated. In another echo of St. Paul, Paine affects to

---

12. Ibid., p. 49.
13. Ibid., p. 53.
14. Ibid., p. 64.
15. Ibid., p. 65.
16. Thomas Paine, *Rights of Man* (New York, NY: Alfred A. Knopf, 1994), p. 15.

perceive in Burke's style a mere sounding gong or tinkling cymbal, censuring "Mr. Burke's periods, with [their] music in the ear, and nothing in the heart."[17] Elsewhere, Paine sees Burke's language as needlessly ornate, "gay and flowery,"[18] and especially as a misapplication of literary treatment to history:

> As to the tragic paintings by which Mr. Burke has outraged his imagination, and seeks to work upon that of his readers, they are well calculated for theatrical representation, where facts are manufactured for the sake of show, and accommodated to produce, through the weakness of sympathy, a weeping effect. But Mr. Burke should recollect that he is writing History, and not Plays; and that his readers will expect truth and not the spouting rant of high-toned exclamation.[19]

The distrust of a dramatic art as a means to truth is evident here, and the images of horror, what Paine calls, "Mr. Burke's horrid paintings,"[20] are condemned in a show of prim, puritanical decorousness. Art, for Paine, is of a piece with the degeneracy that civilization inflicts upon pristine nature:

> Nature has been kinder to Mr. Burke than he is to her. He is not affected by the reality of distress touching his heart, but by the showy resemblance of it striking his imagination. He pities the plumage, but forgets the dying bird. Accustomed to kiss the aristocratic hand that hath purloined him from himself, he degenerates into a composition of art, and the genuine soul of nature forsakes him.[21]

Rather, however, than seeing Burke defeating his own nature through art, we see Paine defeating his art through a misunderstanding of nature. The famous metaphor of the plumage and the dying bird is misapplied. Paine sees the plumage as an image of redundant artifice whereas, of course, the plumage is as essential to the bird's life as is its body, enabling flight, for instance. If anything,

17. Ibid., p. 16.
18. Ibid., p. 19.
19. Ibid., p. 21.
20. Ibid., p. 20.
21. Ibid., p. 21.

plumage could serve as an image of the integration of art and nature that Paine does not recognize.

The truth of Burke's *Reflections* was to be borne out by events, and the hopes that Wollstonecraft and Paine had of the Revolution were not. Burke's visions of terror were far from unreal, heated fantasies, and it is easy to forget, as it is frequently observed, that he was writing before the Terror and the rise of Napoleon. Burke's writing thus possesses a prophetic quality through its integration of art with his knowledge of human nature and history. In particular, his grasp of what he calls the sublime enables him to receive this vision. He is able to look into the abyss, and not avert his eyes, and tell of what he saw. Burke's is the rhetoric of reality, rather than of partiality, in that it is responsive to the whole of man's nature, including his art. Art is the means by which vision is apprehended and conveyed, such that the vision is not so much merely received, like an automatic message, but rather demands all of the artistic, creative power of the author to become incarnated in words. Far from the literary and tragic sense being inappropriate to political or historical writing, in the case of an event of such cataclysmic proportions as the French Revolution it is the only form that is capable of articulating its full reality. The cold language of politics that we are accustomed to hearing in our time, such that human misery is spoken of in terms such as "liquidation" or "ethnic cleansing," has the effect of masking the horrible realities that sanguinary power secretly feasts upon. Burke breaks open the mask, and his "horrible paintings" show the thing itself:

> Plots, massacres, assassinations, seem to some people a trivial price for obtaining a revolution. A cheap, bloodless reformation, a guiltless liberty, appear flat and vapid to their taste. There must be a great change of scene; there must be a magnificent stage effect; there must be a grand spectacle to rouze the imagination....[22]

The diabolical taste for blood is not conceived in the mind of Burke but reflected rather in the mirror of his mind; the title *Reflections*

---

22. Edmund Burke, *Reflections on the Revolution in France,* ed. Conor Cruise O'Brien (London: Penguin, 1968), p. 156. (Hereafter referred to as *Reflections*)

should be dwelt upon. His insight into the sublime makes him capable of showing something that the rationalistic and naturalistic mind cannot (to its undoing as events would eventually bring forth) admit of, that is the evil that reason alone cannot contain.

To be human, Burke reminds us, is to feel revolted, terrified, and disgusted by these "spectacles" of kings led in triumph, and queens outraged, and not because they are above us in the social order but because they represent the personal dimension of authority and society, and bear it up on our behalf. If their humanity is outraged, then so is ours, and it will be further. To give assent to the mistreatment of the French royal family, is "the degenerate choice of a vitiated mind,"[23] not the manifestation of rational virtue. Wordsworth's famous tag on the French Revolution, "Bliss was it in that dawn to be alive,/But to be young was very heaven!"[24] and the poem in which it originally appeared expresses well this inward-looking regard of utopian feelings, replacing an apprehension of a reality in which the sentiments are not permitted to roam freely but inhere in some "sensible object": this Burke provides, as for instance here:

> History will record, that on the morning of the 6th of October 1789, the king and queen of France, after a day of confusion, alarm, dismay, and slaughter, lay down, under the pledged security of public faith, to indulge nature in a few hours of respite, and troubled melancholy repose. From this sleep the queen was first startled by the voice of the centinel at her door, who cried out to her, to save herself by flight—that this was the last proof of fidelity he could give—that they were upon him, and he was dead. Instantly he was cut down. A band of cruel ruffians and assassins, reeking with his blood, rushed into the chamber of the queen, and pierced with an hundred strokes of bayonets and poniards the bed, from whence the persecuted woman had but just time to fly almost naked, and through ways unknown to the murderers had escaped to seek refuge at the feet of a king and husband, not secure of his own life for a moment.

23. Ibid., p. 160.

24. William Wordsworth, "The French Revolution, as it Appeared to Enthusiasts at its Commencement," in *The Poetical Works of William Wordsworth*, ed. Thomas Hutchinson (New York, NY: Oxford University Press, 1933), p. 208.

This king, to say no more of him, and their infant children (who once would have been the pride and hope of a great and generous people) were then forced to abandon the sanctuary of the most splendid palace in the world, which they left swimming in blood, polluted by massacre, and strewed with scattered limbs and mutilated carcases.[25]

In this dramatic recreation, Burke attempts to stimulate a moral response in the reader by working in a tragic idiom, evoking the pity and terror of the sublime. It is an "atrocious spectacle" to which only one response is humane. But, asks Burke,

Why do I feel so differently from the Reverend Dr Price, and those of his lay flock, who will choose to adopt the sentiments of his discourse?—[Such as, we might say, Paine and Wollstonecraft]. For this plain reason—because it is natural I should; because we are so made as to be affected at such melancholy spectacles with melancholy sentiments upon the unstable condition of mortal prosperity, and the tremendous uncertainty of human greatness; because in those natural feelings we learn great lessons; because in events like these our passions instruct our reason; because when kings are hurl'd from their thrones by the Supreme Director of this great drama, and become the objects of insult to the base, and of pity to the good, we behold such disasters in the moral, as we should behold a miracle in the physical order of things. We are alarmed into reflexion; our minds (as it has long since been observed) are purified by terror and pity; our weak unthinking pride is humbled, under the dispensations of a mysterious wisdom.[26]

The use here of the words "plain," "reason" and "natural" ironically echoes, and reappropriates into a traditional usage, the language of the radical school of Rousseau. The passions and the reason work, in the integrated human mind, interdependently, securing the sense of reality of the object. Our reactions are on the moral level, and consist in pity or contempt, depending on the health or otherwise of our own moral condition.

Thus, the integration of art and nature in the mind of Burke,

25. Burke, *Reflections*, p. 164.
26. Ibid., p. 175.

reflective of the complexity of human nature, is the basis of the "moral imagination" that underwrites a healthy politics, as it does a healthy general culture. Nowhere, perhaps, is this better expressed in a passage that goes to the heart of what Burke wants to conserve, and of which he fears, with real terror, the loss:

> But now all is to be changed. All the pleasing illusions, which made power gentle, and obedience liberal, which harmonized the different shades of life, and which, by a bland assimilation, incorporated into politics the sentiments which beautify and soften private society, are to be dissolved by this new conquering empire of light and reason. All the decent drapery of life is to be rudely torn off. All the super-added ideas, furnished from the wardrobe of a moral imagination, which the heart owns, and the understanding ratifies, as necessary to cover the defects of our naked shivering nature, and to raise it to dignity in our own estimation, are to be exploded as a ridiculous, absurd, and antiquated fashion.[27]

We should be careful not to see the word "illusions" as pejorative in Burke's use of it here, any more than his use of "theatre" or "theatric." For, he says with bitter irony, "... the theatre is a better school of moral sentiments than churches, where the feelings of humanity are thus [by Dr. Price's Old Jewry sermon] outraged."[28] The moral imagination chiefly subsists in sympathy—literally, feeling with another—but interdependent with the ethical sense that enables us to see who is really the victim—whether kings and queens, the dispossessed Irish Catholic populace, or heathen Indians. The imagination, and the art it produces, is at the very heart of what it is to be "... Man; whose prerogative it is, to be in a great degree a creature of his own making."[29]

The *Reflections* is the earliest identification, in the idiom of the Burkean understanding of the sublime, of the threat of the Revolution in France to all civil society, but in the years following the French Revolution and the European upheavals of the Napoleonic Wars that it precipitated, the Burkean sublime was to find its way

27. Ibid., p. 171.
28. Ibid., p. 176.
29. Ibid., p. 189.

into other artistic responses to the spirit of the age. J. M. W. Turner's *Snow Storm: Hannibal and his Army Crossing the Alps* (1812) is one of a number of paintings on Carthaginian themes in which the struggle between England and France is seen as prefigured in that between Rome and Carthage. Although Turner's purpose is a Burkean one of the general sublime and moral lessons involved in the contemplation of the fall of human power and imperial ambitions, a particular identification of Hannibal with Napoleon is retrospectively inescapable. (The earlier *The Fall of an Avalanche in the Grisons* (1810) also evokes the Burkean sublime, and in both paintings the Alpine context of overpowering, precipitous darkness is strongly felt.) The human suffering entailed by the irruption of a Tartarean chaos into the order of nature is connected with human pride, and the overtaking of the Carthaginian baggage train, and their brutal slaughter by wild Swiss tribesmen, is given a cosmic significance by the encircling, pelting snow storm. The sun, as a symbol of beneficent order, is obscured, and Hannibal's ambitions made distant and small in the silhouette of his elephants on the horizon: his ultimate defeat is prefigured. The result of Napoleon's ruthless ambition is seen in Turner's *The Field of Waterloo* (1818), where Stygian darkness is shot through with the deathly pale moonlight, or the bloody firelight, and the intermingled corpses of British and French soldiers make us, as in any vision into the sublime, pause in pity and fear.

It is, to reiterate Burke's reminder, natural to pause in this way, and yet most of us would not experience this natural and salutary experience without the intervention of art. Burke's moral imagination sees human upheavals of historical proportions in terms of art, especially drama. In the modern period since the French Revolution, however, life has provided us with many events of terrifying proportions, as overpowering as they are unexpected. In the trenches of the First World War, in the concentration camps, in the gulag, in the fire-bombing or atomic bombing of cities in the Second World War, in the killing fields of Cambodia, and recently in the destruction of two immense, monumental towers, symbols of the power of industrial and commercial Western man: we feel pity and terror at the thought of thousands in the extremity of pain and loss. We feel an unbearable irruption of chaos into order, and a stupefied incomprehension and disorientation. Without a conception of evil, for which we need a system of dogmatic religion, we flounder. The inhumanity of ideology is one of the defining features of late modernity, and it is of this that Burke was prophetic. The "age of chivalry" descends into the cold but sanguinary modernity of the "sophists, economists and calculators"—the scientistic advocates of a new and heartless world. Whether in communism, fascism, Nazism, or the more recent Islamist terror nurtured by fundamentalism, late modernity continues to imitate the paradigm of sanguinary ideology established in the French Revolution. The political response of the West (now a mixture of Christian and post-Christian secular liberalism) insofar as it must oppose "armed doctrine[s]," with global aims, should heed the perennial wisdom in the Christian humanism of Edmund Burke.

There is, of course, considerable mutual antagonism between Christian humanist thought and secular liberalism. Yet it surely becomes increasingly obvious that without the moral conviction, depth of vision and breadth of understanding that comes from religious belief, it is unlikely that the West can sustain itself in the face of ideological assault. In particular, unless the profound connection between religion and law is recognized, law itself will become etiolated, and unable to resist the force of legal positivism on the one hand, and *shari'a* on the other. At that point, a radical disconnection with the past will have occurred; however, it is not at all clear that the majority of the people would want this break to happen. As Burke reminds us in the *Tract on the Popery Laws*:

> Religion, to have any force on man's understandings, indeed to exist at all, must be supposed paramount to laws, and independent for its substance upon any human institution. Else it would be the absurdest thing in the world; an acknowledged cheat. Religion, therefore, is not believed because the laws have established it; but it is established because the leading part of the community have previously believed it to be true.[30]

---

30. Quoted in Stanlis, op. cit., p. 44.

This "leading part of the community" equates to the common mind, that which connects the past with the present, and makes the democracy of the dead the vital patrimony of the living. Burke's Christian humanism exists in a deep sense of his own civilization's roots in history, and its symbiotic growth in and with both religion and law. Like all forms of Christian humanism, it is a vision of society made possible by both knowledge and imagination.

6

The Integrating Imagination
of Samuel Taylor Coleridge

Ulysses: There is a mystery, with whom relation
Durst never meddle, in the soul of state,
Which hath an operation more divine
Than breath or pen can give expressure to.
SHAKESPEARE, *Troilus and Cressida*, III, iii.

If then unanimity grounded on moral feelings has been among the least equivocal sources of our national glory, that man deserves the esteem of his countrymen, even as patriots, who devotes his life and the utmost efforts of his intellect to the preservation and continuance of that unanimity by the disclosure and establishment of principles...Let the scholar, who doubts this assertion, refer only to the writings of EDMUND BURKE....
COLERIDGE, *Biographia Literaria*, 1817

Christendom, from its first settlement on feudal rights, has been so far one great body, however imperfectly organized, that a similar spirit will be found in each period to have been acting in all its members. IBID.

IT IS DIFFICULT, at the best of times, to think of Coleridge, the inveterate opium-eater, as a conservative. Nowadays, the problem is compounded in that the works of Coleridge usually set for study consist of the early poetry of *Lyrical Ballads*, a "levelling" volume as Hazlitt called it, the product of a time when Wordsworth and Coleridge were full of radicalism in letters and in life. The modern tenured radicals of the academy will heave a sigh of disappointment at the disillusionment both poets came to feel for the French Revolution, so it is hardly surprising that they often suggest that the best was over early, especially in Coleridge's case, and that he wrote little poetry thereafter, but much turgid prose. But there is considerably more to later Coleridge than disillusionment, even if the titles of the two volumes of Richard Holmes's biography, *Early Visions* and *Darker Reflections*, seem particularly appropriate. (The word "reflections" also properly suggests the influence of Burke on the later Coleridge.) Moreover, there are, as we shall see, certain continuities of thought between the best poems and the later thinking on the nature of society. This may be summarized, in the words of H.G. Schenk, as "the quest for re-integration,"[1] pursued alike in the soul and in the commonwealth.

First, some reference to the most penetrating critique we have of Coleridge's thought, and that of his opposite, Jeremy Bentham, would be useful. In the course of two essays, one on each of these two philosophers, John Stuart Mill gives us a detailed history of ideas from the eighteenth century to his own time, and an outline of two contrasting modes of thought. These two modes of thought correspond to what we call here the common mind, and its opposite, the disintegrative mind. Where Coleridge was integrative, traditional, religious and poetic, Bentham was skeptical, rational, empirical and prosaic. Coleridge took his view from inside his inheritance; Bentham took his from outside what had gone before. Most importantly, Mill points out the central way in which Bentham's thought is at variance with the common mind:

> His second [disqualification as a philosopher] was the incompleteness of his own mind as a representative of universal human nature. In many of the most natural and strongest feelings of human nature he had no sympathy; from many of its graver experiences he was altogether cut off; and the faculty by which one mind understands a mind different from itself, and throws itself

1. H.G. Schenk, *The Mind of the European Romantics* (Oxford: OUP, 1979), p. 22.

into the feelings of that other mind, was denied him by his deficiency of Imagination.[2]

In Coleridge, by contrast, we see the importance of the imagination not only in his own thought and art, but also as a representative of a continuing theme in the minds of the Christian humanists we consider in this book. Without the imagination, we can say, man is shut up in himself, in the present time, in the material world, and in his logical processes; moreover, he is all the more inclined, without the imagination, to shut up others, too, in his clean and tidy prison. Mill shows how Coleridge, and the German thinkers to whom he was so much indebted, helped to liberate the mind of England from the stale rationalism of eighteenth century thought. We might also add that Coleridge, like the other English Romantics, had no inconsiderable debt to Burke and, as we shall see in the next chapter, without Coleridge there may have been no Oxford Movement. Coleridge made Christianity both intellectually respectable again, and relevant to political thought, society, literature and art.

To return to the two Coleridges, it may be seen that the main thematic continuity between the earlier and the later man is characterized by the metaphorical contrast between an organic and a mechanistic view of life. The essential revolution in Coleridge's thinking was in his rejection of the philosophy of David Hartley. The importance of Hartley to Coleridge is signified by the latter's naming of his first son after the Cambridge physician whose ideas of necessity and the associative workings of the human mind questioned any innate moral sense in man. By 1801, Coleridge had rejected what he saw as the atheistic implications of modern metaphysics, especially in Hartley. Coleridge never lost, in the vagaries of his early radical thought, his Christian convictions, which indeed provided the spring to his concerns for what is commonly called nowadays "social justice." His departure from radicalism, and his embrace of the Tory cause, thus parallels the motives of Swift in leaving the Whigs: the perception that the preservation of mystical Christianity from the depredations of modern rationalism was of

---

2. John Stuart Mill, *Mill on Bentham and Coleridge*, ed. F.R. Leavis (Cambridge: CUP, 1980), p. 61.

paramount importance in the health of society, and that nowhere was this of more practical import than in the defense of the Established Church. Social radicalism was inconsistent with both parts of this goal.

This reaction against rationalism in philosophy was entirely in keeping with Coleridge's earlier reaction against the neoclassical poetry of Pope and his school. Augustan poetry, Coleridge considered, was artificial and mechanical, just like the rationalism of the radicals. Coleridge's ideas of "organic form" in poetry, and his elucidation of the natural qualities of Shakespeare, anticipate his later defense of the organic constitution of Great Britain:

> The form is mechanic when on any given material we impress a predetermined form, not necessarily arising out of the properties of the material, as when to a mass of wet clay we give whatever shape we wish it to retain when hardened. The organic form, on the other hand, is innate; it shapes itself from within, and the fullness of its development is one and the same with the perfection of its outward form. . . . And even such is the appropriate excellence of [Nature's] chosen poet, of our own Shakespeare, himself a nature humanized, a genial understanding directing self-consciously a power and an implicit wisdom deeper than consciousness.[3]

By extension, we may say that rationalism is the imposition of a predetermined, mechanical form of reasoning that does not imitate or correspond to the spirit of nature—what Coleridge calls, in the context of mechanical poetry, "a blind copying of effects instead of a true imitation of the essential principles."[4] The French neoclassical critics and their English followers tended to see Shakespeare as a barbaric genius, and believed that the heroic couplet was the true medium of poetry in a more refined age. The spirit of Voltaire and the spirit of Rousseau come together: the heroic couplet is the literary correlative of an abstract political constitution imposed on any nation, whatever its customs and traditions.

A story that Coleridge liked to tell of his time at Nether Stowey

3. H. Bloom and L. Trilling, eds., *Romantic Poetry and Prose* (New York, NY: OUP, 1973), p. 656.
4. Ibid., p. 655.

illustrates his departure from the philosophical position of the radicals, who inclined to the view that the child's mind is a *tabula rasa* upon which impressions from its environment accumulate. (The idea derives principally, so far as the eighteenth century is concerned, from John Locke.) This being so, a presumption in favor of rationalism follows, as the mind develops under necessary cause and effect, and the implications of this view of the mind for education were developed in Rousseau's *Emile*. John Thelwall, one of the most notorious of the English radicals, and (in a time when the Home Office spies were abroad) rather too obvious a visitor to Coleridge and Wordsworth in Somerset, became the butt of Coleridge's growing disinclination for mechanistic ideas of the human mind:

> . . . Coleridge wittily attacked Thelwall's idea that a child should be brought up as an agnostic until it reached an age of discretion to choose between religion and atheism. "I showed him my garden, and told him it was my botanical garden. 'How so?' said he, 'it is covered with weeds.'—'Oh,' I replied, 'that is only because it has not yet come to its age of discretion and choice. The weeds, you see, have taken the liberty to grow, and I thought it unfair in me to prejudice the soil towards roses and strawberries.'"[5]

Coleridge here opposes a dry, mechanical and rationalistic view of the mind, in which the social environment is restrained and rationally determined, with a view of an imaginative interaction with, and cultivation of, the given. The story neatly encapsulates the importance to Coleridge of religion as a vehicle and treasure-house of the imagination, and its central position in his growing differences with the radical project.

It was about this period of 1797–1798, when he was resident at Nether Stowey, that Coleridge wrote his finest poetry. In addition to the internal revolution occurring in his mind, the outside world was full of immense upheaval. The French Jacobins had executed Louis XVI, ushered in the Terror, and re-consecrated the cathedral of Notre Dame to Reason. England was at war with revolutionary France, which pursued aggressive continental aims, and there was

---

5. R. Holmes, *Coleridge: Early Visions* (London: Harper Collins, 1999), p. 158.

fear of invasion from across the Channel. Pitt's government passed Acts to curb sedition and suspend habeas corpus. Coleridge's poetry of this time reflects the urgent choices he felt obliged to make; his hopes and fears for the future; and the contemplation, on the local scale, of the nature of human social relations. Perhaps most noteworthy, then as now, is the recovery of the sense of the mysteriousness of life and art, so strikingly re-emergent in *Christabel* and the *Rime of the Ancient Mariner*, but it is in the "conversation poems," and in "France: an Ode," that we may principally discern the influence of Burkean ideas of the nature of society as rooted in real, personal affections. These were especially important to Coleridge at this time. As Marilyn Butler puts it:

> The Pantisocratic scheme, which would have made an ideal community, had failed him; the wider radical movement had failed him; all those still suspected of radical opinions were unpopular; his marriage with Sara Fricker brought him scant security or companionship. In his early adulthood Coleridge was experiencing not community but alienation, and his best poetry is the record of it.[6]

This point is well illustrated in "This Lime-Tree Bower My Prison." The poet is prevented from walking out with his friends by a minor accident, and remains in a garden seated under a lime-tree. It is June, 1797. The poem brings into focus, emblematically, the alienation felt by Coleridge, but also the immense importance he attached to friendship. The poet creates a communication, beyond the moment in time, between friends separated in space, through the use of memory and imagination. Although the poem begins gloomily enough, its dominant mood is not melancholy because the poet, after imagining his friends' walk through his memory of the same places, finds a unity of experience in the nature around him. The resolution of disparate feelings, persons and places in an imaginative unity is characteristically Coleridgean:

> Henceforth I shall know
> That Nature ne'er deserts the wise and pure;
> No plot so narrow, be but Nature there,

6. M. Butler, *Romantics, Rebels and Reactionaries* (Oxford: OUP, 1981), p. 83.

No waste so vacant, but may well employ
Each faculty of sense, and keep the heart
Awake to Love and Beauty![7]

Such resolution comes in time, and through contemplation; the poem moves in time almost imperceptibly from morning to evening, always apparently present, always adding to the store of past experience in the memory and imagination that can step outside of time. These faculties enable him to reach into the "One Life" of nature.

In addition, the following February, Coleridge wrote the exquisite "Frost at Midnight." The verdant imagery of summer has been replaced with a winter setting, but there is a similarity to "This Lime-Tree Bower" in both form and content, and in the prevailing intensity of intimate affection, this time focused on his sleeping son, Hartley. The apparently artless, natural, and organic movement of the mind hides a poem that is highly wrought, although reflective of the spirit of nature as outlined in Coleridge's description of organic form quoted above. There are, again, almost imperceptible concentric movements away from the still centre of the poet and his cradled child, and the principle of association that Coleridge took from the philosopher Hartley now takes on more Burkean overtones about the development of association in the social sense. Marilyn Butler points out how these poems accord with Burke's image of the "little platoon . . . the first link in the series by which we proceed towards a love to our country and to mankind."[8] Coleridge's affections in "Frost at Midnight" extend in both space and time, as again he moves back in memory before returning, in a circular motion, to the image of frost preserving the present, as does the poem itself. But the essential unifying force is nature itself, the "eternal language," the creative *logos*, of God.

In that same February, the French invaded Switzerland, and Coleridge responded to this development of the armed revolutionary doctrine with "France: an Ode." Again, there is movement of mind

7. E. Schneider, ed., *Coleridge: Selected Poetry and Prose* (New York, NY: Holt, Rinehart and Winston, 1966), p. 48.
8. Butler, op. cit., p. 84.

in this poem, but here it is a record of the change in Coleridge's feelings from the optimism felt for the fall of the Bastille, to final disillusionment at the invasion of neutral Switzerland. His earlier shame
at Britain's joining the European monarchs' attempt, as he saw it
then, to destroy the new-found French liberty, has been replaced by
a deeper shame at having thought the Revolution served liberty:

> The Sensual and the Dark rebel in vain,
> Slaves by their own compulsion! In mad game
> They burst their manacles and wear the name
> Of Freedom, graven on a heavier chain![9]

Again, there is a circular movement to the poem, as the poet returns
in the final stanza to the open images of natural power on the sea-
shore, identifying the clouds, winds and waves with the spirit of liberty, from which he has never wavered. In vision, he has a feeling of
intense love for all things, which he identifies with the true spirit of
liberty.

This feeling of love for fellow man, promoted by the healing
effect of solitude in natural scenery, also characterizes Coleridge's
most extended meditation connecting personal disturbance with
the wider world: "Fears in Solitude; Written in April 1798, During
the Alarm of an Invasion." "A small and silent dell," an image of
home like the lime-tree bower and the cottage fireside, is the locale
from which the poet's thoughts extend "from east to west" across
the world that Britain has often most shamefully used. In lines that
anticipate Kipling's "Recessional" a hundred years later, Coleridge
sees the all-too-human weakness behind British power, and asks
God's forgiveness for the crimes of his countrymen: "Spare us yet
awhile,/Father and God! O! Spare us yet awhile!"[10] His shame at
aspects of English domestic policy, particularly the disabilities
against Catholics and Dissenters that made light of oath-taking, are
linked with his own shame at being associated with the radical
cause; both released "the owlet Atheism," and the consequent wars,
"And all our dainty terms for fratricide." There is a sense that the

9. Schneider, op. cit., p. 98.
10. Ibid., p. 105.

wrongs done in England's name are reaping a bitter harvest in a war that must nonetheless be prosecuted vigorously:

> Stand forth! be men! repel an impious foe,
> Impious and false, a light yet cruel race,
> Who laugh away all virtue, mingling mirth
> With deeds of murder; and still promising
> Freedom, themselves too sensual to be free,
> Poison life's amities, and cheat the heart
> Of faith and quiet hope, and all that soothes,
> And all that lifts the spirit![11]

As in "France: an Ode," it is against an armed atheism that Coleridge principally reacts, even as his sense of the injustices of old monarchical Europe remain. His patriotism is rooted in his local attachments, to which the poem returns in the circular structure of the conversation poems:

> Homeward I wind my way; and lo! Recalled
> From bodings that have well-nigh wearied me,
> I find myself upon the brow, and pause
> Startled! And after lonely sojourning
> In such a quiet and surrounded nook,
> This burst of prospect, here the shadowy main,
> Dim-tinted, there the mighty majesty
> Of that huge amphitheatre of rich
> And elmy fields, seems like society—
> Conversing with the mind, and giving it
> A livelier impulse and a dance of thought!
> And now, beloved Stowey! I behold
> Thy church-tower, and, methinks, the four huge elms
> Clustering, which mark the mansion of my friend;
> And close behind them, hidden from my view,
> Is my own lowly cottage, where my babe
> And my babe's mother dwell in peace![12]

Marilyn Butler notes the Burkean implications of these lines:

11. Ibid., p. 106.
12. Ibid., p. 108.

It is the demonstration that the little platoon we belong to in society is attachment to society itself. Thus the minutiae of Coleridge's actual life in this rich year were made to illuminate public issues. Hyper-emotional, acutely responsive, he caught the fear in the public mood and availed himself of a moment when his own insecurity could be made the correlative of England's.[13]

External nature, as usual in Coleridge, acts as a healing, *logos*-like medium between God and man. Thus, "the amphitheatre of rich / And elmy fields, seems like society," the "clustering" of the trees around the church-yard an emblem of divinely-ordered human relations, the place of both the poet's God and his friend. The nook where he began has made him ready to return to "Love, and the thoughts that yearn for human kind." For all the "levelling" effect of *Lyrical Ballads*, and some Rousseauistic ideas of nature as expressed in Wordsworth's "The Tables Turned" ("One impulse from a vernal wood / May teach you more of man; / Of moral evil and of good, / Than all the sages can."), we can see the essence of the later Coleridge in this poetical *annus mirabilis*.

The later prose works consider more explicitly the principles by which the individual is integrated with nature and society, and this vision first begins to emerge in the *Biographia Literaria* (1817), something of an intellectual biography in rambling, associative form, full of anecdote and humorous observation. What most concern us here are Chapters X and XIII, in which Coleridge makes his famous distinctions between Reason and Understanding, and Fancy and Imagination, in a discussion that helps us to see clearly the way in which the poetry discussed above gives depth to the later more explicit teachings about the nature of society. Coleridge habitually made distinctions, in paired oppositions, that parallel each other. We have already come across the mechanic-organic distinction, in which the workings of the former are on a lower order of being than the latter. What is particularly interesting in Coleridge's thought is the rescuing of the idea of reason from its equation with rationalism, and hence an implied hostility to the imagination and thus the arts. For Coleridge, reason and imagination are cognate as

13. Butler, op. cit., p. 86.

essentially visionary faculties, whereas the understanding and the fancy are lower, more mechanical—in Hartley's word, associative—modes of mental operation:

> The IMAGINATION then, I consider either as primary, or secondary. The primary IMAGINATION I hold to be the living Power and prime Agent of all human Perception, and as a repetition in the finite mind of the eternal act of creation in the infinite I AM. The secondary Imagination I consider as an echo of the former, co-existing with the conscious will, yet still as identical with the primary in the kind of its agency, and differing only in degree, and in the mode of its operation. It dissolves, diffuses, dissipates, in order to recreate. . . .
>
> FANCY, on the contrary, has no other counters to play with, but fixities and definites. The Fancy is indeed no other than a mode of Memory emancipated from the order of time and space. . . . But equally with the ordinary memory the Fancy must receive all its materials ready made from the law of association.[14]

The higher modes of mental activity essentially consist in vision, the apprehension of the whole rather than a fixation upon parts.

The Imagination-Fancy distinction was cognate with Coleridge's way of seeing the world as a whole, like a living organic being, rather than a sum of working parts, like a machine. It is the distinction between reason and understanding, however, that has more relevance to Coleridge's philosophical considerations of man and society, although the importance of the imagination as a mode of perception in religion and politics was also to have much influence later in the century in the work of Newman and Disraeli, both of whom were directly or indirectly indebted to Coleridge. But Coleridge's fight, as a public controversialist, was with the utilitarian spirit of Bentham, a struggle between two fundamentally different ways of looking at the world, as John Stuart Mill noted. This was a struggle against a philosophy that seemed to sweep all before it, as Basil Willey observed:

14. Schneider, op. cit., p. 268.

In setting up Reason and Imagination above the mind of the flesh, Coleridge was seeking to protect the region of spiritual experience against all attacks from the mere Understanding, that is, against the Zeitgeist.... Understanding, the head disjoined from the heart, the "mere reflective faculty," can only analyse and abstract; it cannot build the parts so separated into a whole; this is the function of Reason, wherein head and heart, light and warmth, are working in unison.[15]

This distinction is also made explicit by Coleridge himself, in tabular form, in his *Aids to Reflection* (1825):[16]

UNDERSTANDING	REASON
1. Understanding is discursive.	1. Reason is fixed.
2. The Understanding in all its judgments refers to some other Faculty as its ultimate authority.	2. The Reason in all its decisions appeals to itself, as the ground and substance of their truth. (Hebrews vi. 13.)
3. Understanding is the Faculty of Reflection.	3. Reason or Contemplation. Reason indeed is much nearer to SENSE than to Understanding: for Reason (says our great HOOKER) is a direct aspect of Truth, an inward Beholding, having a similar relation to the Intelligible or Spiritual, as SENSE has to the Material or Phenomenal.

Thus, religion was fully in accord with reason, and indeed contained its highest reaches. In making this argument, Coleridge was undoing the work of the radicals, utilitarians and liberals who opposed reason and spirituality, and believed that religion and philosophy were therefore also opposed. Religion was in fact largely beneath their notice in the consideration of any matters of real import. Coleridge's reaction was beginning something of a revolution in nineteenth century religious thought:

15. B. Willey, *The English Moralists* (Garden City, NY: Anchor Books, 1967), p. 30.
16. S. T. Coleridge, *Aids to Reflection* (New York, NY: Chelsea House, 1983), p. 148.

That philosophizing could lead to orthodoxy was indeed astonishing to a generation whose philosophers had been mainly scoffers and unmaskers.[17]

Coleridge's "reason" has more in common with the meaning of the word to the seventeenth century divines than the *raison* of the French *philosophes*; the Age of Reason should have been more properly called the Age of Understanding; and what could not be understood was not worth knowing. The limitation of the mind of a rationalist is the lack of imagination and hence of the vision that can alone perceive reality as a whole rather than in part.

In Chapter X of the *Biographia*, Coleridge points to the example of Burke. Coleridge once contrasted Sir James Mackintosh, the Scottish philosopher who had initially defended the French Revolution, unfavorably with Burke. "Burke was a metaphysician, Mackintosh a mere logician,"[18] said Coleridge, in another of his characteristic paired oppositions. Coleridge points out what has often been missed or ignored by Burke's readers, that his opinions on America and on France proceeded from the same principles, and enabled Burke to foresee, correctly, the consequences of those upheavals:

> Whence gained he this superiority of foresight? ... The satisfactory solution is, that Edmund Burke possessed and sedulously sharpened that eye, which sees all things, actions and events, in relation to the laws that determine their existence and circumscribe their possibility. He referred habitually to principles. He was a scientific statesman; and therefore a seer. For every principle contains in itself the germs of a prophecy. ...[19]

Burke thus employed the imagination in the political sphere in order to create a picture of events beyond the present moment.

In the same year that the *Biographia* was published, to delineate Coleridge as a relatively new type (in England) of intellectual man of letters, his second *Lay Sermon*, "Addressed to the Higher and Middle Classes," also appeared. Here, Coleridge adopts the lofty

17. Willey, op. cit., p. 293.
18. Holmes, op. cit., p. 179.
19. Schneider, op. cit., p. 258.

sermonic form that was later to so characterize Victorian public discourse, most notably in the writings of Ruskin and Carlyle. Coleridge consciously invokes the Biblical language of vision in order to develop a picture of England as a Christian society, in order to counter atheistic rationalism. "It is as though Coleridge was born despite himself to be a controversialist. His best years were those of universal political uproar, which were 1792–9, 1815–18, and 1829–32,"[20] writes Marilyn Butler. The years immediately following Waterloo, and the end of the Napoleonic Wars, were of immense economic distress—"hardship, unemployment, agrarian riots, machine-breaking, protest marches and, by 1817, localized insurrection."[21] All these Coleridge addresses in prophetic language, full of Isaiah and Jeremiah, pointing to a need for a return to philosophy, to counter the materialism of the times.

The essential causes of the present discontents are, he says, "resolvable into the overbalance of the commercial spirit in consequence of the absence or weakness of the counter-weights."[22] Coleridge emphasizes that he is not hostile to trade *per se*: quite the contrary, it produces "the largest proportion of our actual freedom, and at least as large a share of our virtues as our vices."[23] But Coleridge points to the need for things like "the ancient feeling of rank and ancestry" as a "counterpoise to the grosser superstition of wealth."[24] Men must also be moved out of the tyranny of the present moment by philosophy, which Coleridge would like to see have a more secure position, and less utilitarian bent, in society at large, for

[a]n excess in our attachment to temporal and personal objects can be counteracted only by a pre-occupation of the intellect and the affections with permanent, universal and eternal truths.[25]

20. Butler, op. cit., p. 88.
21. Ibid., p. 88.
22. S.T. Coleridge, *A Lay Sermon, Addressed to the Higher and Middle Classes* (Burlington, VT: Chauncey Goodrich, 1832), p. 140.
23. Ibid., p. 182n.
24. Ibid., p. 183.
25. Ibid., p. 184.

In this defense of an honorific, philosophical class, Coleridge is seeking a version of the Platonic philosopher-king, who will be able to enact moral virtue within the political constitution. The key qualifier of course is balance. We find no simple-minded Tory sneering at "trade" in Coleridge, but we do find the need for some practical employment in the councils of state of things beyond trade. If commerce were the be-all and end-all, then the merely present and material sphere would, as the utilitarians and their allies in the commercial world implied, be the sum of man. But there is more to human life than efficiency. The material benefits of the industrial revolution, in creating conditions in which a greater number of people could be fed, did not excuse its depredatory effect on the lives of human beings working in the factories:

> I have passed through many a manufacturing town . . . and have watched many a group of old and young, male and female, going to, or coming from, many a factory. . . . Men, I still think, ought to be weighed not counted. Their worth ought to be the final estimate of their value.[26]

The arid calculus of "the greatest happiness of the greatest number" was reductive of the true nature of human beings, and a larger philosophic vision was required to alleviate the ills of the emerging industrial society:

> If we are a Christian nation, we must learn to act nationally as well as individually, as Christians. We must remove half truths, the most dangerous of errors (as those of the poor visionaries called Spenceans), by the whole truth.[27]

This vision of the whole as operating in society is developed at length in Coleridge's final work, *On the Constitution of Church and State According to the Idea of Each* (1830). The Burkean vision of an organic structure that has evolved over time is described in a more theoretic way than Burke himself ever attempted, or was inclined to do, but many of the underlying assumptions are present in Coleridge's earlier prose, especially the second *Lay Sermon*. What is of

26. Ibid., p. 212.
27. Ibid., p. 224.

particular interest in Church and State is another Coleridgean pairing of oppositions, that of Permanence and Progression. In the terms of the *Lay Sermon* these are cognate with the two classes of the gentry/aristocracy and the merchant class, or land and commerce. An associated opposition in Church and State is that between Civilization and Cultivation. As Coleridge put it in the *Lay Sermon*, "To the feudal system we owe the forms, to the Church the substance of our liberty."[28] There is a need for form, system, structure in the state—cognate, we might infer, with art; but there is also a need for substance, movement, life, commerce, and thought—that which corresponds to human nature. Indeed, Coleridge's discussion of the British constitution begins in the nature of man and law. Having dismissed the Lockean social contract as an historical solecism (it is "incapable of historic proof as a fact, and it is senseless as a theory"),[29] Coleridge places the contract, as an idea, in "the very constitution of our humanity, which supposes the social state."[30] The constitution exists as a Platonic idea which is brought into reality within human society as a deposit from tradition, and that is applied by man in society to present circumstances. The English constitution is cognate with common law, as Coleridge shows in quoting the early seventeenth-century jurist, Sir John Davies, on the English constitution, as

> "*Lex Sacra, Mater Legum,* than which (says he), nothing can be proposed more certain in its grounds, more pregnant in its consequences, or that hath more harmonical reason within itself: and which is so connatural and essential to the genius and innate disposition of this nation, it being formed (silk-worm like) as that no other law can possibly regulate it—a law not to be derived from Alured, or Alfred, or Canute, or other elder or later promulgators of particular laws, but which might say of itself—When reason and the laws of God first came, then came I with them."[31]

28. Ibid., p. 215n.
29. S. T. Coleridge, *On the Constitution of Church and State According to the Idea of Each* (London: Dent, 1972), p. 6.
30. Ibid.
31. Ibid., p. 11.

The health of the constitution is thus determined by its nature, which is human nature reified in the political structure and workings of government. When the constitution works according to its nature, civilization is preserved, because its natural roots are cherished. If not, civilization may itself become inhumane:

> But civilization is itself but a mixed good, if not far more a corrupting influence, the hectic of disease, not the bloom of health, and a nation so distinguished more fitly called a varnished than a polished people, where this civilization is not grounded in cultivation, in the harmonious development of those faculties that characterize our humanity. We must be men in order to be citizens.[32]

How might Rousseau have agreed, if he did not know the context in which these words appear! For where Rousseau believed in preserving the child from learning (in the traditional sense), Coleridge believes that in order to become men, and therefore citizens, it is learning that is essential. The difference between Coleridge and Rousseau is all contained in their different sense of "nature"; for Rousseau, this is creation, for Coleridge, the creative principle, the *logos*, which joins man and his Creator. The nation depends crucially on the educated class that Coleridge mentioned in the second *Lay Sermon*, and that he develops more fully in *Church and State* as the *clerisy*.

The need for this clerical class, a more widely defined version of the clergy and thus approaching more closely the sense the word "clerk" had in the Middle Ages, grows out of another pair of opposed ideas, that of the Nationalty and the Propriety. This is Coleridge's attempt to resolve the One and the Many, the community and the individual person. He conceives of both private, inherited estates and national endowments of the church, schools, colleges and universities, as both being part of the same trusteeship that makes up the commonwealth: "The land is not yours; it was vested in your lineage in trust for the nation."[33] Thus both Church and State (of course, another Coleridgean opposition) are parts of the

---

32. Ibid., pp. 33–34.
33. Ibid., p. 40.

same whole, and cannot, in the final analysis, be considered separate. In order that men become citizens, they must be educated by the clerisy into becoming persons capable of civil action. The local schoolmaster and clergyman were essential to the commonwealth, and depended upon some form of national endowment to maintain them. "The proper object and end of the national Church is civilization with freedom,"[34] says Coleridge, and in this object we can see why he makes an important, and interesting distinction between the National Church and the Christian Church as a whole. In fact, the event that spurred his essay was Catholic Emancipation, in 1829, and the consequent debate on how this accorded, or not, with the British Constitution. It is part of Coleridge's genius that he could reconcile within the idea of the traditional constitution both toleration (of which Coleridge was always in favor) and establishment. The salient point, as far as he was concerned, is that without the Church there can be no state, no civility, no commonwealth, for the religious outlook is the basis of all else of human value:

> The commanding knowledge, the power of truth, given or obtained by contemplating the subject in the frontal mirror of the Idea, is in Scripture ordinarily expressed by Vision: and no dissimilar gift, if not rather in its essential characters the same, does a great living Poet speak of, as

> "The VISION and the Faculty divine."

> And of many political ground-truths contained in the Old Testament, I cannot recall one more worthy to be selected as the Moral and L'ENVOY of a Universal History, than the text in Proverbs, WHERE NO VISION IS, THE PEOPLE PERISHETH.[35]

There is much in Coleridge that makes him still a thinker of relevance to us, because that which he fought in the utilitarian *zeitgeist* of his own time continues to menace us. Today, as in his time, a Christian view will detect an "overbalance of the commercial spirit," and a consequent inattention to the principle of permanence in human society. It is presumed, by the ubiquitous managerial class

34. Ibid., p. 43.
35. Ibid., p. 46.

that today has the power that Coleridge once wanted for his clerisy, that human life is guided by "structures," always expressed in mechanical and technological metaphors, and that this machinery can be successfully fiddled with in order to achieve human perfection. On the contrary, Coleridge reminds us of the organic nature of human life and society, against the mechanical and materialistic view. The sense of alienation from his times is one with which we may well sympathize, as we try to make sense of ours. And the fact that this difficult man of letters exercised the kind of influence he did may encourage us to counter the intellectual hirelings of our day. The most hopeful facet of Coleridge's life is that, in evil times, he inspired the revival of dogmatic and supernatural religion that became the saving grace of nineteenth-century England. It is difficult to think of anything that might benefit our times more than such a restoration.

7

John Henry Newman
And the Unity of Truth

There are more things in heaven and earth than are dreamt of in
your philosophy, Horatio.   *Hamlet*, I.v.

Ye cannot halve the Gospel of God's grace;
Men of presumptuous heart! I know you well.
Ye are of those who plan that we should dwell,
Each in his tranquil home and holy place.
        NEWMAN, "Liberalism" [1833], *Verses on Various Occasions*, 1896

The essential principles of Newman's ethic are far from being
peculiar to him alone. They are common to the whole Oxford
Movement: indeed they form part of the common inheritance of
Christianity. But the imaginative power and intellectual subtlety
of Newman's mind revealed them with a clarity which startled the
utilitarian optimism of Victorian culture and the sentimental
humanitarianism of modern religion.
        CHRISTOPHER DAWSON, *The Spirit of the Oxford Movement*, 1933

WRITING OF THE EARLY Romantics in his *Apologia Pro Vita Sua*
(1864), John Henry Newman quoted himself in an article written
many years before, thus:

"While history in prose and verse was thus made the instrument
of Church feelings and opinions, a philosophical basis was laid in
England by a very original thinker, who, while he indulged a liberty of speculation, which no Christian can tolerate, and advocated conclusions which were often heathen rather than Christian,
yet after all installed a higher philosophy into inquiring minds,

than they had hitherto been accustomed to accept. In this way he made trial of his age, and succeeded in interesting its genius in the cause of Catholic truth."[1]

After alluding first to Sir Walter Scott, Newman refers here to Samuel Taylor Coleridge, and his appreciation is as instructive as are his reservations, in this assessment of the grounds of the Oxford revival, in pointing to the way in which Newman is indebted to, and departs from, English Romanticism. On the one hand, there is in Newman a continuity of the opposition, based on a sense of the spiritual nature of man, to the mechanical, rationalistic and utilitarian view of society; on the other, a practical appraisal of the deficiencies of the Coleridgean speculative mind *vis-à-vis* Catholic orthodoxy. But much had happened between Coleridge's death, in 1834, and Newman's *Apologia*. In *On the Constitution of Church and State*, Coleridge was defending the idea of a national and established Church against the reforming spirit that threatened its existence. By the time of the *Apologia*, Newman had acknowledged the victory of the Liberals in the 1832 Reform Act, although out of this apparent disaster a healthier, more spiritual religion emerged, both within the politically diminished Anglican establishment, and in the renewed Roman Catholicism of which Newman became a leading light. More fully, perhaps, than Coleridge, Newman expressed the practical reality of the Church in the human world, and its integral relation to the unseen world. Coleridge's "quest for reintegration" eventually, Newman discovered, requires the abandonment of the national Church for one beyond nations, and ages, and ultimately beyond time.

First, however, Newman felt a sense of alienation not wholly dissimilar to that of Coleridge: it was the alienation of the Christian humanist in a material age. But Newman came from the middle class (his father was a banker) that was most involved with the movement towards political and ecclesiastical reform, and from early in his life, not just from the time when he entered the Catholic Church, his spiritual development involved separation from those

1. John Henry Newman, *Apologia pro Vita Sua* (London: Sheed and Ward, 1979), p. 65.

closest to him. His life inevitably had to conform to an inward sense of the truth in a way that sounds like Wordsworth's "egotistical sublime," and certainly more Protestant than Catholic, if we were to forget that this inwardly perceived reality is also the reality of the Church, the communion of saints, and Christendom. Newman did indeed, as he puts it in "On Liberalism," know well the personal "tranquil home and holy place," but unlike the Liberals, he knew too that this is a common and not a private dwelling. It is perhaps this intensity of the personal on the one hand, and the uncompromising need for a supra-personal authority (that embraces entirely the human and the divine), that makes Newman attractive to both conservatives and liberals in our own time.

However, Newman will always sit more uneasily with liberals, because from the letters on Sir Robert Peel's manifesto given at the Tamworth Reading Room, to his speech on receiving the cardinal's hat, Newman made clear that his lifelong battle was against liberalism. In the political and social sphere, liberalism involved the disintegration of real religion from the mass society that was emerging from the dispensations of the first Reform Act. In the Tamworth speech, Newman makes clear in his *Essay in Aid of a Grammar of Assent* (1870), Peel seemed to be capitulating to the spirit of liberalism in its Benthamite form:

> That doctrine was to the effect that the claims of religion could be secured and sustained in the mass of men, and in particular in the lower classes of society, by acquaintance with literature and the physical sciences, and through the instrumentality of Mechanics' Institutes and Reading Rooms, to the serious disparagement, as it seemed to me, of direct Christian instruction.[2]

Newman goes on to quote himself in a letter written to *The Times* in 1841, in response to Peel's speech, in terms that reveal that he is concerned as much as the Benthamites with practical realities, even as he has a deeper and more reasonable conception of the difference between knowledge and religion:

2. John Henry Newman, *An Essay in Aid of a Grammar of Assent* (Notre Dame, IN: University of Notre Dame Press, 1979), p. 88.

"People say to me, that it is but a dream to suppose that Christianity should regain the organic power in human society which once it possessed. I cannot help that; I never said it could. I am not a politician; I am proposing no measures, but exposing a fallacy and resisting a pretence. Let Benthamism reign, if men have no aspirations; but do not tell them to be romantic and then solace them with 'glory': do not attempt by philosophy what was once done by religion. The ascendancy of faith may be impracticable, but the reign of knowledge is incomprehensible. The problem for statesmen of this age is how to educate the masses, and literature and science cannot give the solution. . . ."[3]

In the first place, then, Newman's objection to liberalism, even in its social and political manifestations, is a philosophical one. It is also, as he makes clear in the note on liberalism in the appendix of the *Apologia*, a theological one. In this note, Newman expands upon his simple definition of liberalism as "the Anti-dogmatic principle":

Whenever men are able to act at all, there is the chance of extreme and intemperate action; and therefore, when there is exercise of mind, there is the chance of wayward or mistaken exercise. Liberty of thought is in itself a good; but it gives an opening to false liberty. Now by Liberalism I mean false liberty of thought, or the exercise of thought upon matters, in which, from the constitution of the human mind, thought cannot be brought to any successful issue, and therefore is out of place. Among such matters are first principles of whatever kind; and of these the most sacred and momentous are especially to be reckoned the truths of Revelation.[4]

Newman's opposition to Peel is a social and political response that has its roots in philosophical and theological principles. While it is difficult to distinguish the two in Newman, since his theology frequently involves practical considerations of the workings of the human mind, the effect is one of great precision of thought and expression. For Newman, as much as for Einstein, God does not play dice.

3. Ibid.
4. Newman, *Apologia*, p. 193.

In 1841, Newman came from a Tory position, that of his Church and his University, to criticize the direction in which Toryism, as Peel's Conservatism, was tending. The disintegration of religion from public life undermines all authority, not just that of the Church, because authority which does not recognize the claims of the Church becomes tyranny, however much it uses the language of liberty. As Christopher Dawson put it,

> Insofar as the Oxford Movement was Tory, its Toryism was not that of the defenders of vested interests, the "Conservatives" who aroused Hurrell Froude's scorn, but that of Southey and Coleridge and the young Disraeli who were among the first to denounce the injustices of the Industrial Revolution and the new Poor Law, and the evils of the factory systems.[5]

Not only the Cavalier spirit of the romantic Froude stood in opposition to the Roundhead spirit of Benthamism and Peelite Conservatism. Further, Newman writes affectionately of John Keble in the aforementioned note in the *Apologia*, in terms that also help us to understand the political outlook of a Movement that harked back to a more integrated society in which authority had not only rights but also duties:

> [Keble] carried his love of authority and old times so far, as to be more than gentle towards the Catholic Religion, with which the Toryism of Oxford and of the Church of England had no sympathy. Accordingly, if my memory be correct, he never could get himself to throw his heart into the opposition made to Catholic Emancipation, strongly as he revolted from the politics and the instruments by means of which that Emancipation was won. I fancy he would have had no difficulty in accepting Dr. Johnson's saying about "the first Whig"; and it grieved and offended him that the "Via prima salutis" should be opened to the Catholic body from the Whig quarter.[6]

Keble, moreover, considering the principles of the 1688 Revolution "too lax," considered those of 1776 and 1789 to be "absolutely and

---

5. Christopher Dawson, *The Spirit of the Oxford Movement* (London: The Saint Austin Press, 2001), p. xi.

6. Newman, *Apologia*, p. 195.

entirely out of keeping with theological truth."[7] But for our purposes here, he illustrates the difficulty in which the Tractarians found themselves in the early years of the Movement and of the Reform Act, and with which conservatives will always, perhaps, find themselves in regard to modernity: namely, how to deal with established authority when that authority turns on itself to undermine the philosophical and theological bases of the authoritative position, whether political, religious, or (to anticipate) educational?

This was the crux upon which the Oxford Movement turned: the nature, and location, of ecclesiastical authority. All the main figures of the Movement were sorely tried in conscience to answer this problem, and each answered in a different form. Whatever that form, however, none could easily square the idea of an integrated constitution of Church and State with the incursions of the secularizing State upon the prerogatives of the Church through the 1832 Reform Act. As priests of the Church of England, the Tractarians had little difficulty in perceiving where their first loyalty lay: not so much to the Anglican Establishment as such, but more to the Catholic Church (rather nebulously conceived at first) and to the Gospel, to Christianity, to the idea of Christendom and Christian society. This they believed to be the only real source of the common life, in a just and ordered society. For Newman, this first loyalty led inexorably to the painful paradox of finding re-integration into the broad tradition of the Catholic inheritance by separating from its reflection in the Anglican Establishment. Quite apart from the pain that this involved for him personally, it was seen by many sympathetic to his outlook (such as, importantly, Benjamin Disraeli) as lamentable for the cause of (in a loose but meaningful sense) the Tory restoration of romantic, medieval England. This regret has been powerfully expressed by the American critic, Paul Elmer More, in the context of a wide-ranging critique of romanticism, and that of Newman in particular. It was, considered More, this aspect of his character that led Newman, in leaving the Church of England, to "[fail] his country in her hour of greatest need":

7. Ibid.

119

But it would be presumptuous to end in such a strain. As we think of the many forces that were shaping the thoughts and ambitions of the [nineteenth] century from which we have just emerged, of its dark materialism, its intellectual pride, its greed of novelty, its lust of change, its cruel egotism and blind penance of sympathy, its wandering virtues and vices, its legacy of spiritual bewilderment—as we think of all these, then let us remember also how the great convert surrendered these things and counted them as dust in the balance beside the vision of his own soul face to face with God. It may be that his seclusion in the Oratory at Edgbaston was not unrelated to the almost inevitable inability of the romantic temperament to live in harmony with society. . . .[8]

While this criticism of Newman takes little account of the range and depth of his involvement in the practical world of affairs from the time of his conversion (for example, editing a review, founding and running two Oratories and a school, and his involvement in the Catholic University of Ireland), More is right to point to Newman's debt to romanticism and to the importance in his life and thought of the sense of his soul alone with God. This is illustrated early on in the *Apologia* in one of its most memorable passages describing the writer's early spiritual apprehensions:

I retained it [the doctrine of final perseverance] till the age of twenty-one, when it gradually faded away; but I believe it had some influence on my opinions, in the direction of those childish imaginations which I have already mentioned, viz. in isolating me from the objects which surrounded me, in confirming me in my mistrust of the reality of material phenomena, and making me rest in the thought of two and two only absolute and luminously self-evident beings, myself and my Creator.[9]

Newman also noted that as a child he had "thought life might be a dream, or I an Angel, and all this world a deception, my fellow-angels by a playful device concealing themselves from me. . . ."[10] But

8. Paul Elmer More, *Shelburn Essays: Eighth Series* (New York, NY: Phaeton Press, 1967), p. 78.

9. Newman, *Apologia*, p. 3.

10. Ibid., p. 1.

however much these striking and fanciful images impressed Newman in his recollection of them, and us in the reading, we should not mistake them for the doctrinal certitude of the mature man. Nor are they particularly egotistical recollections. Apart from the sense of the reality of spiritual phenomena, there is a sense of the other—whether the Creator, or other angels—and it is in this deeply personal relationship with the unseen, *cor ad cor loquitur,* that we find the characteristic Newmanian spirituality, and the essential basis for his grasp of the unity of truth, something that emerges from relationship. We should be wrong, however, to see this other-worldliness of Newman, for example in the translucence of the Millais portrait, as being the final word. It is in him the spring for action in the world, for, as Newman says in the *Grammar of Assent,* "Life is for action."[11] But in the Victorian age, as Paul Elmer More put it, of "dark materialism," it cannot be considered a small service to one's countrymen to attempt to convince them of the reality of the unseen world. More mentions Newman's sermon on "The Invisible World," but we should remember also the extraordinary achievement of "The Dream of Gerontius," and its widespread popularization in Elgar's musical setting. It is no small part of the achievement of this poem that its action consists almost entirely in the experiences of the soul after death, in a spiritual place where poetic imagery, normally reliant on the senses, does not find easy reference points.

We can readily grant, then, that an important part of Newman's special legacy lies in the personal and the other-worldly, and, as John F. Crosby has argued, in a method entirely different to the impersonal objectivity of, for example, St. Thomas Aquinas:

> Newman loved the specific individual and in fact sometimes verges on extreme nominalism in his affirmation of the individual. He is always warning against universals and their tendency to drain the concreteness out of things.[12]

11. Newman, *Grammar,* p. 91.

12. John F. Crosby, "Newman and the Personal," *First Things* (New York, NY: Religion and Public Life, August/September 2002), p. 47.

Newman was not a Scholastic, but rather a Platonist. In a democratic age, he spiritualized the idea of the gentleman, the natural leader, to give new meaning to the aristocratic function. But, to repeat, we would be wrong to see him as a remote, ivory-tower figure. Newman's life was one of action and contemplation, of work among the poor as well as among the leading class. In addition to his Platonic side (or, perhaps more properly, his Neoplatonic side), the sense of the reality of the unseen world, is Newman's no less important strain of English empiricism, and the reality of sublunary existence. Newman does not see himself, in the final analysis, as a man apart. Crosby quotes Newman appositely on St. Paul:

> Newman writes, "Human nature, the common nature of the whole race of Adam, spoke in him, acted in him, with an energetical presence, with a sort of bodily fulness.... And the consequence is that, having the nature of man so strong within him, he is able to enter into human nature, and to sympathize with it, with a gift peculiarly his own." This is also the way it is with Newman.[13]

It is this large, sympathetic humanness that makes Newman so successful at describing the human condition in a range of literature, sermon and treatise, verse and novel, divine and humane. He was concerned with the actual condition of people's lives, as in the *Lectures on the Present Position of Catholics* (addressed to laymen), and with the actual way people come to believe, as in the *Grammar of Assent*. And these were ordinary people. As C.S. Dessain put it, Newman's aim in the *Grammar*,

> ... was to vindicate the right of the ordinary man, and especially the simple, unlearned one, to assent to and have certitude about truths which he never had, and probably never could demonstrate.[14]

Nowhere is the breadth of Newman's human concern better seen than in his attitude to the laity, not only in the social and moral

13. Ibid.
14. C.S. Dessain, *John Henry Newman* (Oxford: Oxford University Press, 1980), p. 153.

condition of their lives but also in their central role in the continuity of the Catholic tradition. In Newman's view, it was the ordinary faithful who preserved Christian orthodoxy, when many bishops of the fourth century were falling into the Arian heresy that denied the divine nature of the Son of God. In his article "On Consulting the Faithful in Matters of Doctrine" (1859), one which caused so much difficulty at the time, Newman writes: ". . . The body of the faithful is one of the witnesses to the fact of the tradition of revealed doctrine, and . . . their consensus through Christendom is the voice of the Infallible Church."[15] As Ian Ker has argued, Newman preferred the word "faithful" to "laity" since the former categorization includes the laity without making the distinction between clergy and lay. He preferred a term that emphasized the unity of "the Church" as all the baptized, not just the clergy, and certainly not just the hierarchy. This is the understanding of the faithful, of consensus, and of Christendom that Thomas More had some three hundred years before Newman, when he, a layman, saw nearly all the English bishops make terms with heresy. The foundation of the extensive authority of the consensus of the faithful is, for both More and Newman, rooted in human nature, and in particular, in conscience:

> Conscience is ever forcing on us by threats and by promises that we must follow the right and avoid the wrong; so far it is one and the same in the mind of everyone, whatever be its particular errors in particular minds. . . . As we have naturally a sense of the beautiful and graceful in nature and art, though tastes proverbially differ, so we have a sense of duty and obligation, whether we all associate it with the same certain actions in particular or not. . . . [C]onscience does not repose on itself, but vaguely reaches forward to something beyond self, and dimly discerns a sanction higher than self for its decisions, as is evidenced in that keen sense of obligation and responsibility which informs them.[16]

15. Quoted in Ian Ker, "Newman on the *Consensus Fidelium* as 'The Voice of the Infallible Church,'" in *Newman and the Word*, T. Merrigan and I. T. Ker, eds. (Leuven, Belgium: Peeters, 2000), p. 69.

16. Newman, *Grammar*, p. 99.

Conscience is the common faculty that enables us, as persons, to reach towards other persons in a responsible way, and is also the foundation of the religious sense: "... the phenomena of Conscience, as a dictate, avail to impress the imagination with the picture of a Supreme Governor, a Judge, holy, just, powerful, all-seeing, retributive, and is the creative principle of religion, as the Moral Sense is the principle of ethics."[17] Moreover, this adherence to conscience illuminated by faith was crucial to Newman's own personal spiritual development, as is illustrated in a letter in the *Apologia*:

> Certainly, I have always contended that obedience even to an erring conscience was the way to gain light, and that it mattered not where a man began, so that he began on what came to hand, and in faith; and that any thing might become a divine method of Truth; that to the pure all things are pure, and have a self-correcting virtue and a power of germinating.[18]

The *Grammar of Assent*, as a work of psychology as much as of philosophy, suggests that, at a foundational level, what is good for the ordinary man is good for everyone. One of the salient features of this work is the way in which such a complex theme is treated in such ordinary words (although the eloquence is extraordinary) and illustrated with such common examples. The *Grammar* is perhaps his most important philosophical counter to the rationalistic, Benthamite spirit of his age, in that it essays a useful and practical purpose, but with considerably higher ends for the human than Bentham could conceive. His "Illative Sense" corresponds to the "Reason" of Coleridge, and also bears similarities with the developed idea of common sense, as a means of perception beyond the merely ratiocinative faculty, in Scottish Enlightenment thinkers such as John Reid. The illative (or inferential) sense is beyond the mere rationalistic, but is far from irrational in its workings or its conclusions. It includes, as Russell Kirk put it,

> ... impressions that are borne in upon us, from a source deeper than our conscious and formal reason. It is the combined product

17. Ibid., p. 101.
18. Newman, *Apologia*, p. 139.

of intuition, instinct, imagination, and long and intricate experience.[19]

The principal similarity of the illative sense to common sense is its consistency with the nature of the human mind and the way in which it works in practice:

> Assent on reasonings not demonstrative is too widely recognized an act to be irrational, unless man's nature is irrational, too familiar to the prudent and clear-minded to be an infirmity or an extravagance. None of us can think or act without the acceptance of truths, not intuitive, not demonstrated, yet sovereign. If our nature has any constitution, any laws, one of them is this absolute reception of propositions as true, which lie outside the narrow range of conclusions to which logic, formal or virtual, is tethered; nor has any philosophical theory the power to force on us a rule which will not work for a day.[20]

The difference, however, between common sense and the illative sense is that the latter depends more on authority than on human nature. In its highest, most developed, and most powerful form it is seen in the capacity of men of genius to express truths about our common human nature that are not normally accessible to common sense, but are consistent with it at its most illuminating. We might make a general inference here of an analogy in the social and political order: that there is a need for authority, or the principle of aristocracy; but it must be cooperative with the democratic claims of the common. The political constitution should reflect the constitution of human nature, and of humane thought.

So important is humane thought that it is the central theme of Newman's idea of liberal education, and of the university in which it is pursued. Newman's *Idea of a University* (1852) counters, on the one hand, the secularizing drift of Victorian education as "useful" subjects excluding the divisive theology (as in Bentham's London University); and, on the other, the Church hierarchy's desire for an Irish university that would teach only Catholic truth, with an

---

19. Russell Kirk, *The Conservative Mind*, Seventh Revised Edition (Washington, DC: Regnery, 1985), p. 285.
20. Newman, *Grammar*, p. 150.

emphasis on divinity, such that the difference between the university and the seminary would be confounded. Between these poles stands Newman's *Idea*, the greatest work of Christian humanism to emerge from the nineteenth century. The human must not be neglected, says Newman, for good religious reasons:

> We [Catholics] have a goodly inheritance. This is apt to cause us—
> I do not mean to rely too much on prayer, and the Divine Blessing,
> for that is impossible, but we sometimes forget that we shall please
> Him best, and get most from Him, when, according to the Fable,
> we "put our shoulder to the wheel," when we use what we have
> been given by nature to the utmost, at the same time that we look
> out for what is beyond nature in the confidence of faith and
> hope.[21]

Newman makes the point in his opening discourse that his opinions on liberal education have not been "got up" for the occasion; rather, they "have grown into my whole system of thought, and are, as it were, part of myself." The principles of liberal education are attainable "by the mere experience of life":[22]

> They do not come simply of theology; they imply no supernatural
> discernment; they have no special connexion with Revelation;
> they almost arise out of the nature of the case; they are dictated
> even by human prudence and wisdom, though a divine illumina-
> tion be absent, and they are recognized by common sense, even
> where self-interest is not present to quicken it; and, therefore,
> though true, and just, and good in themselves, they imply nothing
> whatever as to the religious profession of those who maintain
> them. They may be held by Protestants as well as by Catholics; nay,
> there is reason to anticipate that in certain times and places they
> will be more thoroughly investigated, and better understood, and
> held more firmly by Protestants than by ourselves.
>
> It is natural to expect this from the very circumstances that the
> philosophy of Education is founded on truths in the natural
> order.[23]

21. John Henry Newman, *The Idea of a University* (Notre Dame, IN: University of Notre Dame Press, 1982), p. 4.
22. Ibid.
23. Ibid.

The university should teach and reflect the whole of knowledge, and therefore is not, by definition, a university if it excludes theology. In what Coleridge called the "lecture bazaar" of the utilitarian university, knowledge has become disintegrated and will produce unintegrated people, the opposite of what Newman called "gentlemen," moral aristocrats capable of independent reflection, and guided by the integrated personality itself. Elsewhere, Newman approves the Athenian spirit over the Spartan, the free rather than rule-bound virtue that Pericles speaks of in his funeral oration as given by Thucydides: Newman's gentleman is a Christian Athenian, approaching the fully human.[24]

Newman's objection to the utilitarian approach to education for the mass society being born in his time is a prophetic indictment of a system of mental enslavement rather than of the true liberation that comes with a liberal education. He is not so much protecting a privilege for a particular class as criticizing a system that would come to replace the superior form of education to which the masses could also have access. And Newman helped to keep alive this vision of education even as the darkness of the utilitarian approach has apparently, in our time, become all-encompassing. His *Idea* was thus a great effort to conserve a philosophy of learning that was in danger of being entirely eclipsed, delaying and perhaps even putting off its extinction altogether. Liberal education nurtures the freedom of the human mind without which there can be no active principle to keep human life, on the individual and communal levels, from becoming a prison-house where all is visible precisely because it is desanctified and demystified—a condition rather like Bentham's panopticon. This is life without a dynamic, spiritual principle that enables the change without which comes ossification. Like Burke, Newman saw change as a means of preservation rather than a sign of decay.

This is seen in Newman's *Essay on the Development of Christian Doctrine* (1845) where we hear not only the Burkean note but also the Coleridgean, in the emphasis on the organic growth of ideas. In

24. See Crosby, op. cit.

distinguishing between a corruption and a true development in an idea, Newman notes the idea's "conservative action upon its past":

> A true development, then, may be described as one which is conservative of the course of antecedent developments being really those antecedents and something besides them: it is an addition which illustrates, not obscures, corroborates, not corrects, the body of thought from which it proceeds; and this is its characteristic as contrasted with a corruption.[25]

Newman's religious illustrations of this thesis, including the saying of Jesus that he came to fulfill the Law, not to destroy it, are some interesting analogies from the temporal spheres, of jurisprudence, and modern and ancient history:

> Blackstone supplies us with an instance in another subject-matter, of a development which is justified by its utility, when he observes that "when society is once formed, government results of course, as necessary to preserve and to keep that society in order."
>
> On the contrary, when the Long Parliament proceeded to usurp the executive, they impaired the popular liberties which they seemed to be advancing; for the security of those liberties depends on the separation of the executive and legislative powers, or on the enactors being subjects, not executors of the laws.
>
> And in the history of ancient Rome, from the time that the privileges gained by the tribunes in behalf of the people became an object of ambition to themselves, the development had changed into a corruption.
>
> And thus a sixth test of a true development is that it is of a tendency conservative of what has gone before it.[26]

This conservative aspect of Newman's idea of development is at the heart of his legacy. As Christopher Dawson put it:

> [Newman] realized with exceptional keenness of perception and clarity of vision the new dangers which threatened the Christian faith and the whole traditional order of Christian civilization. And at the same time he discovered and investigated the internal prin-

25. John Henry Newman, *An Essay on the Development of Christian Doctrine* (Notre Dame, IN: University of Notre Dame Press, 1989), p. 200.
26. Ibid., p. 202.

ciple of development in the life of the Church by which what is already implicitly contained in Christian faith and tradition is unfolded and applied to meet the needs of the age. . . .[27]

Newman's doctrine of development, "was inspired by an intense faith in the boundless powers of assimilation which the Christian faith possessed and which made it a unitive principle in life and thought."[28] In an age when the trend towards secularism was being merely disguised by whatever political conservatism could moderate of the advance of liberalism, Newman saw more deeply into the principles through which the Church could continue on her own terms. His separation from the national Church was an essential part of that deeper vision, which involved a deeper communion with the Christian past than the national compromise could accommodate.

The sacrificial nature of Newman's departure from the Anglican project (from its inception, an attempt to come to terms with the secular spirit) bears many similarities with the sacrifice that Thomas More made in cleaving to the creed that Newman also embraced. Both believed in the primacy of a conscience that was far from private judgment; both shied from a tendency towards papal absolutism in favor of the wider authority of historical consensus; both resisted the attempts of the secular power to confine and mitigate the spirit of Christian freedom in the name of liberty; both located this freedom in a Christian humanistic learning that was antipathetic to the kinds of secular absolutism that, different though they were in the cases of Henry VIII and Sir Robert Peel, nonetheless both placed national, secular loyalties and responsibilities above that liberty of the Church to govern herself. This is, after all, merely the corporate reflection of the self-government to which the Christian person is called. Paul Elmer More's conclusion that Newman failed his country suggests that that country was best served within the national Church, but the question for Newman was whether that meant integration with or disintegration from the

27. Dawson, *Spirit*, p. 148.
28. Ibid., p. 151.

Kingdom of Heaven. His conclusion in favor of the latter was no more a triumph of romanticism than was Thomas More's, despite the earthly separations that both endured for it. And the service that both men did for their country has yet to be fully accounted, since it continues still.

8

Orestes Brownson
On Communion and Constitution

[N]o man who has studied the age can, if he have any tolerable powers of generalization, doubt that socialistic principles are those now all but universally adopted. They are at the bottom of nearly all hearts, and at work in nearly all minds.

ORESTES BROWNSON, "Socialism and the Church," 1849

ON FIRST BECOMING ACQUAINTED with the works of the American philosopher, Orestes Brownson, T.S. Eliot wrote to Russell Kirk that, some reservations about the diffuse and wordy Brownsonian style aside, "it is remarkable that a Yankee a century ago should have held such views as his, and depressing that he has been so ignored that most of us had never heard of them."[1] Kirk did much to bring Brownson again to the attention of the American public, in the editing of a reissue of some of his work, but Brownson's Christian humanist conclusions on the nature of political society, and especially on the nature of political constitutions, are both interesting and useful on both sides of the Atlantic. Remarkably, in his time as well as in ours, there was a rooted bias among those who considered themselves thoughtful, or progressive, or benign that liberal or socialist principles were a necessary concomitant and trustworthy path to a happy future; conservatism, especially one rooted in centuries of Christian humanism, was always on the

1. Orestes Brownson, *Selected Political Essays*, ed. R. Kirk (New Brunswick, NJ: Transaction, 1990), p. 7.

defensive. Since the battle of ideas, in which he became a leading figure, continues today, as does the defensiveness of so many conservatives, he can inspire our present thinking on what the principles of a Christian politics may be, from the conservative standpoint. The thought that socialism, as a theory and in practice, is the least suited of the three main political traditions in western society to Christian and humane principles, would still seem counter-intuitive to many Christians, and not only to *bien pensant* intellectuals. If Christian political thinking is to advance at all to meet the challenges of the twenty-first century, there is no more stubborn shibboleth than this: that socialism *is* the politics of Christianity. None has seen the falsity of this idea with more clarity than did Orestes Brownson.

A note on Brownson's intellectual development is in order, given his neglect. Orestes Augustus Brownson was born in Vermont, of Yankee stock, in 1803. He was essentially self-educated, a large, burly, hirsute man dubbed in later life Ursus Major. He came to reject the harsh Calvinism of the Presbyterianism in which he was raised, and moved to the liberal Universalist church, in which he was ordained a preacher. The denial of authority in Unitarianism led Brownson, as he later observed, to become not only non-Christian, but anti-Christian.[2] He lectured and read widely, influenced by socialist schemes, such as those of Owen and Godwin, for social amelioration. During a period of unbelief, he read widely in the works of liberal French Catholic writers such as Lamennais, Lacordaire, and Montalambert. He moved to describing his beliefs as "liberal Unitarianism,"[3] and although his socialist aspirations cooled, he nursed an abiding hatred for modern industrialism, comparing unfavorably the conditions of workers in the northern American cities with those of the Negroes in the South. Brownson was convinced that social progress could not happen without religion, but at this time he was concerned to create a religion of humanity, to substitute for the absence of God. The spirit of Jesus

2. See R. A. Herrera, *Orestes Brownson: Sign of Contradiction* (Wilmington, DE: ISI Books, 1999), p. 8.
3. Ibid.

was the spirit of radical reform,[4] and popular democracy. In spite of Brownson's later association with the Transcendentalists, who included, most notably, Ralph Waldo Emerson and Henry David Thoreau, Brownson never lost this concern for the material condition of the people, or (however vaguely understood) a belief in the Gospel of Christ. It may readily be seen that this idea is not exclusive to Brownson. The apparently obvious logical connection between the Gospel and progressive social reform has long been present in English Nonconformity and Methodism, and persists in all forms of liberal, non-dogmatic Christianity to this day.[5]

Brownson's political opinions reflected, and were intertwined with, his religious outlook. The early Brownson came to identify himself with the Democrats against the Whigs, and during the years that also saw much social and political upheaval in England and on the Continent, Brownson initially supported a radical, Jacksonian program of popular democratic reform. He produced pamphlets supportive of the Democrats, but became disillusioned with popular democracy on the defeat of the Democrats by the Whigs in the 1840 presidential elections. He soon came under the influence of the thought of the Frenchman Pierre Leroux, and withdrew completely from Transcendentalism through a deepening conviction of the reality of sin, with a consequent disillusionment over the possibilities of social progress. Through a study of the Middle Ages, he became drawn towards Catholicism, eventually being received into the Roman Catholic Church in 1844, the year before that of John Henry Newman's reception into the same communion. (Brownson corresponded and argued with Newman, especially over his doctrine of development.) Thereafter, Brownson developed a thesis that Catholicism, or Catholicity as he called it, is the essential principle of liberty, private and public, and ultimately the only enduring preserver of the American Republic, which he came to see as the fullest secular reflection of the Catholic religion. Brownson came to be called "America's Newman," and like Newman, he often had dif-

---

4. Ibid., p. 11.

5. It has often been rightly observed, for instance, that the British Labour Party owes more to Methodism than to Marx.

ficult relations with his religious superiors. Newman wrote appreciably of Brownson's status as the greatest thinker America had produced, despite being at times affronted by Brownson's rudeness, and having reservations about laymen dabbling in theology. In fact, Brownson is more an American Catholic version of a Carlyle or Ruskin—voluminous, verbose, thunderous, and prophetic. He became a confessedly conservative thinker, although in this he anticipates, and resembles, G. K. Chesterton; both came to see in religious orthodoxy the origins and preserving power of the liberty for which they maintained an enduring regard. Neither can be identified with a reactionary defense of the *status quo*, or of powerful economic and financial interests. In a way that distinguishes both Chesterton and Brownson from the Burkean tradition in conservative Christian humanism, both continued in a certain sympathy for the French Revolution.

In another respect, Brownson also anticipates Chesterton's thought, that is, in his critique of modern industrial society from the point of view of a Christian sense of man's nature and potential. In contrast, Brownson notes, to the mechanized slavery of modern industrialism, the Middle Ages were not so dark as they were often presented by the Protestant culture in which he had been raised. In "The Present State of Society" (1843), he looks around him and is filled with a Swiftian *saeva indignatio* at the self-devouring of human kind, and concludes that "men have substituted the worship of Mammon for the worship of God."[6] There has been no unmixed advance in the human condition since the birth of modernity, since "in no three hundred years known to us, since men began to be born and to die on this planet, upon the whole, it has fared worse, for soul and for body, with the great mass of the laboring population":[7]

> We boast of our light; we denounce old feudalism and the middle ages, and fancy it worth a Te Deum that we have got rid of them; and yet, the impartial and clear-sighted historian being asked, what period he lingers on, when, all things considered, it proved best with the great mass of the European population, answers,

6. *Essays*, ed. Kirk, op. cit., p. 32.
7. Ibid., p. 35.

without hesitation, the period when feudalism and the church were in their greatest glory; that is, from the tenth to the end of the fourteenth century. Compare the condition of what Carlyle calls the "workers" of England, the land of our ancestors, during that period, with the condition of the corresponding class at present, and one is almost struck dumb with the contrast.[8]

Brownson was no defender of feudalism as such, as he made clear later in *The American Republic*. The central factor in the relief of man's estate was the Church, in its communication, through the clergy, of the arts of peace and the moral virtues to the wider population. But the subtlety of Brownson's argument lies especially in his being no mere reactionary. He would not return to the Middle Ages, however much he admires them, although even in feudalism he recognizes an important principle:

But even if we would not reconstruct the old feudal and Catholic society, we would have what feudalism and medieval Catholicity sought to realize; and to some extent, though in a rude and imperfect manner, it may be, did realize. We would have men governed, and well governed, let who will be the governors, or what form there may be for selecting them.[9]

The essential achievement of the Middle Ages was, for Brownson, the establishment of a society that worked according to what was given through nature and Revelation as the proper end of man. The norms of medieval culture were fitted, in an exemplary way, to man's nature.

As we have seen, Brownson took some years to be finally satisfied, by what he termed Catholicity, as to what man's nature actually was, but humanism in various forms had always been present in his thinking, being better described as humanitarianism in his earlier period. Even when, later, as a trenchant (although always partly sympathetic) critic of liberalism, socialism and democracy, he asserts the Christian basis of a common humanity:

8. Ibid., p. 36.
9. Ibid., p. 62.

There is something that will not do to sneer at in that free and noble spirit that seeks to break down the artificial barriers which separate man from man and nation from nation, and melt all into one grand brotherhood. If there is any one thing certain, it is that the church has always asserted the unity of the race, and the natural equality of all men. Man equals man the world over, and hence, as Pope St. Gregory I teaches, man, though he has received the dominion over the lower creation, has not received dominion over man, and princes are required to govern as pastors, not as lords; for since all men are equal by nature, the governed are as men the equals and brothers of the governors.[10]

Brownson's assertion of this equality is partly a defense of human nature against the Calvinism with which he was familiar in his Presbyterian upbringing. Calvinism creates a kind of aristocracy of the elect, nullifies human nature as being utterly degenerate, and so founds the political order on grace alone. Only the saints have rights in this order. In contrast to this version of Calvinism, Brownson proclaims the natural law:

The Calvinist does not lie in founding our titles to eternal life on grace and on grace alone, but consists in denying the natural law, that man retains all his original rights in the natural order, and that in the natural order all men have equal rights, which even the elect or those elevated by grace must respect as sacred and inviolable.[11]

Just as Brownson points out the way in which the Calvinist account of Christianity is deficient, he also asserts the deficiency of classical humanism, by pointing to its effect on Christendom during the Renaissance:

The revival and general study of the classics tended by their character to destroy the power of the church of the middle ages, to introduce an order of thought favorable to the supremacy of the civil over the ecclesiastical order, the effect of which is seen in the sudden growth of the monarchical or royal authority. . . .[12]

10. Ibid., p. 141.
11. Ibid., p. 143.
12. Ibid., p. 50.

Catholicism integrates the classical, most importantly in natural law doctrine, with the doctrine of grace; Calvinism and classical paganism work their own process of disintegration in modernity. Catholic Christianity, therefore, is inclusive and unifying on the intellectual and social levels:

> Christianity has taught the world to place a high estimate on the dignity of human nature, and has developed noble and humane sentiments, but under the progress of modern society in losing it, characters have been enfeebled and debased, and we find no longer the marked individuality, the personal energy, the manliness, the force, the nobility of thought and purpose, and high sense of honor, so common in the medieval world, and better periods of antiquity.[13]

Brownson's critique of modernity is essentially a moral one, and his vision of a better future is one that combines nature and grace—or the natural human desire for liberty, with a moral restraint that comes from religion—into a new, and essentially modern, republican synthesis.

Brownson's modernity shows itself in his abiding regard for the spirit of the French Revolution and especially for French liberal thinkers—some Catholic, some not—of the early nineteenth century. Even in his later, avowedly conservative frame of mind, he was always more interested in what they had to say than in conservative monarchists such as De Maistre and the Spaniard, Donoso Cortes. Monarchy was one of the feudal relics that he never wanted to see revived. However, writing in "Socialism and the Church" (1849), a year after that of the revolutions all over Europe, and which threatened to engulf the rest of the western nations, Brownson sought to distance himself from his earlier sympathy for socialism, and Lamennais' doctrine that religion and human liberty were in complete accord. Now, rather than point out the similarities for a positive and inclusive purpose, Brownson prefers to see socialism as a counterfeit of Christianity, its aim to draw Christian adherents even as it undermines their religion. The sly adherents of socialism work

---

13. Ibid., p. 177.

thus, pretending that they are extending, making more catholic, the interpretation of traditional Christianity, which was too narrowly defined:

> The Christian symbol needs a new and a more Catholic interpretation, adapted to our stage in universal progress. Where the old interpretation uses the words God, church and heaven, you must understand humanity, society, and earth; you will then have the true Christian idea, and bring the Gospel down to the order of nature and within the scope of human reason. But while you put the human and the earthly sense upon the old Catholic words, be careful and retain the words themselves. By taking care to do this, you can secure the support of the adherents of Christianity, who, if they meet their old familiar terms, will not miss their old familiar ideas; and thus you will be able to reconcile the old Catholic world and the new, and to go on with humanity in her triumphant progress through the ages.[14]

This kind of "inclusiveness" is dishonest because it retains the language of Christianity while at the same time eviscerating it of its transcendent and supernatural character. "Since it professes to be Christian and really denies the faith, socialism is a heresy...."[15] It will not secure the common good so long as it denies the spiritual and religious, either manifestly or secretly. Where the secular, humanitarian mind is inevitably drawn to a socialist reorganization of society, the Christian tradition has instead "the common good," which is a quite different idea, despite superficial similarities with socialism, a similarity that helps us to understand why, even today, many Christians see socialism as the natural extension of their religion into the political and social sphere. A Christian understanding of democracy, however, should take "the common good" as its reference, not the secular and rationalist idea of socialism:

> [T]his is only what the great doctors of the church have always taught, when they have defined the end of government to be the good of the community, the public good, or the common good of all,—not the special good of a few, nor yet the greatest good of the

14. Ibid., p. 94.
15. Ibid.

greatest number as taught by that grave and elaborate humbug, Jeremy Bentham, but the common good of all, that good which is common to all the members of the community, whether great or small, rich or poor.[16]

At various times and in various political circumstances, Brownson "the weathercock" approved or condemned aspects of liberalism and socialism, in the process moving to a culminating defense of the American republic, more than European monarchy (either constitutional or not) as the great paradigm of Catholic social thought in practice.

To make that defense, however, Brownson's ideas on political constitutions needed some facilitating idea. This he found in the work of the French liberal thinker and socialist Pierre Leroux, whose doctrine of communion Brownson reintegrated with Catholicism. It is with this aspect of Brownson's thought that we are principally concerned here. The conservative character, grounded in his Christian humanist philosophy, of his understanding of society as a community, helps us to wrest this word from the grasp of the liberal and socialist philosophies that have so mischaracterized it as to make the reality of our society at present, in the opinion of so many, deeply offensive to the human spirit. Leroux considered that the social implications of the Gospel had been forgotten in Christianity, and in his doctrine of communion stressed the corporate improvement of humanity, involving a belief in progress. In "Liberalism and Socialism," Brownson frankly acknowledged his debt to Leroux's writings, which, he wrote, "became the occasion of our conversion to Catholicity."[17] But he then goes on to point out Leroux's error, essentially,

> the Eutychian heresy, or the confusion of the human and the divine, and really, though perhaps unconsciously, explains the divine by the human, and thus reduces Christianity to pure humanism or naturalism.[18]

16. Ibid., p. 180.
17. Ibid., p. 125.
18. Ibid.

This is what Brownson had himself done with religion for some time, even though, in the process, he always acknowledged its crucial importance in any schemes of social improvement. His criticism of Leroux, however, is made in the more important context of an analysis of the limited, and ultimately, self-defeating humanism of liberalism and socialism. So far as they go, Brownson can sympathize with secular humanist aims, but he amends Leroux's idea—that man communes with nature through property, with his fellow man through family and the state, and with God through humanity—into a more orthodox formulation that reintegrates religion into human life:

> Man has a threefold nature, and lives by communion with God, man, and nature. He communes with God in religion, with man in society, and with nature in property, and any political or social order that strikes at either [sic] of these, or hinders or obstructs this threefold communion, as Leroux well maintains, is alike repugnant to the will of God and the highest interests of humanity; and efforts made to render this communion free and unobstructed, to give freedom in the acquisition and security in the possession of property, to protect the family as the basis of society, and to break down the barriers to social intercourse interposed by prejudices of birth or caste, and to secure freedom of worship or religion, are in principle great and solemn duties, obligatory alike upon all men.[19]

The essential idea, that human beings must have some object outside themselves with which to commune, came to Brownson from Leroux, and for this Brownson always felt indebted, even when criticizing Leroux. Brownson was always aware of the positive aspects of socialism, even when he had rejected its secular humanitarian bases. The thought of Donoso Cortes helped to provide Brownson with a link between Leroux's idea of communion and the Catholic faith. Just as Burke and Coleridge used the organic metaphor drawn from the natural world as a metaphor for society, Cortes used the supernatural form of the Trinity, both one and many, a community of love, to convey the true nature of human social life.

19. Ibid., p. 156.

Brownson's understanding of man's life in society as a communion on the natural and supernatural levels informs his discussion of political constitutions, and especially that of America. With a clarity that grew through his life until he converted to Catholicism, Brownson knew, with Burke, that man is a religious animal, and inferred that the political order cannot be separated from the religious. Indeed, religion sustains the constitution of a state, as the soul sustains the body, from which it cannot in the final analysis be divorced. As he avers in "Liberalism and Progress," "A nation of atheists were a solecism in history":[20]

> The ancient lawgivers always sought for their laws not only a moral, but a religious sanction, and where the voice of God does not, in some form speak to men's consciences, and bid them obey the higher power, government can subsist only as a craft or as sheer force, which nobody is bound to obey.[21]

Religion, rather than (as in modernity) ideology, provides the moral and spiritual context in which human political society works:

> Politicians may do as they please, so long as they violate no law of right, no principle of justice, no law of God; but in no world, in no order, in no rank, in no condition, have men the right to do wrong. Religion, if any thing, is the lex suprema, and what it forbids, no man has the right to do. This is a lesson liberalism has forgotten.[22]

It might be added that liberalism tends toward the undermining of political authority at the same time that it appears to strengthen the secular order against the spiritual. On the other hand, the circumscribing of the authority of politicians and governments with religion also strengthens their rights, where it underpins the authority of magistrates to govern. (As Brownson puts it, "politicians may do as they please. . . .") Brownson followed Burke and De Maistre, differing from them only in his republicanism, in seeing the constitution of a nation as its soul, and as a Christian and a Catholic he knew that the care of the soul necessitated religion. His argument is

20. Ibid., p. 172.
21. Ibid.
22. Ibid., p. 173.

a humanist one, from the corresponding likeness of the nation to the individual. As Brownson says near the beginning of his major work, *The American Republic* (1865), "Nations are only individuals on a larger scale."[23] They are like human beings, not like machines, or, more pertinently, abstract ideas. Brownson, like Burke, is scathing on the subject of written constitutions:

> [E]xperience has proved that written constitutions, unless they are written in the sentiments, convictions, consciences, manners, customs, habits, and organization of the people, are no better than so much waste paper, and can no more restrain them than the green withes with which the Philistines bound his limbs, could restrain the mighty Samson.[24]

The work of restraint can only be done by something of superhuman origin, that is religion, and so the constitution must be rooted in conscience if it is to enjoy a valid right of obedience and loyalty from the people. The constitution does not derive its authority merely from the convention of those representatives of the people who may have formed it:

> The conventional origin of the constitution excludes its moral or divine right, and therefore denies all obligation in conscience of the people, either collectively or individually to obey it. It has nothing in it that one is morally bound to treat as sacred and inviolable. Its violation is no moral offence, for it is the violation of no eternal and immutable right. Nothing hinders the people, when they find the constitution in the way of some favorite project on which they are bent, from trampling it under their feet.[25]

Brownson, it is important to emphasize, is not here arguing for the people rejecting any constitutional restraints, rather the opposite. Government must be carried on, it has a divine purpose, it is essential for human society, there is a need for order before freedom, but it will be simply natural for a people to reject constitutions that are not rooted both in conscience and custom; the constitution reflects

23. Orestes Brownson, *The American Republic*, ed. Americo D. Lapati (New Haven, CT: College and University Press, 1972), p. 31.

24. *Essays*, ed. Kirk, op. cit., p. 200.

25. Ibid., p. 207.

the traditions of a people, and a people cannot be bent into something that does not fit them.

Conscience inclines people to obey lawful authority, and it is a part of Brownson's critique of liberalism that it weakens the bond between conscience and authority by removing religion from the civil sphere:

> It is the mad attempt to separate the progress of society from religion that has rendered modern liberalism everywhere destructive, and everywhere a failure. It has sapped the foundation of society, and rendered government, save as a pure despotism, impracticable, by taking from law its sacredness, and authority its inviolability, in the understanding and consciences of men.[26]

Insofar as the liberal mind, in pushing political society towards an ever purer form of democracy, breaks the connection between the religious and political orders, it actually turns democracy against conscience, with a consequent effect of demoralizing a people. Then legislation becomes superfluous:

> [L]aws are impotent when the people have become venal, and are easily evaded or openly violated with impunity, when they are not consecrated and rendered inviolable by the national conscience: and it is of the essence of democracy to dispense with conscience, and to attempt to maintain wise and beneficent government, without drawing on the moral order, by considerations of public and private utility alone.[27]

Laws that proceed merely from the supposed will of the majority, which is supposed to represent the democratic mandate under Benthamite, utilitarian ideas, cease to become real laws at all:

> No government that has real authority to govern, can originate in convention [in an assembly to decide *ab initio* or *de novo*] alone; for the convention itself needs to be authorized by a law or an authority superior to itself, since St. Paul teaches, *Non est potestas nisi a Deo.* Where there is no law of nations, which the nation itself is bound to obey, there may be national force, but no national

26. Ibid., p. 174.
27. Ibid., p. 219.

right or authority to govern. Laws that emanate from the people, or that are binding only by virtue of the assent of the governed, or that emanate from any human source alone, have none of the essential characteristics of law, for they bind no conscience, and restrain, except by force, no will.[28]

Although Brownson approved a degree of what we might call conscientious democracy, the constitution, properly formed, represents the conscience of the people in the formal ordering of the republic.

Brownson makes this case, in its most mature and developed form, in *The American Republic* (1865), written partly as a justification of the Union cause in the American Civil War. Notably, Brownson considers the American constitution in its relation to providence, to logic, and to religion, making a strong case that not only does it suit the American people, but is more pleasing to the human and divine reason than any other on earth. In this respect, although it may not easily be transplanted into other countries, it serves as a preeminent example to them. The American political constitution, Brownson says, is reflective of an anterior constitution, which he calls the "providential constitution," that which is given, the customs, traditions, character of the people that, we might say, owes much to the land and the religion from which the people draw their physical and spiritual nourishment. Any formal, written constitution must closely reflect the providential constitution or it is not worth the paper it is written on:

> Thomas Paine would admit nothing to be the constitution but a written document which he could fold up and put in his pocket or file away in a pigeon-hole. The Abbé Sieyès pronounced politics a science which he had finished, and he was ready to turn you out constitutions to order, with no other defect than that they had, as Carlyle wittily says, "no feet, and could not go."[29]

This Burkean understanding of political constitutions should engender a certain humility in a people, a certain wariness about being able to export it wholesale:

28. Ibid., p. 196.
29. *The American Republic*, ed. Americo D. Lapati, op. cit., p. 108.

The English government is no doubt the best practicable in Great Britain, at present at least, but it has proved a failure wherever else it has been attempted. The American system has proved itself, in spite of the recent formidable rebellion to overthrow it, the best and only practicable government for the United States, but it is impracticable everywhere else, and all attempts by any European or other American state to introduce it can only end in disaster.[30]

Insofar as this admonition relates to Americans, Brownson feels it a timely warning, and we can feel the relevance of it to leftist American thinking about the Russian Revolution and the Soviet Union, and about the British Empire, which it wanted dismantled in exchange for American support during the Second World War, among other places before and since:

The democratic Americans are also great political propagandists and are ready to sympathize with any rebellion, insurrection, or movement in behalf of democracy in any part of the world, however mean and contemptible, fierce or bloody it may be; but all this is as unstatesmanlike as unjust: unstatesmanlike, for no form of government can bear transplanting, and because every independent nation is the sole judge of what best comports with its own interests. . . .[31]

Political constitutions, written or otherwise, must reflect the organic nature of the nation they would govern. "Fit your shoes to your feet,"[32] Brownson says pithily.

On the other hand, we sense that part of Brownson that is sympathetic to liberal rationalism when he asserts that there is some logical principle within mankind, ultimately to be identified with the Divine Word or *Logos*, that strives to make its artifacts—including political constitutions—consistent with this inherently reasonable God-created universe. The constitution must reflect the Trinitarian character of created reality. In this respect, the English constitution, with its checks and balances, falls short:

30. Ibid., p. 124.
31. Ibid., p. 125.
32. Ibid.

> The English system, which is based on antagonistic elements, on opposites, without the middle term that conciliates them, unites them, and makes them dialectically one, copies the Divine model in its distinctions alone, which, considered alone, are opposites or contraries. It denies, if Englishmen could but see it, the unity of God.[33]

The English constitution is unsettled, always subject to shifts of power among crown, lords and commons, satisfying nobody. Unlike in the American constitution, there is no settled division of powers that gives direction to power, rather than nullifying it, as in the English system. The American constitution, Brownson tells us, reflects the order of the universe, as revealed by Catholic truth, and it is in this version of American exceptionalism that America finds its role on the world stage. The Greco-Roman civil system worked over time to rid itself of its barbaric, tribal elements until it was eventually overcome by barbarians from outside its walls: the Germanic tribes in the West, and the Turks and Tartars (much later) in the East. It is in America that this Roman civil system has been most successfully revived, and Europeans need to imitate it by ridding themselves of their barbaric, feudal elements, to find their own appropriate forms of the civil, republican system.

America has a religious dimension to this destiny and mission, which is to "render practicable and to realize the normal relations between church and state."[34] In Europe, the Church has been made, in different ways, the creature of the State, corrupting both. In America, each operates freely in its proper sphere, both reflecting in their different realms, natural and spiritual, the inherent "catholic" nature of the universe. So long as both Church and State operate according to Catholic principles, there can be no conflict between them. Brownson emphasizes that the non-establishment of religion in the United States is part of the Church's freedom.

Brownson is a stimulating thinker, devoted to the idea of America while being an intelligent critic of it in practice. In particular, he

---

33. Ibid., p. 236.
34. Ibid., p. 242.

appreciates what in his time was the potential perversion of the idea (in our time, a misdirection more fully and regrettably pursued) by the spirit of liberal democracy combined with the commercial spirit (of which there has been, in Coleridge's phrase an "overplus" in America, as in Britain). In a curious echo of Samuel Johnson's critique (although for different reasons) of America, Brownson regrets the hold of Whiggery on the country:

> In a word, the business classes, according to the "urban party" of the time of Swift or Addison, or of Queen Anne's reign, have permanent possession of the government, and use it to further their own interests, which is a damage; for this country is fitted to be, and really is, a great agricultural country.[35]

American democracy creates a passion for wealth that, in Brownson's analysis, causes misery and crime, and arises from a sense that poverty is a disgrace. In this respect, America is removed from what it should be as a "catholic" nation, for the Catholic Church teaches that poverty is something to be honored, and the virtuous poor respected. One has a sense, reading Brownson's critique of his times and his country, of liberalism, and socialism, that the same struggle continues between Christian humanism and modernity. To paraphrase T. S. Eliot, the battle is not won, but then neither is it lost, and for us there is only the trying.

Orestes Brownson, writing on communion and constitution, has much to say to us today in a time when the liberal interpretation of the relationship between Church and State is causing much constitutional upheaval, such that the nature of America as a religious nation is being threatened by a militant secularism. Constitutional reform in Britain is being led, too, by liberal thinking to which conservatives often seem to have few ideas with which to respond. The movement towards European integration, a "United States of Europe," for example, is also being led by leftist political thinking, and Brownson's warning that constitutions cannot be imported and imposed could be a salutary word of warning before a paper-made

---

35. *Essays*, ed. Kirk, op. cit., p. 210.

house of cards falls apart, a victim of its own inherent instability. In a time, too, when the United States and Britain are involved in "nation-building" elsewhere in the world, Brownson's ideas could provide a useful guide to what they can and cannot do.

9

Benjamin Disraeli's One Nation

This blessed plot, this earth, this realm, this England,
This nurse, this teeming womb of royal kings,
Fear'd by their breed, and famous for their birth,
Renowned for their deeds as far from home,
For Christian service and true chivalry.
Richard II, II, i.

Art is order, method, harmonious results obtained by fine and
powerful principles. I see no art in our condition. The people of
this country have ceased to be a nation. They are a crowd, and
only kept in some rude provisional discipline by the remains of
that old system which they are daily destroying.
DISRAELI, *Tancred*, 1847

In comparison with Gladstone [Disraeli] was a philosopher and
statesman; he was a genius as opposed to a man of great talent—as
it is fair to say that conservatism is in general the intuition of
genius, whereas liberalism is the efficiency of talent.
PAUL ELMER MORE, "Disraeli and Conservatism," 1915

BENJAMIN DISRAELI is remarkable in the history of English literature for being, thus far, the only instance of a novelist turning politician and eventually becoming Prime Minister of Great Britain. He
was also the first former Prime Minister to publish a novel, *Lothair*,
in 1870. Insofar as he thus uniquely combines public life and letters,
he is worthy of our attention. More importantly, however, he combined public life, letters, and an unusual, not to say idiosyncratic,
religious perspective. He is the only British Prime Minister to have
been born in the Jewish faith, a remarkable fact in what was then a

self-consciously Christian nation, but his thoughts on the importance of traditional Christianity in the life of the nation, imaginatively explored in his novels, mean that he may meaningfully be considered within the Christian humanist tradition. In Disraeli, literature, politics and religion work together to form a clear philosophy of social integration in a time when national disintegration was a widespread fear. As we shall see, the imagination is at heart of this Disraelian project, conceived, like Newman's, as a counter to the rise of utilitarianism. In important ways, Disraeli is the counterpart in the political sphere of Newman in the religious, except that Disraeli wrote more on religion than Newman ever did on politics. This fact alone shows us how important it was to Disraeli, and both literature and religion provided the materials with which he regenerated national myth. As will be seen, there are some remarkable contemporary echoes of the war between Disraelian Tory romanticism and the utilitarian "sophisters, economists and calculators" of the previous generation, and suggestions that renewal may not, therefore, be a vain hope.

As many scholars and readers have suggested, Disraeli's political philosophy (except in its imperial elements) was formed and expressed early in his career, and most clearly demonstrated in his *Vindication of the English Constitution* (1835), and in the Young England trilogy of novels: *Coningsby* (1844), *Sibyl* (1845), and *Tancred* (1847). These are the principal works that we examine here, and they form the essentials of Disraeli's critique of whiggery, and more particularly, its contemporary manifestation as utilitarianism. In his *Vindication*, Disraeli argues a Tory interpretation of history, and in the Young England trilogy, brings this creed into imaginative life. The imagination is the cornerstone of the Disraelian attack on utilitarianism, and on the Peelite amalgamation with the spirit of the age. In his biography of Lord George Bentinck, Disraeli weighed Peel as "gifted" and "accomplished," but he "had a great deficiency: he was without imagination."[1] (Paul Elmer More notes that what Disraeli says of Peel was equally true of Gladstone.) The importance

---

1. Paul Elmer More, *Shelburn Essays: Eighth Series* (New York, NY: Phaeton Press, 1967), p. 173.

of this deficiency to Disraeli is explained by his comment written in his diary in 1833: "The Utilitarians in politics are like the Unitarians in religion; both omit imagination in their systems, and imagination governs mankind."[2] This is a startling conviction, entirely opposed to the spirit of liberalism, and the religion of progress, which depend on a rationalism purged of anything that smacks of fancy, faith or intuition. But Disraeli does not argue that the imagination is superior to the reason; he observes what he takes to be a fact of human nature, that the imagination is a more powerful force than reason as an impulsive, or compulsive, agency in the private and public affairs of humanity; therefore, the wise statesman takes it into account in the development and prosecution of national policy.

Disraeli's writings attest to and restate the English myth, as it resides in the national imagination, to be brought out by a successive generations of new story-tellers. First, in his *Vindication*, a sweeping account of English history, Disraeli counters the rationalism of the utilitarians, whose ideas he characterizes satirically as a form of the worst aspects of medieval scholasticism, of reason disconnected from life:

> And now we have an a-priori system of politics. The schoolmen are revived in the nineteenth century, and are going to settle the state with their withering definitions, their fruitless logomachies, and barren dialectics.[3]

Disraeli follows Burke in opposing those whose object is to

> ... form political institutions on abstract principles of theoretic science, instead of permitting them to spring from the course of events, and to be naturally created by the necessities of nations.[4]

Respect for precedent, prescription and antiquity, despised so much by the utilitarians, arise, in Disraeli's view, from a "profound knowledge of human nature,"[5] and government is not a science, in the

---

2. Quoted in ibid., p. 171.
3. Benjamin Disraeli, *Vindication of the English Constitution* (London: Saunders and Otley, 1835), p. 15.
4. Ibid.
5. Ibid., p. 23.

modern sense of the word; on the contrary, "a State is a complicated creation of refined art,"[6] but an art that is consonant with human nature, and that works with the grain of the English people. Those of our wise ancestors who steered the State through its difficult times, "would not tolerate nature struggling with art, or theory with habit"[7]—as happens when abstract systems are imposed on a people. Reason, as the word came to be understood in the eighteenth century, has its limitations. The stability of the English State, for instance, is in its foundation upon prescription, which is "placed above law, and held superior to reason."[8] France, on the contrary, is in a "Laputan state,"[9] where Swift's mad scientists have "divided it into equal geometrical departments,"[10] in spite of nature, destroying the ancient provinces with their differences of soil, population, manners and temperaments.

Utilitarianism, then, is not only whiggery, but also Jacobin scientism. Against this abstract political theorizing, in which rationalistic forms of government may be imposed, disastrously, on any people anywhere, Disraeli argues that the English constitution has grown out of the law of the land, based on custom, and the respect for prescription. Even constitutional upheavals appeal to some ancient principle of right:

> In short, all our struggles for freedom smack of law. There is, throughout the whole current of our history, a most salutary legal flavour. And arbitrary monarchs and rebellious parliaments alike cloak their encroachments under the sacred veil of right, alike quote precedent and cling to prescription.[11]

Even at their worst, England's upheavals are quite different from those of France: "An English revolution is at least a solemn sacrifice: a French revolution is an indecent massacre."[12] The constitution is a

---

6. Ibid.
7. Ibid., p. 25.
8. Ibid.
9. Ibid., p. 29.
10. Ibid.
11. Ibid., p. 22.
12. Ibid., p. 45.

creation of the genius of the place, and Disraeli (like Orestes Brownson, sometime later) points to the folly of trying to impose the English constitution on other countries, such as poor, afflicted France: "I am only surprised that the ludicrous imposture lasted so long."[13] Neither can the American constitution be exported to those South American countries where it has been tried, and where it has failed:

> [T]he constitution of the United States had no more root in the soil of Mexico, and Peru, and Chili [sic], than the constitution of England in that of France, and Spain, and Portugal: it was not founded on the habits or the opinions of those whom it affected to guide, regulate, and control.[14]

In contrast to such folly is the innate conservatism of the English practice, in which

> ... a wise statesman will be careful that all new rights shall, as it were, spring from out old establishments. By this system alone can at the same time the old be purified and the new rendered permanent.[15]

Disraeli's conception of the English constitution being based in the common law is emphasized by his broad understanding of the constitution as including the law and the courts:

> Throughout these observations, in speaking of the English constitution, I speak of that scheme of legislative and executive government consisting of the King and the two Houses of Parliament; but this is a very partial view of the English constitution, and I use the term rather in deference to established associations, than from being unconscious that the polity of our country consists of other institutions, not less precious and important than those of King, Lords and Commons. Trial by Jury, Habeas Corpus, the Court of King's Bench, the Court of Quarter Sessions, the compulsory provision for the poor, however tampered with, the franchises of municipal corporations, of late so recklessly regarded by short-

13. Ibid., p. 34.
14. Ibid., p. 57.
15. Ibid., p. 50.

sighted statesmen, are all essential provisions of the English constitution. . . . The political institutions of England have sprung from its legal institutions. They have their origin in our laws and customs.[16]

Disraeli states that, like custom, and the common law, the constitution is an artifact that issues naturally from incorporated human nature, and we can infer that its authority derives ultimately from the natural law that comes from God; similarly, the constitution is authoritative, and has a claim on our allegiance, insofar as it accords with these prescriptive and transcendent authorities.

All this is prelude to Disraeli's Tory narrative of one nation represented by the constitution, rather than, in the Whig story, the people being (to a greater or lesser extent, depending on the tide of progress) represented by the House of Commons. The House of Commons is not the house of the people anyway, argues Disraeli, but the house of the knights, the lesser nobility, the equestrian order that gradually admitted into its ranks the burgesses—to form that peculiarly English order,

> . . . the gentlemen of England; a class of whom it is difficult to decide, whether their moral excellence or their political utility be most eminent, conspicuous and inspiring.[17]

To be precise, Disraeli says, English law does not recognize "nobility," which he characterizes as a useless, parasitic French class, to be contrasted with the English "peers" and "commons," who saw "their rank was a political institution for the public weal, and not a privilege for their private gratification."[18] In order to establish his case against the modern Whigs, and to remove them from their pretended role as defenders of the people, he shows how the Whig nobility grew from those supporters of Henry VIII who benefited from the despoliation of monastic lands at the time of the Reformation. This class was eventually to dominate the monarchy and install a "Venetian" system, in which the king was merely a limited figure

16. Ibid., pp. 67–68.
17. Ibid., p. 86.
18. Ibid., p. 87.

ruling at the pleasure of the aristocracy. Thus was the constitution subverted by one class, as the Commons had done during the Civil War. Some of Disraeli's most telling points are made in drawing parallels between these upheavals of the seventeenth century, and those of Disraeli's own time; they are not without relevance, either, to ours:

> The Bishops expelled from the House of Lords, the King defied, then imprisoned, and then decapitated, the House of Lords disregarded, and then formally abolished, voted "a nuisance, and of no use"—you see, my Lord, there were Utilitarians even in those days,—behold the great object at length consummated of concentrating the whole power and authority of the government in one estate of the realm.[19]

This usurpation of the constitution was made on the basis that the House of Commons represents the people, the Commons having declared, "that the people are the origin of all just power," an axiom to which any person may annex any meaning of his fancy."[20] Disraeli then points out the tyranny that followed the Civil War, order only coming with Cromwell's military despotism. All this was more than a century before the French Revolution and Terror, the parallels with which we cannot help but consider. The aristocracy, Disraeli reminds us, restored liberty with the Revolution of 1688, but thereafter the Whigs established far too much control over the monarchy, making him a Venetian Doge.

In contrast to this model, Disraeli presents us with a Tory union between people and king that is truly democratic. The Whig supremacy was overturned:

> [E]ncouraged by the example of a popular monarch in George III, and a democratic minister in Mr. Pitt, the nation elevated to power the Tory, or national party of England, under whose comprehensive and consistent, vigorous and strictly democratic system, this island has become the metropolis of a mighty empire, its Sovereign at the same time the most powerful and its people the most free. . . .[21]

19. Ibid., pp. 117–118.
20. Ibid., p. 118.
21. Ibid., p. 173.

But at the time that Disraeli was writing his *Vindication*, the Whigs had returned to power, to continue their dismantling of the constitution, and thus the nation, in ways that may remind us of the governments of our own time:

> [T]he Whigs are an anti-national party. In order to accomplish their object of establishing an oligarchical republic, and of concentrating the government of the state in the hands of a few great families, the Whigs are compelled to declare war against all those great national institutions, the power and influence of which, present obstacles to the fulfilment of their purpose. It is these institutions which make us a nation. Without our Crown, our Church, our Universities, our great municipal and commercial Corporations, our Magistracy, and its dependent scheme of provincial policy, the inhabitants of England, instead of being a nation, would present only a mass of individuals governed by a metropolis, whence an arbitrary senate would issue the stern decrees of its harsh and heartless despotism.[22]

Disraeli's Toryism stands against that malignant, ever-present political spirit that makes use of those with grievances in order to increase its own power; that has no love for those local and dispersed centers of authority that would frustrate at any level its purposes; and that would replace the fertile national myth with a banal cult of novelty. But Disraeli's approach is not simply defensive. The most remarkable feature of the *Vindication* is in the way it builds towards its main thrust of argument, that is, to show that the Tory party is the real democratic party, despite the appropriation of that role by the Whigs and Liberals. (This would be similar to an as yet wholly imaginative case of the modern Tory party arguing, on the basis of the defense of traditional British institutions, that it is the really European party.) Democracy, for Disraeli, is about ends rather than means, and he understands the term empirically rather than abstractly:

> The Tory party in this country is the national party; it is the really democratic party of England. It supports the institutions of the country, because they have been established for the common

22. Ibid., pp. 181–182.

good, and because they secure the equality of civil rights, without which, whatever may be its name, no government can be free, and based upon which principle, every government, however it may be styled, is, in fact, a Democracy.[23]

Moreover, those aspects that are generally recognized as being characteristic of democracy, especially freedom and equality, Disraeli perceives as being established in the English system, more successfully and enduringly than anywhere else, because, not in despite, of a constitution in which natural hereditary power is given public duties. Disraeli neatly distinguishes French equality from English equality; the former makes no one privileged, the latter makes everyone privileged:

> Thus the meanest subject of our King is born to great and important privileges; an Englishman, however humble his birth, whether he be doomed to the plough or destined to the loom, is born to the noblest of all inheritances, the equality of civil rights; he is born to freedom, he is born to justice, and he is born to property. There is no station to which he may not aspire; there is no master whom he is obliged to serve; there is no magistrate who dares imprison him against the law; and the soil on which he labours must supply him with an honest and decorous maintenance. These are rights and privileges as valuable as King, Lords and Commons; and it is only a nation thus schooled and cradled in the principles and practice of freedom, which, indeed, could maintain such institutions. Thus the English in politics are as the old Hebrews in religion, a "favoured and peculiar people."[24]

Disraeli's sense of English exceptionalism is reinforced by the comparison with a Hebraic sense of religion, the importance of which he was to elaborate later in *Tancred*. Anglo-Saxon politics and Judeo-Christian religion have in them a common quality that speculative and abstract modes of thought lack, as Disraeli points out in this remarkable insight:

> English equality governs the subject by the united and mingled influences of reason and imagination; French equality having

23. Ibid., pp. 182–183.
24. Ibid., pp. 204–205.

rejected imagination and aspiring to reason, has[,] in reality, only resolved itself into a barren fantasy. The constitution of England is founded not only on a profound knowledge of human nature, but of human nature in England; the political scheme of France originates not only in a profound ignorance of human nature in general, but of French human nature in particular.[25]

The integrated constitution is a reflection of an integrated view of human nature, where reason and imagination combine, as do rights and duties. Finally, Disraeli's understanding of equality and freedom derive from his religious sense of their relationship with law, which develops over time in the context of a particular people in a particular place.

Disraeli's thought is ever reaching after this paradoxical combination of universality in particularity, always seeking for an inclusive understanding of an apparently exclusive English constitution. In *Coningsby*, the first of his "Young England" novels, Disraeli resists what Toryism had declined into, and criticizes the successors of Pitt for turning Toryism into a by-word for the excluding of sections of the population from the constitution:

> Impudently usurping the name of that party of which nationality, and therefore universality, is the essence, these pseudo-Tories made Exclusion the principle of their political constitution, and Restriction the genius of the commercial code.[26]

Disraeli sees Pitt as representing the authentic Tory vision, one that involves a liberal extension of rights to various groups which would demonstrate loyalty to the Crown, and liberal policies in commerce; the restriction of constitutional rights went hand in hand with a restriction of commerce, and both were alien to the "manners and customs of the English people."[27] We hear in Disraeli's discussion of Pitt an early note of "Tory democracy," as well as his sympathy for the plight of Catholics:

---

25. Ibid., pp. 206–207.
26. Benjamin Disraeli, *Coningsby*, ed. T. Braun (London: Penguin, 1983), p. 95.
27. Ibid., p. 101.

A widening of our electoral scheme, great facilities in commerce, and the rescue of our Roman Catholic fellow-subjects from the Puritanic yoke, from fetters which have been fastened on them by English Parliaments in spite of English Sovereigns; these were the three great elements and fundamental truths of the real Pitt system.[28]

The characters in the novel, of the Catholic landowner, Eustace Lyle; the northern manufacturer, Millbank; and the Jewish financier, Sidonia—all disaffected from the cult of Utility, but inspirational to the young Coningsby—represent the breadth of Disraeli's inclusive sweep of those he wishes to see granted a recognized place in the ancient English constitution. They are distinguished by their religious vision, their imagination, and their attachment to real human beings rather than abstract ideas: all oppose "the frigid theories of a generalizing age."[29] In particular, Disraeli recognizes the instinctive conservatism (or, in Disraeli's preferred term, Toryism) of both Jews and Catholics, both of which manifestations of the Judeo-Christian tradition are supportive of monarchy and traditional religious values. The essence of Toryism for Disraeli is a free monarchy and free traditional religion. Both direct the course of a nation through a profound effect on the human imagination, and point upwards towards the divinity that is the heart of our humanity. Sidonia reminds us that Reason is not responsible for any of the great achievements of man—not even the French Revolution: "Man is only truly great when he acts from the passions; never irresistible but when he appeals to the imagination. Even Mormon counts more votaries than Bentham."[30]

In contrast to a broad national constitution that enables the fruitful expression and transmission of natural human vitality, especially faith, is the dead hand of Utility (novel, rational schemes giving rise to a whole new class of bureaucrats and managers). In his response to Peel's Tamworth Manifesto, the appeasement of utility and liberalism that also crucially stimulated John Henry New-

28. Ibid.
29. Ibid., p. 495.
30. Ibid., p. 262.

man to action, Disraeli sees the dangerous prospect of an evisceration of the constitution, such that the dead body would be animated, as it were, by a mechanical technique. It would be "Tory men and Whig measures":

> The Tamworth Manifesto of 1834 was an attempt to construct a party without principles; its basis therefore was necessarily Latitudinarianism; and its inevitable consequence has been political Infidelity.[31]

The Peelite evisceration of Toryism in favor of the new liberalism would mean an evisceration of the constitution; hence Coningsby's famous question, one that typifies Disraeli's knack for turning words round, as he does with "democracy," on those who misuse them by looking at mere forms: "What do you mean to conserve? Do you mean to conserve things or only names, realities or merely appearances?"[32] Rather as Newman resisted the move away from a vital religious faith as the basis of the national Church, so Disraeli resisted the movement away from political faith in the living spirit of the English constitution. This settlement joined king and people through the exercise of gentlemanliness, an idea that Newman defined and in which Disraeli too believed. The Young England novels, which have been described as the political counterpart of Tractarianism, are full of Newman's ideal. Coningsby himself evinces a character close to that of Hurrell Froude, whom Newman identified as the spiritual founder of the Tractarian movement:

> His was a mind that loved to pursue every question to the centre. But it was not a spirit of scepticism that impelled this habit; on the contrary, it was the spirit of faith. Coningsby found that he was born in an age of infidelity in all things, and his heart assured him that a want of faith was a want of nature. But his vigorous intellect could not take refuge in that maudlin substitute for belief which consists in a patronage of fantastic theories. He needed that deep and enduring conviction that the heart and the intellect, feeling and reason united, can alone supply. He asked himself why gov-

31. Ibid., p. 125.
32. Ibid., p. 343.

ernments were hated, and religions despised? Why loyalty was dead, and reverence only a galvanized corpse?[33]

It is this movement of faith that was to be so successful in renewing both traditional Christianity in the nineteenth century and making political Conservatism Disraelian rather than Peelite.

Sybil is a more dramatic book than *Coningsby*, has more varied and vivid characters, and a deeper social theme. The satire is, if anything, more piercing, and amusingly anticipates the worlds of Oscar Wilde and Evelyn Waugh. ("I rather like bad wine," said Mr. Mountchesney; "one gets so bored with good wine.")[34] The religious theme established in *Coningsby* becomes more developed, particularly in its relationship to the condition of the English people. The English Reformation is presented more closely as an immense disaster, mainly for the poor who benefited from the relief and improvement given by the monasteries, although not all the Catholics in the novel are entirely praiseworthy: for the ideal landowner, Trafford, there is the scheming fabricator of pseudo-aristocratic pedigrees, Hatton. (Disraeli is an imaginative enough novelist not to deal in schematic characterization, and can make characters with opposing views to his own not unsympathetic.) But the spirit of the pre-Reformation Church is represented by Aubrey St. Lys, a type of the Anglican priest (to become more and more evident with the spread of Tractarian ideas) faithful to the ancient forms of the Church, and devoted to the improvement of the spiritual and material condition of the people. Industrial society is contrasted with the integrated world of the Middle Ages:

> "As for community," said a voice which proceeded neither from Egremont nor the stranger, "with the monasteries expired the only type that we ever had in England of such an intercourse. There is no community in England; there is aggregation, but aggregation under circumstances which make it rather a dissociating than a uniting principle."[35]

---

33. Ibid., pp. 149–150.
34. Benjamin Disraeli, *Sybil* (Ware, Herts: Wordsworth Editions Ltd., 1995), p. 4.
35. Ibid., p. 57.

This comes from the socialist Morley, who refers to community of property, but the distinction between community and aggregation is one that Disraeli intends us to accept; he makes a similar distinction between a "nation" and a "mere crowd" in *Tancred*. But Disraeli shows us that religion is the basis of community, not a redistribution of wealth. St. Lys laments the separation between the English Church and the people:

> "I blame only the Church. The Church deserted the people; and from that moment the Church has been in danger, and the people degraded. Formerly, religion undertook to satisfy the noble wants of human nature, and by its festivals relieved the painful weariness of toil. The day of rest was consecrated, if not always to elevated thought, at least to sweet and noble sentiments. The Church convened to its solemnities, under its splendid and most celestial roofs, amid the finest monuments of art that human hands have raised, the whole Christian population; for there in the presence of God, all were brethren."[36]

In its inclusiveness, Disraeli seems to see in the Church the model for the political constitution of the nation. Moreover, his conception of the Church is profoundly sympathetic to those, like Catholics and Jews, who cling to their ancient traditions, while being less so to those sectarians who cut themselves off from tradition. "Christianity is completed Judaism, or it is nothing," says St. Lys. "Christianity is incomprehensible without Judaism, as Judaism is incomplete without Christianity."[37] If anything, however, the constitution can be more inclusive than a particular religious tradition. (The effortlessly superior Sidonia can be an English subject and a practicing Jew, since he can give an appropriate and sincere loyalty to both ancient traditions.)

The Church is to blame for disconnecting itself from the people, as is the aristocracy. While the main characters of Disraeli's novels are aristocratic, the aristocracy comes in for a good deal of satirical treatment for failing to live up to their role of leadership of the people, and declining into self-interest. The satire against the acquisi-

36. Ibid., p. 96.
37. Ibid., p. 97.

tion of bogus ancient pedigrees by those wishing to advance themselves in the peerage, is only one part of an attack that includes the unprincipled and greedy Lord Marney, whose lands were taken from the Church at the Reformation. Lord Monmouth in *Coningsby* is a similar study in self-absorption. Disraeli is concerned with the younger generation, however, and the renewal of a sense of duty in the aristocracy, as in all orders of society; no class should cut itself off from the others; each has a duty to perform that benefits the whole. The connection between the aristocracy and the people is essential, as Egremont says to Sybil:

> "The new generation of the aristocracy of England are not tyrants, not oppressors, Sybil, as you persist in believing. Their intelligence, better than that, their hearts, are open to the responsibility of their position. But what is before them is no holiday-work. It is not the fever of superficial impulse that can remove the deep-fixed barriers of centuries of ignorance and crime. Enough that their sympathies are awakened; time and thought will bring the rest. They are the natural leaders of the people."[38]

Too often the leaders who emerge from the people come to betray them, says Egremont. The alternative to class duties, suggests Disraeli, is class warfare, through which the people suffer most. The Disraelian project of national re-integration and re-enchantment requires a revitalizing of the traditional orders and classes, and the substitution of faith for a skeptical and mutually hostile suspicion and antagonism. Only then will the two nations of *Sybil*'s subtitle become one again.

Disraeli was proud of the way he both belonged and was alien to the country in which he was born, and into whose religion he was baptized. Another remarkable facet of his integrating imagination is the combination of the importance of the English national party (the Tories) and "the great Asian mystery"—Sidonia's phrase in *Tancred* that became satirically applied by one wit to Disraeli himself. Certainly, part of Disraeli's aim to re-enchant his times through a deeper appreciation of the imaginative and mysterious

---

38. Ibid., p. 237.

character of the Christian religion involved putting himself in the role of the initiated, and thus giving his story the force of prophecy. (He was by no means the only Victorian, however, to play this role; it was an age of patriarchal, bearded prophets.) *Tancred* begins in a penetrating critique of an England fallen away from itself, rather like John of Gaunt's speech in *Richard II* in its imagination of an ideal England grubbily descended and dispossessed, like Gaunt's "tenement or a pelting farm." The young aristocrat, Tancred, laments the age's lack of faith, either political or religious, and determines to go on pilgrimage to the Holy Land to discover the principle behind both. England, Tancred tells Sidonia, has lost religious inspiration; it is "divided between infidelity on one side and an anarchy of creeds on the other."[39] (Later in the novel, another character explains Tancred's pilgrimage by saying that "the English are really neither Jews nor Christian, but follow a sort of religion of their own, which is made every year by their bishops.")[40] Tancred laments that, "Nobody now thinks of heaven. They never dream of angels. All their existence is concentrated in steamboats and railways."[41] Civilization has been rejected in favor of money and comfort. Sidonia recognizes in Tancred "not a vain and vague visionary, but a being in whom the faculties of reason and imagination were both of the highest class."[42] With a suggestion of symbolic significance, the Jewish financier makes possible the spiritual renewal of the young aristocrat by giving him contacts for his journey in the Holy Land.

Tancred rather peters out, ending on a memorably inconclusive line announcing the arrival of Tancred's parents in Jerusalem. But the novel is full of interesting insights into Disraeli's political ideas, especially, as we have seen, on the relationship between politics and religion, but also between politics and opportunity. The burden of this chapter is that Disraeli was a man of profound, if idiosyncratic, principle and yet he is often dismissed as an opportunist. In a certain

39. Benjamin Disraeli, *Tancred* (London: Peter Davies, 1927), p. 126.
40. Ibid., p. 215.
41. Ibid., p. 135.
42. Ibid., p. 127.

way, however, he was both. Rather as Burke's political philosophy involves a sophisticated understanding of the relationship between principles and circumstances, so also is Disraeli's. "Opportunity is more powerful even than conquerors and prophets,"[43] writes Disraeli in the narrative voice of *Tancred*. It is a part of political prudence, which involves the imagination, for the successful statesman to further the common good in circumstances as they arise. It is important that he not be confined by schema, ideological dogmata, or rash promises; a certain mystery should hang about his art like that of any artist, politics being indeed an art rather than a science. He should be free to exercise a moral imagination in human things, such that they remain human, and not become removed into the realm of arid abstractions, and mechanical metaphors. Edgar Feuchtwanger has suggested that the unprincipled and scheming Fakredeen resembles Disraeli, in "what he wanted to be and what he feared he really was."[44] But there is an interesting dialogue between the idealistic Tancred and the skillful operator Fakredeen that suggests another possibility. Tancred says,

> "I do not believe that anything great is ever effected by management. All this intrigue, in which you seem such an adept, might be of some service in a court or in an exclusive senate; but to free a nation you require something more vigorous and more simple. This system of intrigue in Europe is quite old-fashioned. It is one of the superstitions left us by the wretched eighteenth century, a period when aristocracy was rampant throughout Christendom; and what were the consequences? All faith in God and man, all grandeur of purpose, all nobility of thought, and all beauty of sentiment, withered and shrivelled up.... If you wish to free your country ... you must act like Moses and Mahomet."[45]

Tancred is as much a part of Disraeli as is Fakredeen. No one can doubt that Disraeli enjoyed intrigue and the great game of politics, but it would be the opposite of the case to suppose that he was without faith, like Fakredeen. Disraeli had the high purpose of attempt-

---

43. Ibid., p. 389.
44. Edgar Feuchtwanger, *Disraeli* (London: Arnold, 2000), p. 70.
45. Benjamin Disraeli, *Tancred*, p. 266.

ing to marry imaginative ideals with human reality, both in himself and in the nation.

It is this integrative approach that principally characterizes Disraeli's politics, which were, writes J. P. Parry,

> reactive and restorative rather than reactionary. He tackled specific challenges; he was a practical politician, not a visionary ... the aim was always to re-establish an organic unity out of chaos, to build a synthesis out of conflict—to make England a nation again, to reunite her church, to resolve tensions in her great landed interest, to realize her national role in the world, to save her empire.[46]

Disraeli's approach to the British Empire is beyond the scope of this chapter, although we may note in passing that his sense of the imagination, and the oriental imagination, was central to his moving that Queen Victoria be given the title "Empress of India." Although the nation was central to Disraeli's vision of England, he cannot be described in a narrow sense as a nationalist. As his religious vision was neither reductively latitudinarian or diffusely catholic, but deeply rooted in an ancient and world-wide tradition,[47] so did his sense of the purpose of the English nation mean that it could not be narrowly confined in a small island. Disraeli was a mythmaker whose literary mind was an important part of his political vision, and it is no small part of his considerable success in saving his party and his country from a total capitulation to that other, materialistic, scientific, reductive, inhumane and grey world that is the other side of Victorian England. The Conservative Party still has its grey, Peelite, conservative side in tension with its colorful, Tory, Disraelian side. Disraeli was not a visionary, but he was a man with vision. His written record of that vision can still inspire and teach, and may help to recall both England and the Conservative Party to some central human and divine truths.

---

46. J. P. Parry, "Disraeli and England," *The Historical Journal*, 43, 3 (2000), p. 705.

47. It is intriguing to note, in a phrase that the Anglican Disraeli could have written, Pope Pius XII once affirmed that "spiritually speaking, we are all Semites."

10

G. K. Chesterton
And the Authority of Common Sense

THESEUS: The lunatic, the lover, and the poet,
Are of imagination all compact:

....

And, as imagination bodies forth
The forms of things unknown, the poet's pen
Turns them to shapes, and gives to airy nothing
A local habitation and a name.
A Midsummer Night's Dream, V.i.

A page of statistics, a plan of model dwellings, anything which is rational, is always difficult for the lay mind. But the thing which is irrational any one can understand. That is why religion came so early into the world and spread so far, while science came so late into the world and has not spread at all. History unanimously attests the fact that it is only mysticism which stands the smallest chance of being understood of the people. Common sense has to be kept as an esoteric secret in the dark temple of culture.

G. K. CHESTERTON, *Heretics*, 1905

G. K. CHESTERTON has been appropriately called the "apostle of common sense."[1] The words "common sense" frequently recur in his writings, and could be used to describe both the form and the content of the writing itself. As Roger Scruton has noted, Chesterton's stylistic mannerisms are quite similar to those of his opponent, George Bernard Shaw; that is, "an opinionated tone, an

1. This appellation was first given, I believe, by Dale Ahlquist.

affectation of common sense, and an effrontery which lent zest to his love of paradox."[2] But there is more than affectation in Chesterton's attachment to common sense, although an inquiry into what he meant by the words might be useful, given that the idea is more often appealed to than understood. Common sense might, in fact, be termed the central Chestertonian idea, since other important concepts to which he was attached can be seen to cohere about this central one. Orthodoxy, Catholicism, sanity, the ordinary, the normal, the "centric," myth and fairy tale, democracy, liberalism, revolution, distribution, proportion, and imagination: all these ideas Chesterton somehow connects with "common sense." In another way, too, common sense is central to Chesterton's work and achievement. John Henry Newman, late in his long life, mentioned liberalism as the central idea against which he had fought, and insofar as we can similarly sum up Chesterton's life work in a word, we might say that it was the fight against skepticism. As Benjamin Disraeli in various places suggested, it is faith that is the creative and integrating principle in human life; by contrast, we might say that it is skepticism that is the destructive and disintegrating principle, in religion and in society, in the soul and in the mind. Common sense, then, is at the heart of Chesterton's battle against skepticism.

Before we consider common sense as Chesterton used and understood the term, some context—of usage antecedent of and contemporary with him—will help to clarify this elusive idea. The medieval *sensus communis* is similar to consensus (and also "consent"), what is generally believed, admitted and held to be true. In this sense, its authority is quantitative, and derives from the overwhelming number of persons, or nations, who hold to, or have held, a particular creed or doctrine or opinion. *Securus judicat orbis terrarum*, says Augustine. This authority is consistent with the idea of natural law, since it implies that all the faithful are capable of judgment if their opinion is to be valued. Conscience, then, is a vital part of the *sensus communis*, and it is easy to see how the Christian civilization of the Middle Ages leads to the authority of human rea-

2. *Conservative Texts: An Anthology*, ed. Roger Scruton (London: Macmillan, 1991), p. 59.

son and democracy in succeeding ones. Common sense is in opposition to *gnosis*, that knowledge that is only revealed to a few, and is
hidden from the multitude, and insofar as heresy is a form of *gnosis*,
a special revelation of truth, common sense is orthodoxy. It is an
inclusive rather than exclusive principle, and associative rather than
sectarian. Its authority is God and the community, rather than God
and a solely-inspired individual.

After the Reformation, common sense seems rather to go into
abeyance. It does, however, enjoy something of a revival in the eighteenth century, where it is associated with the simplicity and purity
of human reason, as among the English radicals. It was also an
important source of authority for Edmund Burke, their principal
opponent. It is at this time that common sense receives some qualitative, philosophical consideration, most notably from the Scottish
Enlightenment thinkers. For the radicals, such as Mary Wollstonecraft and Thomas Paine ("Mr. Common Sense" as he became
known on the streets of Philadelphia), common sense is the obvious, the lowest common denominator of thought; it cuts through
the falsities of art and rhetoric, and it is unmixed with the untrustworthy imagination. Wollstonecraft and Paine seem to have mis-
trusted the imagination quite as much as the earlier neoclassicals,
and in this respect, "common sense" can be found in the context of
rationalistic thought that leads subsequently to utilitarianism.
Common sense can often mean, especially in the English context, a
straightforward, honest practicality, exclusive of the higher reaches
of intellectual speculation, complex ratiocination, and artistic imagination, to all of which it is hostile. For the Rousseauistic radical,
common sense is a natural faculty of perception that resides in the
common people, where it is unpolluted by learning or corrupt manners. Jacksonian Democracy, and the post-1812 war Era of the Common Man, owed something to this radicalism. Jackson distrusted
the Jeffersonian "natural aristocracy," believing that all a statesman
needed was common sense. However short-lived Jackson's Common Man Era, the twentieth century would be dedicated to the
common man, and the appeal to common sense still occasionally
makes itself felt in (usually conservative) political campaigns.

In the Scottish Common Sense School of the eighteenth and early nineteenth century, a philosophy of common sense developed in reaction to Hume's skepticism and Berkeley's idealism, both of which tended to dissociate the individual mind from the external world, including other people. For Thomas Reid (as we have seen, a leading member of this school), perception of external objects involves a belief in qualities belonging to them. An excessive emphasis on ideas as premises leads to absurdities, as reality is made to submit to those ideas. (We recall Dr. Johnson's commonsense reply to Berkeley when he kicked the stone, and in an appropriate, or ironic, twist of events, the Scottish philosophy became the official philosophy of France from the early nineteenth century up until 1870.) The Scottish philosophy of common sense is also associative, in that it implies a continuity between subject and object that opposes the Cartesian split between mind and matter; the subject has something in common with the world of which he is a part. In the twentieth century, the Cambridge philosopher, G.E. Moore, also defended common sense, and turned academic philosophy towards an analysis of commonly held certainties. Nowadays, common sense still popularly carries authority, in an age when all authority is questioned, and it is quite possible that the absurdities of the postmodernist thinkers are preparing the ground for its reappraisal, as once did eighteenth-century skepticism. It remains one of the few philosophical concepts possessed of all kinds of people, although it is seldom elaborated upon, or thoroughly examined. Perhaps that is as it should be, but it certainly bears thinking about in the context of G.K. Chesterton's thought, and in the context of a fragmented world in need of an understanding of the bases of community.

To summarize, we may say that common sense is an active principle of both quantitative and qualitative authority, and operates on the general and the particular level. On the general level, it means the consensus, the field within which my opinion may or may not lie, insofar as I think with the common, integrated mind, or with the individual, and singular mind. Some people have more common sense than others; some possess the mind of the group, or the community, the nation, the Church, the culture, the civilization, more than do others. It depends on their immersion in the traditions of the group, their awareness of the present conversation of the group, and their commitment to the perpetuation of the group. It is characteristic of our own time, of course, to pursue the original, the strange, the *outré*, rather than the things of the common mind. On the level of the particular, we fail to see ourselves as part of a community, tradition, or culture; we fail to use our common sense in the way that it is a faculty of perception by which the subject enters into communion with the objects around him. We are fascinated by stories that suggest that there is no "reality" outside us, that it might be computer-generated, a reflection that so many of us live our lives as fantasies in machine-made screen-worlds of one kind or another. "Virtual reality" is no longer an oxymoron, but fully consistent with the postmodern subjectivism. It means the loss of reality, and the atomization of individuals, the acceptance and celebration of alienation. Common sense sounds dull in comparison.

In *Orthodoxy* (1908), Chesterton's first major assault on philosophical skepticism, he accepts this use of the term, while at the same time exploring its deeper significance:

> We have all forgotten what we really are. All that we call common sense and rationality and practicality and positivism only means that for certain dead levels of our life we forget that we have forgotten. All that we call spirit and art and ecstasy only means that for one awful instant we remember that we forget.[3]

Chesterton is concerned with challenging this notion of common sense, rather as elsewhere he challenges the notion of conservatism. Both ideas, says Chesterton, have become a stale crust over the deeper sources of vitality, or a tired acceptance of a dead *status quo*. To the extent that common sense and conservatism are words sometimes used unreflectively, we can readily see what he means. But the same chapter, "The Ethics of Elfland," is one of Chesterton's most important considerations of common sense, and of a genuinely conservative idea of society that we can recognize as being remarkably similar in all important details to that of Burke, and even more so of Disraeli, who incorporated the idea of democracy into Burke's thought. Chesterton memorably expresses the idea of

---

3. G.K. Chesterton, *Orthodoxy* (New York, NY: Doubleday, 1990), p. 54.

common sense as consensus, which he here links with his Liberal and democratic politics:

> I was brought up a Liberal, and have always believed in democracy, in the elementary liberal doctrine of a self-governing humanity. If any one finds the phrase vague or threadbare, I can only pause for a moment to explain that the principle of democracy, as I mean it, can be stated in two propositions. The first is this: that the things common to all men are more important than the things peculiar to any men. Ordinary things are more valuable than extraordinary things; nay, they are more extraordinary. Man is something more awful than men; something more strange. The sense of the miracle of humanity itself should be always more vivid to us than any marvels of power, intellect, art, or civilization.[4]

The essential miracle of human life, Chesterton shows, inheres in the common: "This is the first principle of democracy: that the essential things in men are the things they hold in common, not the things they hold separately. And the second principle is merely this: that the political instinct or desire is one of these things which they hold in common."[5] Chesterton tells us that his belief in liberal democracy led him to Christian orthodoxy, in a reverse of the historical process by which Christian orthodoxy led Western civilization to liberal democracy, through the doctrine of equality.

Where of course Chesterton departs from the current of liberal thought—that seeks to cut itself off from the grip of an inferior past—is in his conservative vindication of tradition, which he sees as the extension both of democracy and common sense. A little disingenuously, perhaps, he says,

> I have never been able to understand where people got the idea that democracy was in some ways opposed to tradition. It is obvious that tradition is only democracy extended through time. It is trusting to a consensus of common human voices rather than to some isolated or arbitrary record.... Tradition may be defined as an extension of the franchise. Tradition means giving votes to the

4. Ibid., pp. 46–47.
5. Ibid., p. 47.

most obscure of all classes, our ancestors. It is the democracy of the dead. Tradition refuses to submit to the small and arrogant oligarchy of those who happen to be walking about.[6]

There is much that is playful about this memorable statement, and it makes a very telling point, but it does present problems if we take it literally. The "extension of the franchise," we should remember, is metaphorical; dead people cannot vote. But Chesterton reminds us, as does Disraeli, that democracy, rightly ordered, and meaning more than just voting, may be as useful a means of conservation as is aristocracy. Chesterton also reminds us that the nature of the human race requires us to include, in any question of moment, those who have gone before us, and (remembering Burke) those who are yet unborn. Democracy, like any other important human thing, does not exist solely in the present.

Having established the link between common sense and democracy and tradition, "The Ethics of Elfland" also connects common sense with myth and fairy-tale, in the striking formulation: "Fairyland is nothing but the sunny country of common sense."[7] Like tradition, fairy-tale is the distillation of commonly held truths, with the added authority of the common people, whom Chesterton is inclined to trust more than other classes:

> I have always been more inclined to believe the ruck of hard-working people than to believe that special and troublesome literary class to which I belong. I prefer even the fancies and prejudices of the people who see life from the inside to the clearest demonstrations of the people who see life from the outside.[8]

Here, the "special" is contrasted with the common, and it is connected with Chesterton's preference for the amateur over the professional, and his suspicion of presumptuous and disconnected élites, particularly scientists and aristocrats. Part of the authority of myth and fairy-tale is quantitative, in that it has been tested and affirmed by many generations of individuals, but it is also qualita-

---

6. Ibid., p. 47–48.
7. Ibid., p. 49.
8. Ibid., p. 48.

tive, in that it is a more trustworthy means of perception into the reality of things, because it is imaginative. In absorbing fairy-tales as children, we see life in imagination before we experience it. As Chesterton puts it: "I knew the magic beanstalk before I had tasted beans; I was sure of the Man in the Moon before I was certain of the moon."[9] Common sense is the integrated wisdom of the group, but also the wisdom of the integrated person, and in both involves the imagination as an aspect of the perception of truth. The imagination is a part of true Reason—as Coleridge would have said, and as Chesterton says in "The Maniac," the second chapter of *Orthodoxy*. Here again Chesterton resists the use of "common sense" as pure rationalism, or the scientific intellect, which he rather associates with madness:

> That unmistakable mood or note that I hear from [the lunatic asylum at] Hanwell, I hear also from half the chairs of science and seats of learning to-day; and most of the mad doctors are mad doctors in more senses than one. They all have exactly that combination of an expansive and exhaustive reason with a contracted common sense. They are universal only in the sense that they take one thin explanation and carry it very far.[10]

This definition of madness corresponds with heresy, the unbalanced emphasis of one apparently all-encompassing half-truth. Science and reason narrowly defined, exclusive of the imagination, are less able to express reality than literature and art, which at their best involve both imagination and reason. (Much of Chesterton's discussion of fairy tale in chapter 5 involves the unbreakable "laws" of fairy land.) Imagination is not opposed to common sense, but is a part of it:

> There is a notion adrift everywhere that imagination, especially mystical imagination, is dangerous to man's mental balance. Poets are commonly spoken of as psychologically unreliable; and there is vague association between wreathing laurels in your hair and sticking straws in it. Facts and history utterly contradict this

9. Ibid., p. 49.
10. Ibid., p. 22.

view.... Imagination does not breed insanity. Exactly what does breed insanity is reason.[11]

The excessive and exclusive emphasis on reason, and the absence of the balance that imagination helps to bring, causes the loss of proportion that is sanity: "The madman is not the man who has lost his reason. The madman is the man who has lost everything except his reason."[12] True common sense involves a vision of wholeness, which means integrity and interconnectedness: "[M]ost things of common sense come ... rather vaguely and as in a vision—that is by the mere look of things."[13]

Orthodoxy came out of Chesterton's early struggle with certain ideas current in the literature and art of his time, one of which was literary realism. The attack on the materialist assumptions of literary realism is a theme running through a number of Chesterton's works in the first decade of the twentieth century. His defense, in *Charles Dickens* (1906), of the great Victorian against the attacks of those who accused him of being untrue to life, involves the idea of "the common mind" that includes the greatest and most ordinary minds in a normative reflection of real human nature, a reflection conveyed in story and through myth. Dickens's greatness, observes Chesterton, lies in his being a mythologist rather than merely a novelist. Dickens, however, following Carlyle, did not understand the French Revolution, and so gives a false picture of it in *A Tale of Two Cities*. For Chesterton, the Revolution was about the recovery, on the social level, of sane norms of human nature:

> We, the modern English, cannot easily understand the French Revolution, because we cannot easily understand the idea of bloody battle for pure common sense; we cannot understand common sense in arms and conquering. In modern England common sense appears to mean putting up with existing conditions. For us a practical politician really means a man who can be thoroughly trusted to do nothing at all; that is where his practicality

11. Ibid., pp. 16–17.
12. Ibid., p. 19.
13. G.K. Chesterton, *Eugenics and Other Evils* (London: Cassell and Co. Ltd., 1922), p. 120.

comes in. The French feeling—the feeling at the back of the Revolution—was that the more sensible a man was, the more you must look out for slaughter.[14]

This is a Liberal and democratic view, rather than a conservative one, of the French Revolution, but it embodies an essentially conservative idea of revolution as restoration. (The Glorious Revolution of 1688, and the American Revolution of 1776, can both be seen as conservative revolutions intended to protect the existing order against change that threatened that order, but if we follow Burke then we will not see the French Revolution, any more than the Bolshevik Revolution of 1917, in this light.) "The best men of the Revolution were simply common men at their best,"[15] believed Chesterton, and he seems to think of them as he did of William Cobbett, who "did not feel exactly that he was 'in revolt'; he felt if anything that a number of idiotic institutions had revolted against reason and against him."[16] It is in this way that Chesterton understood the revolutionary principle, which he always preferred to the evolutionary one—always and gradually becoming but never suddenly being. Revolution is a kind of conversion towards right order that comes in a flash rather than gradually:

> To the orthodox there must always be a case for revolution; for in the hearts of men God has been put under the feet of Satan. In the upper world hell once rebelled against heaven. But in this world heaven is rebelling against hell. For the orthodox there can always be a revolution; for a revolution is a restoration. At any time you may strike a blow for the perfection which no man has seen since Adam.[17]

For Chesterton, common sense is the ability of any person to

14. G. K. Chesterton, *Charles Dickens* (London: House of Stratus, 2001), p. 101.
15. Ibid., p. 4.
16. Ibid., p. 101. Cobbett's *A History of the Protestant Reformation in England and Ireland* (written between 1824 and 1827) is a profoundly conservative, even reactionary, revisionist account of the Reformation, in favor of the *status quo ante*. It bears comparison with Eamon Duffy's more recent *The Stripping of the Altars*. Chesterton's biographical study *William Cobbett* (1925) makes "the old Radical" a proto-distributist.
17. Chesterton, *Orthodoxy*, p. 110.

think according to his natural reason and in his own conscience. He can have confidence in the authority of conscience illuminated by revelation; then he will be guided to the normal, the ordinary, the lawful, the sane—those things which connect him to the broad current of his fellow men. Chesterton opposed the usurpation of this common authority by the specialist. The problem with rule by the specialist is not so much that he knows more about something than other people, but rather that he sees everything through that one thing which he knows, however well. Chesterton sees that, more and more in the modern world, the idea that ordinary people should, so far as possible, rule themselves, is losing ground to the fact that more and more facets of human life are being put into the hands of specialists. Following the skepticism about whether God exists, there arises a profound skepticism that human beings exist, at least in the traditional sense of man before modernity, and a skepticism about man involves a skepticism about common sense. Everything, including man, is redefined by modern science, which has been placed above man, where before man was above science. This is well illustrated in *Eugenics and Other Evils* (1922), much of which was written in response to the eugenic Mental Deficiency Act of 1913. Chesterton's book shows how science (in the limited sense of the empirical method applied to measurable, and often unmeasurable, things) has entirely arrogated to itself the authority by which we know anything. This might serve as a definition of scientism, directly antithetical to common sense, in which knowing is open to the many and not just the few. Scientism leaves no room for instinctive knowledge, an important dimension of common sense, as is shown for example in this passage from the first essay in the book, "What is Eugenics?":

> Dr. S. R. Steinmetz, with that creepy simplicity of mind with which the Eugenists chill the blood, remarks that "we do not yet know certainly" what were "the motives for the horror of" that horrible thing which is the agony of Oedipus. With entirely amiable intention, I ask Dr. S. R. Steinmetz to speak for himself. I know the motives for regarding a mother or sister as separate from other women; nor have I reached them by curious researches. I found them where I found an analogous aversion to eating a baby for breakfast. I found them in a rooted detestation in the human soul

to liking a thing in one way, when you already like it in another quite incompatible way.[18]

The specially-qualified scientific advisor to an overweening government gives dubious counsel on the basis of which the State usurps the proper role of common sense:

> If something which has been discovered at last by the lamp of learning is something which has been acted on from the first by the light of human nature, this (so far as it goes) is plainly not an argument for pestering people, but an argument for letting them alone. If men did not marry their grandmothers when it was, for all they knew, a most hygienic habit; if we know now that they instinctly [sic] avoided scientific peril; that, so far as it goes, is a point in favour of letting people marry anyone they like.[19]

Eugenics, now seen as a pseudo-science rather than real science, and despite its affinities with modern "bioethics," did suggest that it would be better for humanity if people were bred on scientific principles, rather than free choice. The extension of the definition of "mental deficiency" threatened to put all of humanity under the lunacy laws, said Chesterton, and this idea was given some philosophical force by those psychological theories, current throughout the twentieth century, that suggest we are all at least a bit mad, and "normality," quite as much as common sense, non-existent.

Insofar as scientism involves the attempt to reduce the whole of reality to a single aspect of truth, it is one heresy among the many that have multiplied unchecked in modernity. Chesterton's very use of the words "orthodoxy" and "heresy" involves an adoption of a pre-modern idea of an integrated and balanced view of the world that might not unfairly be called medieval. Thus, the idea of a "common mind" finds its fullest realization in medieval civilization, the greatest philosophical expression of which is Thomism. Aquinas was, for Chesterton, the philosopher of common sense. As he put it in his biography *St. Thomas Aquinas* (1933), and as we saw in the first chapter of this book:

---

18. G. K. Chesterton, *Eugenics and Other Evils*, op. cit., pp. 8–9.
19. Ibid., p. 9.

Since the modern world began in the sixteenth century, nobody's system of philosophy has really corresponded to everybody's sense of reality; to what, if left to themselves, common men would call common sense. Each started with a paradox; a peculiar point of view demanding the sacrifice of what they would call a sane point of view. That is the one thing common to Hobbes and Hegel, to Kant and Bergson, to Berkeley and William James. A man had to believe something that no normal man would believe, if it were suddenly propounded to his simplicity; as that law is above right, or right is outside reason, or things are only as we think them, or everything is relative to a reality that is not there. The modern philosopher claims, like a sort of confidence man, that if once we will grant him this, the rest will be easy; he will straighten out the world if once he is allowed to give one twist to the mind.[20]

Insofar as modern philosophy is modern philosophies, it reflects and assists the breakdown of reality, the disintegration of belief and the fragmentation of society. The common mind, however, is accessible to everyone, and belongs to all, being in no sense a private quality, even when it is expressed in substantial, subtle, memorable and sometimes sophisticated terms only by a few. (This is quite different from the idea of an élite of specialists, professionals, bureaucrats, politicians, scientists, or academics who make decisions for other people deemed incapable of making them; it is the difference between leadership and management.) Aquinas's conclusion, for instance,

> ... is what is called the conclusion of common sense; ... it is his purpose to justify common sense, even though he justifies it in a passage which happens to be one of uncommon subtlety. The problem of later philosophers is that their conclusion is as dark as their demonstration; or that they bring out a result of which the result is chaos.[21]

Thomism is the philosophy of sanity since it is integrative, universal, sensible, and reiterative of the common understanding of expe-

20. G.K. Chesterton, *St. Thomas Aquinas* (London: Hodder and Stoughton, 1933), pp. 172–173.
21. Ibid., p. 178.

rience rooted in the senses and refined by reason. For Chesterton, as for Aquinas, an objective reality does not merely exist as a remote dogma, but may be apprehended by all sane human beings via the senses and reason, both bases of common sense. Sanity is a universal wholeness that connects man and God, matter and mind, heart and soul. The difference, says Chesterton, between St. Thomas and Hegel is simple: "St. Thomas was sane and Hegel was mad," and "the Thomist philosophy is nearer than most philosophies to the mind of the man in the street."

Since at least as early as *Heretics*, Chesterton was possessed of the idea that it is religion, rather than science, that protects the conditions, both mental and cultural, in which common sense can exist. As a philosophy of common sense, Thomism embodies the two aspects that we have previously noted, common sense in the general and in the particular, or in its quantitative and qualitative authority; common sense is what is generally held to be true of matters in which it is competent to judge, and common sense is the faculty of perception in the individual by which he is able to make such judgments. The decay of religion leads to a skepticism not merely confined to the existence or otherwise of God. Once religion goes, all things are doubted, including man. One of the most important aspects of Chesterton's religious thought is his apprehension of the miraculous nature of man. In later life, secure within the precincts of his Catholic faith and religion, the fullest expression of the common mind of the West, Chesterton considered the question, "Is Humanism a Religion?" (By "humanism" he meant the secular religion, the "New Humanism" of Irving Babbitt, but aspects of what he says are applicable also to the quite different humanism of John Dewey and the later twentieth century "humanists.") Chesterton acknowledges that in his time (1929), there is a need to defend the human, which is threatened by science reducing man to a clever animal driven by unconscious compulsions:

> This fight for culture is above all a fight for consciousness: what some would call self-consciousness: but anyhow against mere subconsciousness. We need a rally of the really human things; will

which is morals, memory which is tradition, culture which is the mental thrift of our fathers.[22]

But Chesterton does not agree with the conservative humanists, such as Babbitt, who think that this rally can be brought about without religion: "I do not believe that Humanism can be a complete substitute for Superhumanism."[23] All the good things that the humanists want to preserve ultimately trace their course to something beyond the human:

> The fact is this: that the modern world, with its modern movements, is living on its Catholic capital. It is using, and using up, the truths that remain to it out of the old treasury of Christendom; including, of course, many truths known to pagan antiquity but crystallized in Christendom.[24]

Included among these old pagan truths are insights into the nature of man, the law of his nature for example, but, Chesterton reminds us, these ideas "wither very quickly in modern hands," having been snatched out of ancient and medieval ones. Chesterton goes on to note the death of liberalism, and "the old republican view of human nature," that he saw revived in the French Revolution, and as having had a salutary effect on the nineteenth century. The sense of the sacredness of man has disappeared in the harsh modernity that he sees, for example, in eugenics, and Mencken:

> Here is a monumental remark by Mr. H.L. Mencken: "They (he means certain liberal or ex-liberal thinkers) have come to realize that the morons whom they sweated to save do not want to be saved, and are not worth saving."[25]

The trend in humanism that Chesterton opposes here is the movement away from a faith in democracy to a new aristocratic élite who will govern the mass of humanity, for good or ill. The liberal mood has vanished but, Chesterton says, "while it has evaporated as

---

22. G. K. Chesterton, *The Thing* (London: Sheed and Ward, 1931), p. 22.
23. Ibid.
24. Ibid.
25. Ibid., p. 25.

a mood, [it] still exists as a creed."[26] That creed is Catholicism, the religion of common sense.

In contrast to Christianity, this secular humanism, says Chesterton, is not likely to take hold on people, and therefore will not last. Its problem is the same as that of Matthew Arnold's project for culture in the nineteenth century. Humanism will founder on its own skepticism about human nature, as much as its doubts of a superhuman source. It is essentially egregious:

> In short, I distrust spiritual experiments outside the central spiritual tradition; for the simple reason that I think they do not last, even if they manage to spread. At the most they stand for one generation; at the commonest for one fashion; at the lowest for one clique. I do not think they have the secret of continuity. For an antiquated, doddering old democrat like myself may be excused for attaching some slight importance to that last question; that of covering the common life of mankind.[27]

In his faith in the common, Chesterton stands at the opposite pole to Nietzsche, the type of the intellectual madness that in hailing the death of God, leads to the destruction of man:

> Nietzsche, who represents most prominently this pretentious claim of the fastidious, has a description somewhere—a very powerful description in the purely literary sense—of the disgust and disdain which consume him at the sight of the common people with their common faces, their common voices, and their common minds.[28]

Chesterton points out that the irony is that it is Nietzsche who is weak, and advocates an "aristocracy of weak nerves." The common man has become separated from those who govern him, and the paradoxical consequence, Chesterton says, is that in the century of the common man, as in the course of modernity generally, the common man is persecuted:

---

26. Ibid.
27. Ibid., p. 32.
28. *Heretics*, p. 185.

[M]odern emancipation has really been a new persecution of the Common Man. If it has emancipated anybody, it has in rather special and narrow ways emancipated the Uncommon Man. It has given an eccentric sort of liberty to some hobbies of the wealthy, and occasionally to some of the more humane lunacies of the cultured. The only thing that it has forbidden is common sense, as it would have been understood by the common people.[29]

This is the consequence of the disappearance of common sense, as an operative idea, that as the banners of the various "isms" of the disintegrated truths proliferate, so does persecution, as humanity is made to fit into abstractions. This can become a bloody and terrible business, but perhaps in the long run the effect of skepticism is as a kind of negative corrective, as Chesterton puts it in this prophetic passage:

We who are Christians never knew the great philosophic common sense which inheres in that mystery until the anti-Christian writers pointed it out to us. The great march of mental destruction will go on. Everything will be denied. Everything will become a creed.[30]

This is even more true of the postmodernism of our time than it was of his, and perhaps the more society disintegrates, the more it cultivates the desire for integration, and eventually its rebirth.

In a sense, the common man is the opposite of the privatized man to whom modernity has given birth, and rather as common sense sits insecurely in modernity, so does the common man. (Chesterton notes that, despite the much vaunted "freedom" of modernity, "the Common Man does not in the least want to found a sect. He is much more likely, for instance, to want to found a family.")[31] Nowadays, the privatized man is concerned with himself rather than others, with his rights rather than his duties, with his own life rather than his family's, with his own fulfilment rather than the community's. He is undemocratic, since he is incapable of, or

---

29. G.K. Chesterton, *The Common Man* (New York, NY: Sheed and Ward, 1950), p. 1.
30. *Heretics*, p. 305.
31. *The Common Man*, p. 1.

uninterested in, the exchange of views that democracy requires. He does not bother to vote. There are many like him, but perhaps he is much less universal than is supposed. Perhaps he is merely fashionable, and in view. If that is so, then the common man remains the norm, although he is not entertainingly strange, and he does not serve to illustrate or promote the philosophy of the day, as it is manifested in the media and other redoubts of the postmodern worldview. Were he to hear the truth that he is still sane, rather than one kind of madman living in a mad world, he would be a force to be reckoned with.

11

T. S. Eliot
From Fragmentation to Unity

HAMLET: What piece of work is a man, how noble in reason, how infinite in faculties, in form and moving how express and admirable, in action how like an angel, in apprehension how like a god: the beauty of the world, the paragon of animals—and yet, to me, what is this quintessence of dust? Man delights not me....

Hamlet, II. ii.

Common sense does not mean, of course, either the opinion of the majority or the opinion of the moment; it is not a thing to be got at without maturity and study and thought. The lack of it produces those unbalanced philosophies, such as Behaviourism, of which we hear a great deal. A purely "scientific" philosophy ends by denying what we know to be true....

T. S. ELIOT, "Francis Herbert Bradley," 1927

And the fire and the rose are one.

T. S. ELIOT, "Little Gidding," 1942

IT TOOK SOME TIME before G. K. Chesterton and T. S. Eliot overcame their antipathy towards the other's literary style. Chesterton mistook Eliot's early poetry for a manifestation of *fin de siècle* decadence, a sick recoiling from life, and an absence of the healthy vitality that Chesterton wanted to affirm, as in his riposte to Eliot's "The Hollow Men":

> Some sneer; some snigger; some simper;
> In the youth where we laughed, and sang.

And they may end with a whimper
But we will end with a bang.[1]

Following Eliot's reception into the Church of England in 1927, something of a rapprochement began between them, as Eliot and Chesterton (and C.S. Lewis, as we shall see) found themselves in increasingly common territory. In a sense, however, this was an understanding that they always had been together in addressing (albeit in different ways) the fragmented consciousness and disintegrated world of modernity. Eliot, more than Chesterton, recognized aspects of the divided Western consciousness in himself, and Chesterton had determinedly placed himself in opposition to it, from his own conversion onwards. But it is a mistake to see Eliot's early poetry as simply a confessional expression of his interior predicament, however much the poetry draws on his own experience. More formally than this, Eliot places himself in an objective philosophical position, and is always trying to escape the merely personal.[2] His early poetry speaks powerfully for a generation largely because he seeks to express a widespread malaise through the impersonal (so far as the poet is concerned) dramatic monologue. The original title of The Waste Land, "He Do the Police in Different Voices," stands for the whole of Eliot's early poetry; the poet brings the decadent city (polis rather than police) to life—ironically, often a death in life—through different voices that can never be identified (at least wholly) with the poet himself, in an exercise in poetic ventriloquism.

The poetry allows room for the reader to speak through the poetry, too, and its endless fascination ultimately resides in its spiritual depth, in which the reader can see his own spiritual development running parallel with Eliot's speaking for him. In this way, it has become typical for readers of Eliot to trace through the collected works a journey from the heart of darkness to the heart of

1. Chesterton in his last radio broadcast, quoted in Joseph Pearce, Literary Converts: Spiritual Inspiration in an Age of Unbelief (San Francisco, CA: Ignatius Press, 1999), p. 188.

2. See "Tradition and the Individual Talent," Selected Prose of T.S. Eliot, ed. F. Kermode (London: Faber, 1975), p. 37.

light. It is a suggestion that Eliot himself makes with the arrangement of *Selected Poems* (1954) made by himself, implying a search for meaning in a fragmented and etiolated world. Fragmentation, in the early poems, usually takes the form of non-communication, at the verbal and emotional level. Always, there is a sense of the ambiguity of the personal and the general, as if philosophical problems are being enacted in dramas of the individual human consciousness. What unites the various personae in, say, "Prufrock," or the young man in "Portrait of a Lady," or the various voices of *The Waste Land*, is a search that is ultimately a religious quest: in terms of Eliot's life, this finds completion in orthodox Christianity and a perspective of the wider culture as springing from it. Philosophical viewpoints become the ground of an emerging religious sense, as being the only possible sphere in which personal and communal integration is possible. This theme of integration is reflected in the whole of Eliot's *oeuvre*: of philosophy, poetry and social criticism; the integration of the private and the public; subject and object; mind and matter; individual talent and literary tradition; language and reality; thought and feeling; time and eternity; soul and commonwealth. The persona of the gloomy skeptical poet, locked in himself, that Chesterton found so unappealing, becomes the "smiling public man" of the later years.

While the early poetry strikes us, initially, as presenting a late Romantic sense of emotional non-communication, it is helpful, as Benjamin Lockerd[3] has shown, to see Eliot's early poetry also in the context of his doctoral studies. Eliot's studies involved the criticism of scientific materialism by F. H. Bradley, Bergson and Whitehead. Bradley's *Appearance and Reality* (1893), in particular, was the subject of Eliot's thesis. Bradley attacked any attempt to make physics into metaphysics, and showed that in contrast to science, poetry and religion "deal with direct experience."[4] Eliot, like Bradley, concluded that "when science is taken as the whole of truth, one misses essen-

---

3. In Benjamin Lockerd, *Aethereal Rumours: T. S. Eliot's Physics and Poetics* (Cranbury, NJ: Associated University Presses, 1998). I am particularly indebted, in this chapter, to this excellent book.
4. Ibid., p. 22.

tial elements of the truth."[5] This is not to say that Eliot despised scientific inquiry. The whole tenor of his writings is to achieve, in literature, the precision of expression, feeling and logical thought, as in the analogy, drawn from science, that Eliot uses in "Tradition and the Individual Talent," of the poet's mind compared to a platinum filament used as a catalyst for a reaction between two gases. The possibilities of science, as well as a sense of its inherent limitations to the material sphere, intrigued Eliot. His own quest, that which he embarked upon at Harvard, was to answer the question of how the spiritual heart of the universe relates to its material embodiment; or, how does human life cohere in its physical and spiritual aspects? A significant part of the answer involves the way we, both as individuals and as a civilization, understand the nature of matter itself.

The dualism of objectivity and subjectivity, which both Bradley and Eliot found unsatisfactory, and which is behind Eliot's famous formulation of "the dissociation of sensibility,"[6] finds philosophical roots in the Cartesian split between mind and body. From Descartes onwards, Western philosophy had been composed of those who emphasize the exclusive reality of matter, and those who emphasized that of subjective experience. In symbolism, Eliot found a poetics that could express the continuity of subject and object, and which would reflect the notions of reality that Eliot had absorbed in his study of the pre-Socratic philosophers, and also Aristotle. Symbolism implied the unity of the signifier and the signified; the supreme example, and one which foreshadows Eliot's later conversion, is the Eucharistic sacrament, in which the Host does not merely represent the body of Christ, it *is* the body of Christ. The connection between the natural world and the spiritual, implied in a sacramental symbolism, places a gulf between Eliot and poststructuralism, in which all signs are arbitrary. Although he would have agreed that words are arbitrary signs, he knew that symbols point to a continuity in relations within the natural world.

The symbolism of the early poems is pointing towards a hidden truth in the world that the persona, and to an extent Eliot himself,

5. Ibid., p. 23.
6. Kermode, op. cit., p. 266.

188

find elusive. *Prufrock and other Observations* (1917) reveals the soul of man under the pressure of scientific materialism. Prufrock speaks of himself as "etherized upon a table,"[7] "pinned and wriggling on the wall,"[8] "as if a magic lantern threw the nerves in patterns on a screen"[9]—X-rayed, dissected, bereft of freedom and faith in an emotional life by a materialist, scientistic universe. Prufrock represents, as do other voices in the 1917 volume, the soul of man trapped in, and reduced by, a materialist vision, one which does not recognize his spiritual nature, and thereby reinforces a false dualism, a disintegrated consciousness that cannot connect. As Benjamin Lockerd puts it, "Scientific materialism both cuts modern man off from nature and reduces him to it."[10] In this regard, Eliot's early poems, albeit obliquely, make the same point that C.S. Lewis was to make in *The Abolition of Man*: the final victory over nature for scientistic man is the reduction of himself to mere matter.

Prufrock and the other "consciousnesses" in the 1917 poems inhabit a "smoky" universe from which they are dissociated, and which reduces, dirties and oppresses them. The soul itself becomes "yellowed," a physical, skin-like substance, "stretched tight across the skies,"[11] the universe consisting of "worlds" that "revolve like ancient women/ Gathering fuel in vacant lots."[12] The image here is of the emptiness between atoms, or within atoms themselves, human beings essentially working as deterministically as simpler forms of matter. The separated consciousness sees only material objects in "the spaces of the dark":[13]

> I could see nothing behind that child's eye.
> I have seen eyes in the street
> Trying to peer through lighted shutters,
> And a crab one afternoon in a pool,

7. T.S. Eliot, "The Love Song of J. Alfred Prufrock," *The Complete Poems and Plays of T.S. Eliot* (London: Faber, 1969), p. 13.
8. Ibid., p. 14.
9. Ibid., p. 16.
10. Lockerd, op. cit., p. 96.
11. Eliot, op. cit., p. 23.
12. Ibid.
13. Ibid., p. 24.

> An old crab with barnacles on his back,
> Gripped the end of a stick which held him.[14]

The eyes are without vision in an essentially dead universe, and as when Prufrock imagines himself as "a pair of ragged claws/ Scuttling across the floors of silent seas,"[15] there is no apparent difference between humans and the creatures of the "protozoic slime"[16] from which we emerged at the beginning of the evolution narrative. Random associations of particles exist in a dark emptiness, and move deterministically within it. In these urban landscapes, human beings exist with the four elements, which are polluted and polluting. The human consciousness, or soul, is weighed down and desperate, confusedly unable to connect with a world composed only of dead matter.

The 1920 volume develops the picture of the disintegration that is consequent upon the modern philosophical positions of materialism on the one hand, or idealism on the other. Gerontion believes he will be like the other strange faces in the poems, "whirled/ Beyond the circuit of the shuddering Bear / In fractured atoms."[17] In dramatizing a life and death, the poem provides a curious contrast to Newman's "The Dream of Gerontius," and represents the view of man in modernist philosophy as opposed to Catholic Christianity. Both Gerontion and Gerontius are Everyman, seen from radically different viewpoints, and both conscious of themselves in different ways. In the 1920 volume, as in the 1917 poems, there is a backward movement in a view of man, as he heads back to the "protozoic slime" via a range of animals, but particularly apes and monkeys: "goats and monkeys" is in the epigraph to "Burbank with a Baedeker: Bleistein with a Cigar," and, infamously, Bleistein is in an apelike pose:

> A saggy bending of the knees
> And elbows with the palms turned out.[18]

14. Ibid., p. 25.
15. Ibid., p. 15.
16. Ibid., p. 40.
17. Ibid., p. 39.
18. Ibid., p. 40.

But it is a Boston Irishman, rather than a Chicago Jew, who is Eliot's most developed image of devolving man, Sweeney Erect, a figure both hilarious and terrible. He is a creature of impulses, grossly physical and propelled by a violent, sexual energy, seen rising out of water, like Prufrock's "ragged claws" that he still essentially is, at least on the spiritual level. The world of religion, implied in the epigraph to "Burbank": *"nil nisi divinum stabile est; caetera fumus,"*[19] is remote from the world of the 1920 volume. Priests are "caterpillars,"[20] Christ is a "tiger";[21] the Church is a "hippopotamus,"[22] "in the old miasmal mist."[23] The image of smoke (or fog, or mist) stands for the materialist universe of atoms with nothing between. The early poems suggest not what Eliot himself thought of humanity, but what humanity makes of itself when it fails to make sense of its spiritual reality. (In this sense, John Carey's reading of Eliot in *The Intellectuals and the Masses* seems very wide of the mark.)

Where in the 1920 volume Eliot reduces, satirically, the pretensions of materialism, and shows some of the forms, both hideous and absurd, that humanity takes when it come to believe in such an isolated fragment of the truth, in *The Waste Land* we see a constructive project, a building up of a view of man towards some divine revelation. The poem is a heap of fragments, of broken (and, in C.S. Lewis's word, discarded) images. In anthropological terms, as Frazer had used myth to show us why Christianity is not true, we see Eliot doing the opposite, using old stories to show how man developed glimpses of the truth. Eliot moves out of the city and the urban mental landscapes of the early poems, into the desert, returning to nature. The voices from the city continue, however, to be overheard. Science there makes false teeth and abortions (see "A Game of Chess"), and intensifies the separation between man and nature. The natural process, the rhythm of the seasons, is one from which the inhabitants of the waste land are alienated: "April is the cruellest

19. Ibid.
20. Ibid., p. 54.
21. Ibid., p. 37.
22. Ibid., p. 49.
23. Ibid., p. 50.

month."[24] The constant presence of the four elements reiterates the reality of matter and whereas in the early poems the four elements are constantly dissociative, muddied and polluting, in *The Waste Land* they move towards integration. The five parts of *The Waste Land* suggest not so much tragedy but, as Benjamin Lockerd has shown, Eliot's use of the pre-Socratic philosophers to find a way of knowing beyond the scientific empiricism confined to matter. The pre-Socratic philosophers debated which was the primary element. For Heraclitus, the most important of them, it was fire.[25] Fire corresponds to energy in modern physics. The ancients also spoke of a fifth element, or quintessence, a kind of rarefied air ("pneuma," which means, also, spirit) sometimes seen as fire. The fifth element was known as the aether, and the "aethereal rumours"[26] in the final part of *The Waste Land* are representative of intimations of a spiritual dimension without which matter is oppressive and ultimately destructive of human consciousness.

With the aether, Eliot is able to oppose the atomistic notions inherent in materialism, notions which held that between atoms there is only a vacuum, an emptiness at the heart of things. It is an idea that lends itself to nihilism, but paradoxically turns atomistic materialism into a kind of idealism: as Evelyn Underhill put it in *Mysticism*, for the atomistic materialist, "matter is not more solid than a snowstorm."[27] For Eliot, not only is materialism hopeless, it is essentially flawed as a way of looking at the physical universe, and it is the subject of Eliot's satiric eye in the 1917 and 1920 volumes. *The Waste Land* has moved considerably beyond an essentially negative critique of the times, and established rumours of a spiritual revelation, either Western or Eastern, and the necessity of some kind of spiritual and religious view of the world, that would fill the dehumanizing vacancy of materialism. Eliot at the time was thinking of conversion to Buddhism. Images of Christ's death and resurrection

---

24. Ibid., p. 61.
25. Cf. Gerard Manley Hopkins' poem, "That Nature is a Heraclitean Fire, with the Promise of the Resurrection."
26. Eliot, op. cit., p. 74.
27. Lockerd, op. cit., p. 125.

suggest that the physical presence is not so straightforward as we think. Finally, Eliot's use of Hindu myth suggests that, indeed, the world of matter is considerably more mysterious than materialism suggests.

In the *Four Quartets*, Eliot's major poetic works of a consciously Christian mind, the elements, and the quintessence, become present throughout, having been merely "rumoured" in *The Waste Land*. Heraclitus is an important presence here, too. The first epigraph to "Burnt Norton" is an expression of the common mind as opposed to the disintegrated tendencies of subjectivism: "Although the Logos is common, the many live as if they had a private understanding."[28] For Heraclitus, neither the individual elements, which are really different forms of the same quintessence, nor individual human beings, are ever really separate:

> Heraclitus's emphasis on the underlying unity of the elements goes with an emphasis on the unity of knowledge in an objective natural law ordained by the divine Logos.[29]

Paradoxically, the ancient Heraclitus allows Eliot to engage with the modern, in the form of post-Newtonian physics. In the Newtonian universe, with its causal laws of thermodynamics, force (or energy) acts upon inert matter; it is essentially dualistic. Eliot was aware that Einstein, with relativity theory, and Planck, with quantum theory, were showing that at the extremes of the physical world matter and energy are the same. This new physics, making the material world appear mysterious again, resonated in Eliot's mind with Heraclitus, for whom physics and metaphysics were not wholly separate—something which is very different from the tendencies in nineteenth-century materialism (and in those who still adhere to its tenets today) to make physical science substitute for metaphysics.

Where *The Waste Land* affirms the necessity of a spiritual revelation, and the presence of the resurrected Christ is prophetic of an understanding of the human being as being a part of, but not

28. Ibid., p. 200.
29. Ibid.

confined to, the world of matter, *Four Quartets* expands philosoph-
ically on the meaning of the Incarnation. The four poems move
repeatedly about the same themes, deepening (or heightening—
significantly, it does not matter which) the sense of meaning, and
the approach to some ultimate truth beyond words. Time, and the
spatial world of nature, embody this deeper truth. As Lockerd puts
it:

> *Four Quartets* hints that everything in one world is an incarnation
> of spiritual reality. This notion is consistent with the thought of
> Heraclitus, for whom physics is not separate from metaphysics, as
> well as with Christian thinking about the physical world.[30]

Incarnation, Eliot says in "The Dry Salvages," is where "the impossible union/ Of spheres of existence is actual."[31] Insofar as relativity
theory and quantum theory suggest that at some level matter and
energy are the same, the language of post-Newtonian physics is not
unlike theological language in being able to resolve dualities. Nineteenth century scientistic determinism, relying on paradigms of
causality, with forces acting on inert matter, and implying a dualistic world of subjects and objects, is seen to be undermined by science itself. The resolution of the Cartesian mind-matter dichotomy
is also a resolution of the split between the arts and the sciences,
which should, like the different seasons of *Four Quartets*, be revelation, in different modes, of the same reality.

Like Coleridge, Eliot becomes a poet who turns prophet and, like
Coleridge, he opposes the disintegrative tendencies of his time,
from the standpoint of the Christian humanist. Eliot's prose continues, in the public sphere, the project of reintegration begun in the
1917 volume. *The Idea of a Christian Society* (1939) expertly echoes
Coleridge's use of the word "idea" in *On the Constitution of Church
and State*; and it is the Anglican model of a nation in which Church
and State, and to some extent soul and commonwealth, are formally
integrated, that Eliot has in mind. Eliot's conversion to (as he saw it)
the Anglican form of Catholicism should be seen as a sign of what

30. Ibid., p. 225.
31. Eliot, op. cit., p. 190.

he refers to in his writings on culture, society and religion: an understanding that these form a whole, and are more fully integrated when connected by the common language of English. Eliot's *Idea* is influenced importantly, as he says, by Christopher Dawson and Jacques Maritain ("especially his *Humanisme Intégral*"),[32] and represents the work of someone not primarily a theologian, or a political philosopher, or an economist: in short, the "common reader," like other subjects of this book. *The Idea of a Christian Society* is a particularly useful example of what constitutes a reflection of the common mind:

> I am not writing for scholars, but for people like myself; some defects may be compensated by some advantages; and what one must be guided by, scholar or no, is not particularized knowledge but one's total harvest of thinking, feeling, living and observing human beings.[33]

Where Eliot's poetry provides a critique of the disintegrative tendencies in scientific materialism, his social criticism counters similar tendencies in liberalism. As such, it continues the work of Coleridge and Newman:

> That Liberalism may be a tendency towards something very different from itself, is a possibility in its nature. For it is something which tends to release energy rather than to accumulate it, to relax, rather than to fortify.[34]

Eliot sees the advance of the industrial, utilitarian project seen in the nineteenth century by his predecessors, in words that remain applicable, and prophetic, today:

> By destroying traditional social habits of the people, by dissolving their natural collective consciousness into individual constituents, by licensing the opinions of the most foolish, by substituting instruction for education, by encouraging cleverness rather than wisdom, the upstart rather than the qualified, by fostering a

---

32. T. S. Eliot, *The Idea of a Christian Society* (London: Faber, 1982), p. 42.
33. Ibid., p. 43.
34. Ibid., p. 49.

notion of getting on to which the alternative is a hopeless apathy, Liberalism can prepare the way for that which is its own negation: the artificial, mechanized or brutalized control which is a desperate remedy for its chaos.[35]

For "collective consciousness" one can, to an extent, read "common mind," the antithesis of not only "individual constituents," the atomized world of the early poems and *The Waste Land*, but also of the "control" that modern political systems, openly in the East or surreptitiously in the West, have attempted since World War II. So, although the liberal project involved the freeing of the human from the constraints of tradition, it ends in the dehumanizing consequences of the industrialism and materialism that fostered, and were fostered by, liberalism:

> The more highly industrialized the country, the more easily a materialistic philosophy will flourish in it, and the more deadly that philosophy will be. Britain has been highly industrialized longer than any other country. And the tendency of unlimited industrialism is to create bodies of men and women—of all classes—detached from tradition, alienated from religion, and susceptible to mass suggestion: in other words, a mob. And a mob will be no less a mob if it is well fed, well clothed, well housed and well disciplined.[36]

This is the ironical end of liberal individualism: a drab, mindless, sensual, acquisitive—a dehumanized—populace.

Another aspect of the critique of his times in *The Idea of a Christian Society* is Eliot's emphasis on the relationship between humanity and nature. Eliot makes explicit here what is implicit in the poetry such that the *Idea* can act as a commentary on Eliot's poetry:

> We may say that religion, as distinguished from modern paganism, implies a life in conformity with nature. It may be observed that that natural life and the supernatural life have a conformity to each other which neither has with the mechanistic life.[37]

35. Ibid.
36. Ibid., p. 53.
37. Ibid., p. 80.

The human lives separated from the elements in the early poetry may thus be seen as symptomatic of a society ultimately disconnected from the source of nature:

> I mean only that a wrong attitude towards nature implies, somewhere, a wrong attitude towards God, and that the consequence is an inevitable doom. For a long enough time we have believed in nothing but the values arising in a mechanized, urbanized way of life: it would be as well for us to face the permanent conditions upon which God allows us to live upon this planet.[38]

Eliot's observation is not merely ecological, a concern for an objective, external nature with which, according to the modern environmentalist, we are in conflict. Eliot is beyond the subject—object distinction, and rather sees man in relation to nature, and in relation to his own nature, in a way that is bound up with the environment:

> The struggle to recover the sense of relation to nature and to God, the recognition that even the most primitive feelings should be part of our heritage, seems to us to be the explanation and justification of the life of D. H. Lawrence, and the excuse for his aberrations.[39]

It is also an explanation for the prevalence of myth in the early poems, and especially *The Waste Land*, the recovery for urbanizing man of his spiritual roots in nature, however much this might be an unwelcome and painful process.

It is, for Eliot, the interrelations between religion and nature that produce a culture, as he shows in his *Notes Towards the Definition of Culture* (1948). "Culture is the one thing that we cannot deliberately aim at,"[40] says Eliot, in spite of the machinations of the post-war planners, with their faith in "control." Culture, in the individual or in society as a whole, relies on the integration of a number of things—manners, education, intellect, sensibility—that taken on

---

38. Ibid., p. 81.
39. Ibid.
40. T.S. Eliot, *Notes Towards the Definition of Culture* (London: Faber, 1962), p. 19.

their own cannot confer or create culture. Moreover, the culture of an individual is mutually dependent on that of society:

> Cultural disintegration may ensue upon cultural specialisation: and it is the most radical disintegration that a society can suffer.[41]

Following Dawson, Eliot makes clear that religion is the source of a culture, and, again, the later prose can be seen to illuminate the earlier poetry. Culture is the physical, material embodiment of what religion makes possible:

> We may go further and ask whether what we call the culture, and what we call the religion, of a people are not different aspects of the same things: the culture being, essentially, the incarnation (so to speak) of the religion of a people.[42]

Without religion, culture disintegrates, and without religion or culture, humanity is left in the "boredom and despair"[43] that we remember in the early poems. Without the religious ties that bind both knowledge and society, there is a fragmentation into specialists and élites that do not possess the common mind. In this respect, the liberal secular society, of a controlling socialist bent, will merely directly control atomized individuals, and fail to produce the community of mind and culture that a shared religion produced indirectly. Both *The Idea of a Christian Society* and *Notes Towards the Definition of Culture* are instructive analyses of the states of mind that produce politics that encourage the "boredom and despair" of a people separated from nature, religion and the source of both.

Eliot constantly tells us in his prose what he does not mean and he is careful not to be reduced to a pigeon-hole that expresses part of the truth. To describe him, however, as a Christian humanist is precise without being reductive. Eliot's early humanism is as important as his Harvard studies in F. H. Bradley, and it proceeds from the same place and time. At Harvard, Eliot was influenced by the humanism of Irving Babbitt and Paul Elmer More. Like More, and

41. Ibid., p. 26.
42. Ibid., p. 28.
43. Ibid., p. 34.

unlike Babbitt, Eliot moved from humanism to Christianity, without abandoning his humanism:

> I'm not attacking humanism: I should be more hostile toward a catholicism without humanism; I only mean that humanism is an ingredient, indeed a necessary one, in any proper catholicism.[44]

Evelyn Waugh said of his novel *A Handful of Dust*, a novel that takes its title from *The Waste Land*, that "It was humanist and contained all I had to say about humanism."[45] For Waugh, it was not enough for a man to embody the graces of a post-Christian gentleman, without an understanding of Grace itself. Finally, Waugh's hero, Tony Last, is left as naked and shivering before the abyss as are any of the characters of *The Waste Land*. Waugh shared Eliot's position. Similarly, Babbitt's humanism was larger, more integrative than the liberal, secular humanism of our own time, which Babbitt would have called "humanitarianism":

> Against the humanist, Babbitt set the humanitarian. The humanist struggles to develop by an act of will, the higher nature within man; the humanitarian, on the contrary, believes in "outer working and inner laissez faire," material gain and emancipation from moral checks. What the humanist desires is a working in the soul of man; but what the humanitarian seeks is the gratification of appetites. Francis Bacon represented for Babbitt the utilitarian aspect of humanitarianism, the lust for power over man and over physical nature; Rousseau stood for the sentimental side of humanitarianism, the treacherous impulse to break what Burke had called "the contract of eternal society" and to substitute for moral obligation the worship of a reckless egoism.[46]

Babbitt's mind was integrative but fell short of a religious confession. Eliot, however, was to continue the critical tradition he took from Babbitt, to enrich in turn the tradition of integrative, Christian humanism.

---

44. Russell Kirk, *Eliot and His Age* (Peru, IL: Sherwood Sugden and Co., 1984), p. 140.

45. *The Essays, Articles and Reviews of Evelyn Waugh*, ed. Donat Gallagher (London: Methuen, 1983), p. 304.

46. Kirk, op. cit., p. 29.

In this sense, it is, as we have seen, useful to consider Eliot's writings as a whole. Just as we can see the early poetry of Coleridge (whom Eliot consciously resembles) as developing—naturally, as it were—into a prose that comments upon many of the themes in the poetry, so it is with Eliot. In his essential ideas, whether philosophical, religious, literary or social, Eliot's works manifest a continuity, such that change (for example, his conversion) when it occurs, is a product of mature thought building upon what has been previously known. Change is not reversal but fruition, and as such Eliot's thought reflects, in the individual mind, the common mind of, say, the Church in Newman's doctrine of development. The common mind, in which Eliot shared, is integrative of truth, rather than dualistic. This is evident, more than in any other book on Eliot, in Russell Kirk's *Eliot and His Age* (1971). Kirk demonstrates the wholeness of Eliot's thought, and also how it stands, in its integrity and wholeness, as antithetical to the "bent time" of the twentieth century.

12

C. S. Lewis
And the Nature of Man

For Aquinas, as for Bracton, political power is never free and never originates. Its business is to enforce something that is already there.

C. S. Lewis, *English Literature in the Sixteenth Century*, 1954

Part of the reason for Lewis's popularity is his assumption that almost all good men who have ever thought honestly share universal convictions which may differ in detail but not in substance. He felt that the amorality, agnosticism, and atheism of much of twentieth-century culture, and especially of the culture of modernism, amounted to an aberration within the historical tradition of common sense, and that its adherents were, in the terms of Augustine whom he quotes, "divorced by some madness from the *communis sensus* of man."

MICHAEL D. AESCHLIMAN, *The Restitution of Man:*
C. S. Lewis and the Case Against Scientism, 1983

THE CHRISTIAN HUMANIST, deeply aware of the living past, looks with a critical eye on the times in which he lives. He recognizes that the Golden Age, the happy place, will always here remain an idea only, and attempts to make this state real on the sublunary plane will be forever frustrated by man's fallen condition. Christian humanism, then, confines itself to a project of conservation of that which is good in the social, political and religious tradition, and includes the task of amelioration where transformation is impossible. Indeed, the attempt to transform fallen human nature through social and political means, as in so many "progressive" projects of the twentieth century, either ignores or attempts to coerce the intractable realities of humanity; the response is therefore to attempt the remaking of the human, and force its accommodation to the ideal. A traditional understanding of human nature, and its law, and a traditional disposition towards nature (or creation) as a whole, makes the Christian humanist skeptical of what T.S. Eliot called "systems so perfect that no one will need to be good."[1] Insofar as a belief in the power of these systems represents a lack of imagination, Christian humanism shows the importance of the moral imagination in any conception of, and response to, the mysterious reality of human society.

C.S. Lewis shared this imaginative capacity with T.S. Eliot, despite their marked differences in temperament and, importantly, in their attitude to modernity. Lewis was, like G.K. Chesterton, always more obviously critical of modernism in art and literature than was Eliot. Eliot aligned himself with Classicism (despite some late-Romantic aspects, especially in the early poems), whereas Lewis identified himself with Romanticism (despite his being steeped in the classics, both literature and philosophy). Like Eliot, however, Lewis's early training was primarily in philosophy, and like Eliot, he came to Christianity through rediscovery. They came to share an Anglican public position, but their differences illustrate the fact that Christianity, and Christian humanism, is inclusive of much human variation, as well as being inclusive of the grounds for a common belief. Lewis and Eliot shared a powerful imaginative faculty that was evoked by the challenge of the Western breakdown precipitated by the Great War, in which Lewis fought. They both continued to address the causes, and analyze the symptoms of, the Western breakdown, into and beyond the Second World War. Between them they addressed different sides of the Western mind: the American Eliot, more hieratic and aristocratic, appealed to the European consciousness; the Anglo-Irish Lewis, bluff and homespun, has found an even more devoted following in America than at home. Both Anglicans, Lewis appeals more to Evangelicals and Eliot to Catholics.

1. T.S. Eliot, "Choruses from The Rock," *The Complete Poems and Plays of T.S. Eliot* (London: Faber, 1969), p. 159.

The conduct of war in the twentieth century, as a motive force for controversy with the spirit of the age, is as significant for Lewis (and also for his friend, J. R. R. Tolkien) as it was for Edmund Burke at the time of the French Revolution. The Nazi-Soviet pact appeared to Evelyn Waugh, another Christian writer, as "the modern age in arms,"[2] in a phrase that echoes Burke's characterization, in the "Second Letter on a Regicide Peace," of Jacobinism as an "armed doctrine." It is in the context of the Second World War that some of Lewis's most effective considerations of natural law were produced. Lewis began giving the radio talks that became collected as *Mere Christianity* (1952) in 1941, and the last was given in 1945. *The Abolition of Man* (1945), probably finished in 1943, was complementary to the sequence of novels that became known as the Space Trilogy. Together with *English Literature in the Sixteenth Century* (1954), a large portion of which Lewis had finished by the time he gave the Clark Lectures at Cambridge in 1944, and the essay "On Ethics," which also touch on nature and natural law, the works mentioned show Lewis as a master of different forms and idioms, explicating a subject that clearly exercised him greatly, at a time when traditional ideas of nature and natural law seemed under severe threat, and when a reconsideration would be salutary. For Lewis, as for Tolkien, the Second World War was a continuation of the militant modernity they had both faced, and survived, in the trenches of Flanders.

Tolkien objected to Lewis's setting himself up as an amateur theologian, believing as he did that such things should be left to the professionals. However, in speaking as a lay Christian to a general audience, Lewis reminds us that, within the common mind, not only is a lay teacher able to speak in an effective and informed way of spiritual things, but the ordinary person is also interested and able to listen. Lewis speaks as a common man speaking to common men and women. He speaks in a common but not demotic language, showing consummate skill in logical argument and the ability to render complex matters in plain language, and with clarity of

2. Evelyn Waugh, *Men at Arms* (London: Penguin, 1964), p. 12.

thought. As we have seen, this is particularly characteristic of the Christian humanist tradition in English, the tradition of Thomas More, Jonathan Swift and of Samuel Johnson, Lewis's hero. It is also in the tradition of English common sense. As Michael Aeschliman has put it:

> Lewis was convinced that every person was in essence homo sapiens, the moral and philosophical knower, meant to live happily and considerately—happy because considerately—in community with his fellows, and that this was the elementary "natural" tendency with which every human creature was endowed by his Creator, however much it might be weakened or blighted by sinful egotism, by excessive claims for the self.[3]

Lewis's integrating mind operated on the social level, inclusive and democratic, in the Chestertonian sense. *Mere Christianity* epitomizes this aspect of Lewis's work.

There are echoes of the Chestertonian style in the first book of *Mere Christianity*, "Right and Wrong as a Clue to the Meaning of the Universe." Although plainer than Chesterton's style, with perhaps less use of the cumulative power of paradox, there is the same note of common reason, in plain language, and the colloquial character of a personal voice speaking to another person. The context of a war for civilization also makes itself felt:

> This law was called the Law of Nature because people thought that every one knew it by nature and did not need to be taught it. They did not mean, of course, that you might not find an odd individual here and there who did not know it, just as you find a few people who are colour-blind or have no ear for a tune. But taking the race as a whole, they thought that the human idea of decent behaviour was obvious to everyone. And I believe they were right. If they were not, then all the things we said about the war were nonsense. What was the sense in saying the enemy were in the wrong unless Right is a real thing which the Nazis at bottom knew as well as we did and ought to have practised? If they had had no notion of what we mean by right, then, though we might still have

3. Michael D. Aeschliman, *The Restitution of Man: C.S. Lewis and the Case Against Scientism* (Grand Rapids, MI: Eerdmans, 1998), p. 6.

had to fight them, we could no more have blamed them for that than for the colour of their hair.[4]

Here we see the simple language, the clear thinking, the commonplace illustration and the argumentative power that distinguish Lewis the teacher, in relation to his audience. His approach is integrative of all human beings—including those in his audience, the wartime enemy, and the civilizations of the past, in an argument more fully developed in *The Abolition of Man*: "If anyone will take the trouble to compare the moral teaching of, say, the ancient Egyptians, Babylonians, Hindus, Chinese, Greeks and Romans, what will really strike him will be how very like they are to each other and to our own."[5] Like Eliot, Lewis argues that in reality there is Civilization rather than civilizations, and its enemy is barbarism in many forms.

Here also Lewis also counters the new idea of human nature that creates so much modern barbarism:

> Now this Law or Rule about Right and Wrong used to be called the Law of Nature. Nowadays, when we talk of the "laws of nature" we usually mean things like gravitation, or heredity, or the laws of chemistry. But when the older thinkers called the Law of Right and Wrong "the Law of Nature," they really meant the Law of Human Nature. The idea was that, just as all bodies are governed by the law of gravitation and organisms by biological laws, so the creature called man also has his law—with this great difference, that a body could not choose whether it obeyed the law of gravitation or not, but a man could choose either to obey the Law of Human Nature or to disobey it.[6]

Further, Lewis makes the point that the word "law" when used of gravitation, for instance, is being used metaphorically. It is really descriptive of what things in nature necessarily do. A version of this idea is also applied to human beings nowadays: man merely acts as a thing of necessity, being essentially a thing like a stone acting under the compulsion of gravitation. For Lewis, however, reading

4. C.S. Lewis, *Mere Christianity* (New York, NY: Macmillan, 1981), p. 5.
5. Ibid.
6. Ibid., p. 4.

Natural Law as one of the last remnants of "Old Western Man," the moral law points us towards the reality of the universe, and the personal mind behind it. His final sentences in the first book of *Mere Christianity* again draw the parallel with the mid-century conflict over certain basic moral truths: "Most of us have got over the pre-war wishful thinking about international politics. It is the time we did the same about religion."[7] The implication here is that Lewis has a sense of warfare at the very heart of the universe.

The Abolition of Man (1944) makes allusions to enemies and the context of war, but goes far beyond the identification of the "enemy" with the Nazis. As well as being, again, a defense of the traditional idea of natural law, this book is an analysis of the pervasive totalitarianism present not only in the Nazi and Soviet systems, but also closer to home:

> I am not here thinking solely, perhaps not even chiefly, of those who are our public enemies at the moment. The process which, if not checked, will abolish Man goes on apace among Communists and Democrats no less than among Fascists. The methods may (at first) differ in brutality. But many a mild-eyed scientist in pince-nez, many a popular dramatist, many an amateur philosopher in our midst, means in the long run just the same as the Nazi rulers of Germany.[8]

Lewis is opposing a general drift away from the Old West, especially in education, where a new kind of value-less utilitarian conditioning is replacing the traditional induction into inherited values. Subjectivism is replacing the continuity of subject and object (that so much concerned T. S. Eliot) and a sense of right responses to objects such as the human person. The whole idea of the natural law is seen by Lewis as being central to the modern problem of man, in a world where he is seen as essentially a part of a naturalistic view of the universe, where there is nothing beyond physical reality: the nature of man is not, except in complexity, essentially different from the nature of animals, vegetables and minerals. Without the idea of the

7. Ibid., p. 28.
8. C.S. Lewis, *The Abolition of Man* (New York, NY: Harper Collins, 2001), pp. 73–74.

natural law, the law for man's nature, man is at the mercy of the "conditioners," the "innovators"—the modern version of Burke's "sophisters, economists and calculators."[9] Like Burke in the *Reflections*, Lewis argues from the remote consequences of the terrible things happening in his own time. He looks into futurity and prophetically views a totalitarian, scientist state with complete control over the physical condition of its human inhabitants. It is a nightmare vision that preoccupied science-fiction writers throughout the twentieth century, and, as we shall see, was to be treated fictionally by Lewis in *That Hideous Strength*.

Like Chesterton, writing on modern heretics and heresy, Lewis shows that modern thinking involves the extraction from the whole of aspects of the truth, the real nature of things (for which Lewis uses the Chinese word, *Tao*), and elevating them into the whole truth:

> There has never been, and never will be, a radically new judgment of value in the history of the world. What purport to be new systems or (as they now call them) "ideologies," all consist of fragments from the *Tao* itself, arbitrarily wrenched from their context in the whole and then swollen to madness in their isolation, yet still owing to the *Tao* and to it alone such validity as they possess.... The rebellion of new ideologies against the *Tao* is a rebellion of the branches against the tree: if the rebels could succeed they would find that they had destroyed themselves.[10]

The *Tao* is Lewis's word for an integrated reality, involving the true nature of man and of the universe, and the right relationship between the two. Developments in the understanding of the *Tao* may be compared to developments in language:

> A great poet, who had "loved, and been well nurtured in, his mother tongue," may also make great alterations in it, but his changes of the language are made in the spirit of the language itself: he works from within. The language which suffers, has also inspired the changes. That is a different thing—as different as the

---

9. Edmund Burke, *Reflections on the Revolution in France* (London: Penguin, 1968), p. 170.
10. Lewis, *The Abolition of Man*, p. 43.

works of Shakespeare are from Basic English. It is the difference between alteration from without: between the organic and the surgical.[11]

One might add, as Lewis elsewhere implies, that this is true also of the development of the human body, of the human mind and of culture and civilization. The *Tao* is also the *Logos* itself, without which there can be no reason, language, communication or understanding:

> An open mind, in questions that are not ultimate, is useful. But an open mind about the ultimate foundations either of Theoretical or Practical reason is idiocy. If a man's mind is open on these things, let his mouth at least be shut. He can say nothing to the purpose. Outside the *Tao* there is no ground for criticizing either the *Tao* or anything else.[12]

Lewis's resolute pre-modernism is entirely opposed to the post-modern, and he would agree with Roger Scruton on "deconstruction":

> When at last the veil is lifted, we perceive a wondrous landscape: a world of negations, a world in which wherever we look for presence we find absence, a world not of people but of vacant idols, a world which offers, in the places where we seek for order, friendship and moral value, only the skeleton of power. There is no creation in this world, though it is full of cleverness—a cleverness actively deployed in the cause of Nothing. It is a world of uncreation, without hope or faith or love, since no "text" could possibly mean those transcendental things. It is a world in which negation has been endowed with the supreme instrument—power and intellect—so making absence into the all-embracing presence. It is, in short, the world of the Devil.[13]

The Abolition of Man, written by a pre-modernist in modernity, points to the late developments of modernism, or the early developments of the postmodern. The world of the post-modern becomes the world of the post-human. The end of the Baconian project, the

11. Ibid., p. 45.
12. Ibid., p. 48.
13. Roger Scruton, *An Intelligent Person's Guide to Modern Culture* (London: Duckworth, 1998), pp. 127–128.

conquest of nature, is the uncreation of the nature of man himself, by men who have rejected and worked against their own humanity:

> Stepping outside the *Tao*, they have stepped into the void. Nor are their subjects necessarily unhappy men. They are not men at all: they are artefacts. Man's final conquest has proved to be the abolition of man.[14]

The natural law put man above nature; its removal, in the name of the conquest of nature, paradoxically reduces man to nature, and therefore nature conquers him. There are political implications for all this philosophical shift:

> I am very doubtful whether history shows us one example of a man who, having stepped outside traditional morality and attained power, has used that power benevolently. I am inclined to think that the Conditioners will hate the conditioned.[15]

As Thomas More also knew,

> Only the *Tao* provides a common human law of action which can over-arch rulers and ruled alike. A dogmatic belief in objective value is necessary to the very idea of a rule which is not tyranny or an obedience which is not slavery.[16]

For all George Orwell's antipathy for C. S. Lewis, and his Christianity, their visions of a scientific, totalitarian future, composed at the time of the Second World War, were not very different. Orwell's violent vision of the future, "a boot stamping on a human face—forever,"[17] the Nietzschean will to power crushing the human values of pity, compassion, sympathy, and so on, is remarkably close to Lewis's in *The Abolition of Man*, and in *That Hideous Strength*. (As we shall see in the next chapter, however, Orwell's humanism lacks the Christian dimension.)

Lewis subtitled *That Hideous Strength*, "A Modern Fairy-Tale for Grown-Ups." It has affinities with a number of twentieth-century

14. Lewis, *The Abolition of Man*, p. 64.
15. Ibid., p. 66.
16. Ibid., p. 73.
17. George Orwell, *Nineteen Eighty-Four* (London: Penguin, 1954), p. 215.

writers, in addition to Orwell's *Nineteen Eighty-Four*. As political satire, and as science fiction, it is like the "scientific romances" of H.G. Wells, with cosmic battles played out in domestic, everyday, even Home Counties' settings. As a novel of ideas, it is also akin to Chesterton's romances, such as *The Flying Inn*, and in that it involves the supernatural breaking in upon the everyday, it is like Charles Williams's novels, and, of course, Lewis's own Narnia stories. Taking a longer perspective, we see the influence of More's *Utopia* and Swift's *Gulliver's Travels*, as satires of ideology and of society. Further back still, there are connections to be made with the literature of the Middle Ages, and the dream visions of alternative realities, such as *Piers Plowman*, with their mixture of fantasy and real life, including the state of society.

As Walter Hooper notes,[18] Lewis had enjoyed science fiction since reading Wells and Verne as a boy, and Lewis's space trilogy shows the influence of David Lindsay (*Voyage to Arcturus* [1920]), Olaf Stapledon and J.R.S. Haldane. The central theme of the space trilogy is a response to the philosophical position of the last two writers mentioned: the naturalistic approach to the universe, and the ideology (or heresy) of scientism, the modern tower of Babel, by which Man will achieve mastery of the heavens and earth, and all who therein lie. We see here another strand to Lewis's writing, from radio talks, to university lectures, to science fiction. Like others of the great exponents of the Christian humanist tradition, Lewis is a master of various forms, with an integrated understanding of, and skill in, different branches of literature.

Much of the action of *That Hideous Strength* takes place at Bracton College, in the fictional English midlands University of Edgestow, ironically "founded in 1300 for the support of ten learned men whose duties were to pray for the soul of Henry de Bracton and to study the laws of England."[19] Names of places and persons in this novel are significant. In *English Literature in the Sixteenth Century*, Lewis shows how, at that time, the absolutist doctrine of the

---

18. Walter Hooper, *C.S. Lewis: The Companion and Guide* (London: Harper Collins, 2005), p. 205ff.

19. C.S. Lewis, *That Hideous Strength* (London: Harper Collins, 2005), p. 6.

divine right of kings came to replace the older medieval polity based in natural law, and as we have seen in our earlier discussion of Thomas More, the thirteenth-century Henry de Bracton's *De Legibus et Consuetudinibus Angliae* (*On the Laws and Customs of England*), written at the time of the upheavals between the barons and King John, asserted the obligations of the ruler to listen to his subjects, and that the law provides limits to what the king can do. As Lewis writes:

> Thus for Aquinas, as for Bracton, political power (whether assigned to king, barons or the people) is never free and never originates. Its business is to enforce something that is already there, something given in the divine reason or in the existing custom. By its fidelity in reproducing that model it is to be judged. If it tries to be original, to produce new wrongs and right in independence of the archetype, it becomes unjust and forfeits its claim to obedience.[20]

Bracton College represents this older, medieval model of England, against which the N.I.C.E. works, as power abstracted from all that makes it humane. Bracton is the scene of a battle between the relics of a customary, humane civilization, and a system of education, and modernity in totalitarian form. Lord Feverstone, whom we know from *Perelandra* as Weston's accomplice Dick Devine, is keen to draw up the battle lines:

> "But it is the main question at the moment: which side one's on—obscurantism or Order. It does really look as if we now had the power to dig ourselves in as a species for a pretty staggering period, to take control of our own destiny. If Science is really given a free hand it can now take over the human race and re-condition it: make man a really efficient animal."[21]

The presentation of Bracton College involves a satire, too, on the state of education in Lewis's time, and the debates occurring on whether the traditional or modern, technical and scientific subjects

---

20. C.S. Lewis, *English Literature in the Sixteenth Century, Excluding Drama* (Oxford: OUP, 1973), p. 48.
21. Lewis, *That Hideous Strength*, p. 42.

were more important. It is not unlike the Ancients versus Moderns debate in Swift, and Lewis's concern, like Swift's, is what constitutes a humane education.

Opposite poles in the novel are Belbury, and St. Anne's-on-the-Hill. Belbury, the Head Quarters of the N.I.C.E., is "a florid Edwardian mansion which had been built for a millionaire who admired Versailles. At the sides, it seemed to have sprouted into a widespread outgrowth of newer cement buildings. . . ."[22] It is a false extension of modern plutocracy, with brutalist concrete additions. St. Anne's, on the other hand, is a traditional English village, named after the mother of the Blessed Virgin, and the manor house there, with a garden, is the headquarters for the Company, who oppose the N.I.C.E. The language of the places is different, too: rough, ill-mannered, scheming at Belbury; courteous, humorous and deferential at St. Anne's manor. There is warfare against nature at Belbury, and harmony with it at St. Anne's, which is like the Last Homely House, the House of Elrond, in Tolkien's *The Lord of the Rings* (the name "the Company" also echoes Tolkien), a place of peace and natural order.

Language, especially that of Wither, the Deputy Director of N.I.C.E., is used to hide meaning, defer meaning constantly, so that Mark Studdock is kept ignorant of his standing, his salary, and his purpose as a member of the N.I.C.E. Wither's language is a masterly satire on the language of professional evasion, among politicians, officials, and managers at all levels of modern society. Here, there are echoes again of the Orwellian language of *Nineteen Eighty-Four* and even of a Kafkaesque nightmare state where the evasions of language are used for political control, and the creation of a meaningless world in which only power exists.

The treatment of Nature in *That Hideous Strength* illustrates the point that in Lewis's mind, as in the mind of Tolkien, there is a profound interconnection in the way that man treats his own nature and the "external" nature of living things, particularly, the earth, trees and animals. The despoliation of Bragdon Wood, within the confines of Bracton College (and the resting place of Merlin), and the destruction of the village of Cure Hardy, represent the "liquida-

22. Ibid., p. 57.

tion of anachronisms" at the hands of the modern, mechanistic, bureaucratic projects, with which Studdock's sociology finds itself in some (albeit uneasy) agreement:

> "I say, you know, there'll be the devil of a stink about this. Cure Hardy is famous. It's a beauty spot. There are the sixteenth-century almshouses, and a Norman church, and all that." [says Mark]

> "Exactly [replies Cosser]. That's where you and I come in. We've got to make a report on Cure Hardy. We'll run out and have a look round tomorrow, but we can write most of the report today. It ought to be pretty easy. If it's a beauty spot, you can bet it's insanitary. That's the first point to stress. Then we've got to get out some facts about the population. I think you'll find it consists almost entirely of the two most undeniable elements—small *rentiers* and agricultural labourers."[23]

The satire here functions on a number of levels. The violation of the scientific method, by those who consider themselves scientists, in the interests of a political agenda, is noticeable. There is also the contradiction involved in the improvement of humanity in the destruction of all that is humane in culture and civilization: as such, the passage goes to the heart of the contradiction within modernity itself. A "new model village" (one thinks here of the British post-war "new towns," all highly-efficient but soulless, and built for cars rather than people) will be built when the old is eradicated. One might think also of Isengard, after the corruption of Saruman, in Tolkien's *The Two Towers*. It is significant that Saruman is destroyed by the Ents, who symbolize the spirit of nature turning on its tormentor.

The freeing of the animals, kept for vivisection by the N.I.C.E, in the reverie that comes at the climax of the book, and the animals who freely cohabit St. Anne's manor, symbolize the harmony that extends outwards when man is in harmony with his own nature. This is seen also in the admixture of men, and anthropomorphic animals in the Chronicles of Narnia, and proceeds from a coherent idea. As such, it is not "chaotic" as Tolkien thought. Insofar as the opposition to the law of his nature means death, it is the death not

---

23. Ibid., p. 105.

only of himself, but of all living things that follows. Man's contempt for himself ends in contempt for all creation—and vice versa.

That Hideous Strength, although a ragged concoction to some critics, is a remarkably fertile and stimulating novel. As A.N. Wilson has said:

> If *That Hideous Strength* lacks the imaginative cohesion of Lewis's later fiction, it yet remains a great achievement. There are so many moments which are not merely "good" but which are distinctly Lewisian and which come from the depths.... Though Lewis's cooking may be rough, you never forget its flavour.[24]

The characteristic structural pattern of war and conflict involves also an opposition between past and future. Along with Lewis's profound imaginative grasp of the essence of the modern predicament is his profound imaginative grasp of the pre-modern mind. The medieval cosmic model he describes so sympathetically and fully in *The Discarded Image* is resurrected along with the pre-modern outlook of Merlin, that makes for such trenchant satire and keen humor. (Unlike most dystopian fictions, Lewis's does have humor.) Lewis substitutes an animated vision of nature for a mechanical one, returning to the sensibility that still existed in the sixteenth century:

> Behind all the literature studied in this volume lies the older conception of Nature. Davies's *Orchestra* gives us the right picture of the Elizabethan or Henrican universe; tingling with anthropomorphic life, dancing, ceremonial, a festival not a machine.[25]

Lewis goes so far as to say that this sensibility works more deeply than we may suppose when we read the images of Nature in Shakespeare or Wyatt: they are not just metaphors or conceits, rather spiritual realities in a different order of perception than our mechanistic one. When we read Lewis on nature, we feel that the pre-modern model of the universe has not been discarded by him at all. Nature is a thing alive.

Insofar as humanism is an aspect of modernity, from the six-

---

24. A.N. Wilson, *C.S. Lewis: A Biography* (New York, NY: W.W. Norton and Co. Inc., 2002), p. 4.
25. Lewis, *English Literature in the Sixteenth Century*, p. 4.

teenth century onwards, Lewis found it distasteful, and it may seem perverse to describe him as any kind of humanist, Christian or otherwise. (The word "humanist" for Lewis, like the word "conservative" for Chesterton, seems to have provoked a kind of reflex protest.) As Lewis argued in *English Literature in the Sixteenth Century*, those sixteenth century authors we call, in retrospect, humanists were united in a rejection of scholasticism, and a preference for classical Latin authors over medieval ones. The preference for Augustan Latin over the medieval was, in many ways, a Puritan inclination, rather than being opposed to Puritanism: "the puritans and the humanists were quite often the same people."[26] In many ways, Lewis disturbs our categories in this work, pointing out for example that not all Puritans were Protestants: "More and Fisher had these ['puritanical'] traits in a much higher degree than most Protestants."[27] He also warns us not to divide the sixteenth century into "two camps, the conservatively superstitious and the progressive or enlightened: even, possibly, to suppose that they would have agreed with our dichotomy."[28] The distinction between magic and science, for instance, is not always applicable: Baconian science was similar to magic in pursuing the same end—control of nature, to make her do man's bidding. The word "humanist" also implies a preference for "humane" letters over "divine" writings, again implying writing of the pagan rather than Christian era, and of course Lewis did not accept the English humanists' estimation of themselves, and did not accept their view of the inferiority of medieval writing to classical. The pagan, cerebral, anti-medieval aspects of humanism, together with its cold "northerness," are all present in the American humanism of Irving Babbitt and T. S. Eliot, that Lewis also found distasteful. The humanists, essentially, are too rational. The Afterword to *The Pilgrim's Regress* echoes the conclusions of *The Abolition of Man* on the reality of human nature:

With both the "North" and the "South" ["the smudging of all frontiers, the relaxation of all resistances, dream, opium, darkness,

26. Ibid., p. 18.
27. Ibid.
28. Ibid., p. 5.

death, and the return to the womb"] a man has, I take it, only one concern—to avoid them and hold the Main Road. We must not "hearken to the over-wise or to the over-foolish giant." We were made to be neither cerebral men nor visceral men, but Men. Not beasts nor angels but Men—things at once rational and animal.[29]

Lewis's disturbance of stale categories, while it involves the invention of categories of thought, is creative, and reflective of the power of his imagination, quite Coleridgean in its creative reach, and always integrative of new wholes.

It is in this sense that C. S. Lewis is one of the greatest of the Christian humanists writing in English. He makes no false distinctions, and is not content with stale modes of thought. Lewis is a *microcosmos* himself, because man is such: all things are interconnected, and interrelated. The word "humanist" in his case, applies as well to his interest in the nature of man, and to his interest in humane letters (both as scholar, and as creative writer). As a pre-modern, it did not occur to him that he was excluded from the domain of divine letters, any more than it occurred to Thomas More; both laymen, they were both able to write from a similar conception of conscience. Like More, Lewis's mind was essentially medieval, and like T. S. Eliot in *Four Quartets*, Lewis points us towards a respiritualized vision of material reality, an image of nature as alive not only in an organic sense but, somehow, like man, sharing in the spiritual nature of God. Man's difficulty, particularly with the increasing development of science and technology, has been to distinguish, on the one hand, between those aspects of his control over nature that develop and enhance both him and her together, and so reflect a creative co-operation with the Creator; and, on the other hand, those aspects of his control over nature that diminish and impoverish both him and her, and thus reflect a co-operation with the Devil. The writings of C. S. Lewis provide an invaluable guide, when man's potential for either good or ill is even greater than it was in his time.

29. C.S. Lewis, *The Pilgrim's Regress* (Grand Rapids, MI: Eerdmans, 1992), p. 207.

13

Russell Kirk

And Adventures in Normality

All the super-added ideas, furnished from the wardrobe of a
moral imagination, which the heart owns, and the understanding ratifies, as necessary to cover the defects of our naked shivering nature, and to raise it to dignity in our own estimation, are
to be exploded as a ridiculous, absurd and antiquated fashion.
BURKE, Reflections on the Revolution in France, 1790

As it will be in the future, it was at the birth of Man
There are only four things certain since Social Progress began.
That the Dog returns to his Vomit and the Sow returns to her Mire,
And the burnt Fool's bandaged finger goes wabbling back to the Fire;

And that after this is accomplished, and the brave new world begins
When all men are paid for existing and no man must pay for his sins,
As surely as Water will wet us, as surely as Fire will burn,
The Gods of the Copybook Headings with terror and slaughter
return!   KIPLING, "The Gods of the Copybook Headings," 1919

WHAT IS UNIQUELY VIVID in the life and work of Russell Kirk is the
thoroughly considered identification of Christian humanism with a
conservative political philosophy. Whereas in, say, C.S. Lewis and
J.R.R. Tolkien, with both of whom Kirk has so much in common,
the word "conservative" is avoided (in a way no less significant than
in Chesterton's explicit rejection of the word), for Kirk "conservative" sums up and stands for a whole attitude to life, including the
religious, philosophical, political, literary and the everyday. In this
analysis, however, conservatism is the integration of the Christian

humanist mind with political theory, rather than with a particular political program. For Kirk, conservatism is the natural political position of the common man, guided by common sense, faith and, especially, by what Kirk calls, borrowing from Burke, his "moral imagination." Amid all the recurring phrases, and embedded quotations, that are so much a feature of Kirk's engaging style, none is more important than this. In Kirk, most powerfully, we see the Christian humanist emphasis on the imagination brought to bear on the business of living and thinking, in a particularly prudential way. In many ways closer to Eliot, than to Lewis or Tolkien, in his conservative political understanding, Kirk developed this understanding more fully than Eliot, or any other Christian humanist of the twentieth century.

We have seen, in an earlier chapter, how Burke's use of the phrase "the wardrobe of a moral imagination"[1] comes in the context of an extended theatrical allusion. Burke is able to say that "Man['s] prerogative it is, to be in a great degree a creature of his own making"[2] because he knows, and Kirk follows him in this, that it is in the imagination that the human being begins his self-fashioning, a process that leads in Christian terms, to his redemption, a co-creative act with God. The self-fashioning we see especially in Burke and Eliot[3] we also see in Kirk. All use rhetorical personae; all enact a public role; all have an imagination of themselves that to misunderstanding contemporaries could appear false. Yet nothing could be further from the truth, if we understand their self-fashioning in terms of play. For the Christian humanist, unlike the post-modernist, play is not transgressive or subversive. The rules of the game, the script of the drama, or the role we undertake, are givens to be recognized as an external authority. The game, or the drama, thus lifts the player into a recreative process, a product of the tension that occurs between the limits of the rules, and the freedom of the player. It is in this playing of parts and roles that the Christian

1. Edmund Burke, *Reflections on the Revolution in France* (London: Penguin, 1968), p. 171.
2. Ibid., p. 189.
3. See also More and Disraeli.

humanist engages with himself and others to bring about, in another of Kirk's favorite phrases, order in the soul and in the commonwealth.

Kirk's sense of play is also in the Romantic tradition of the re-enchantment of a deadened world. Like Eliot, he identifies boredom as a salient feature of human experience in modernity:

> The spectre of a colossal planned boredom—classless, frontierless, rootless, deprived of poetry, of historical consciousness, of imagination, and even of emotion; a Waste Land governed, if governable at all, by an "élite" of dull positivists and behaviourists and technicians, knowing no standards or aspirations but those of their own narrow trade; a world utterly impoverished in spirit, and therefore soon to be impoverished in flesh—this apparition stalks through the calm admonitory pages of *Notes Towards a Definition of Culture*.[4]

The twentieth century sees the culmination of the hopes of Rousseau, Bentham and Marx, in a world rid of the customary, the spiritual and, ultimately, the human. Left with only the material and the sensational, Man quickly tires of these things, and can only wish for self-annihilation. In contrast to this, Kirk posits a life of enjoyment, grounded not in sensationalism but in the higher pleasures of culture. He liked to quote Bagehot:

> The essence of Toryism is enjoyment. Talk of the ways of spreading a wholesome Conservatism throughout this country: give painful lectures, distribute weary tracts...; but as far as communicating and establishing your creed are concerned—try a little pleasure. The way to keep up old customs is, to enjoy old customs.[5]

Kirk's sense of pleasure is a creative one, evident especially in his literary style, his various personae and in his fiction. It is in his novels and short stories that we can, perhaps, best see Kirk's moral imagination at work in a creative and enjoyable engagement with moder-

4. Kirk, *Eliot and His Age* (Peru, IL: Sherwood, Sugden and Co., 1984), p. 337.
5. Walter Bagehot, *Literary Studies*, Vol. II, ed. R.H. Hutton (London: Longmans, 1898), p. 13.

nity. This is where Kirk's (albeit never painful or weary) lectures and tracts, those works in the history of ideas that made him famous, tend and find fulfilment in a cultural product. Kirk's life was a redemptive work of art: the man of letters in his Italianate mansion, built in the depressed village of Mecosta in the denuded "stump country" of central Michigan, giving, or attracting to himself, resonant titles and colorful personae: "the father of modern American conservatism"; the "Bohemian Tory"; a "Crepuscular Romantic"; the "Ghost Master or Wizard of Mecosta"; walking with his broad-brimmed hat, cape and stick in an attempt to keep grey modernity at bay —all these are features of an essentially literary rather than political consciousness. The improbability of Russell Kirk is part of the way in which he opens up vistas of cultural possibility, that involve the restoration of the means of a healthy enjoyment of life.

Before we consider Kirk's literary achievement, it might be useful to consider him in the context of his literary criticism. Kirk's strength as a literary critic, rather as his strength as a political theorist, is his grasp of the history of ideas. Both Kirk's politics, and his criticism, is given perspective by an understanding of the normal, the common, the laws of human nature. This is made particularly clear in *Enemies of the Permanent Things: Observations of Abnormity in Literature and Politics* (1969).[6] The book neatly illustrates the Kirkian and Christian humanist connection between literature and politics, and reminds us that the writer's critique of his time provides a perspective on society that should be indispensable to politicians. And yet, in modernity, there is frequently both an inclination and practical attempt to establish the abnormal: "For the most part, I am concerned here with the modern defiance of enduring standards in literature and politics. Although now and again I shall suggest means for the restoration of true standards, my primary purpose is diagnostic."[7] Kirk also considers in this book how some

6. See also Kirk, "The Perversity of Recent Fiction," in *Redeeming the Time* (Wilmington, DE: ISI Books, 1998).

7. Russell Kirk, *Enemies of the Permanent Things* (Peru, IL: Sherwood Sugden and Co., 1984), p. 15.

writers such as Tolkien, Lewis, Charles Williams, and the science
fiction writer Ray Bradbury, use fantasy and myth to remind people
of the norms from which their society departs. (We might add here
that the use of fantasy is especially characteristic of many literary
works in the Christian humanist tradition, beginning with More's
Utopia.) Usefully, Kirk locates norms in a discussion of custom and
common sense:

> Common sense is "consensus" or general agreement on first prin-
> ciples—a word somewhat tarnished by politicians in recent years.
> In the vast majority of our normative decisions, we defer to the
> consensus of mankind—that is, we feel ourselves bound to think
> and behave as decent men always have thought and behaved. Con-
> formity to custom—call it prejudice, if you will—makes a man's
> virtue his habit, as Burke expressed this idea. . . . Custom and
> common sense constitute an immemorial empiricism. . . .[8]

Literature and politics (especially ideology) in modernity work
against the norms, which they see as intellectually exploded, and
therefore irrelevant. Where the nineteenth-century writers
"assumed that the writer is under a moral obligation to normality:
that is, explicitly or implicitly, bound by certain enduring standards
of private and public conduct," in modernity, writers tend to look at
man

> as if he were a brute only—or, at best, brutalized by institutions. In
> our own time, and especially in America, we have seen the rise to
> popularity of a school of writers more nihilistic than ever were the
> Russian nihilists: the literature of merds, of disgust and denuncia-
> tion.[9]

Kirk here echoes Chesterton, who wrote of Ibsen and the nineteenth-century "realists" (in contrast to Christian writers of the
past):

> Now we have fallen a second time, and only the knowledge of evil
> remains to us. . . . A great silent collapse, and enormous unspoken

8. Ibid., p. 35.
9. Ibid, p. 43.

disappointment, has in our time fallen on our Northern civilization.[10]

This is still the prevailing trend that Kirk sees, and it leads ultimately to boredom in readers and citizens.

The vision of hell that modernity, and especially political ideology, opens up for us can be described effectively by humane writers
such as George Orwell in *Nineteen Eighty-Four*. But the final message of that powerful and insightful book is one of despair:

> Orwell saw the Church in disrepute and disorder, intellectually
> and morally impoverished; and he had no faith. He could not say
> how the total corruption of man and society would be produced;
> he could not even refer to the intrusion of the diabolical [in
> O'Brien's terrifying vision of the future of humanity]; but he could
> describe a coming reign of misrule wonderfully like the visions of
> St. John the Divine. He saw beyond ideology to the approaching
> inversion of humanitarian dogmas. All the norms of mankind
> would be defied and defiled. Yet because he could not bring him-
> self to believe in enduring principles of order, or in an Authority
> transcending private rationality, he was left desperate in the end.[11]

The Christian humanist writer, as opposed to the liberal humanist
that Orwell essentially was, is saved from the vision of despair—"the
picture of the future ... a boot stamping on a human face—forever"[12]—by the knowledge that the way leads up from hell through
purgatory to heaven. And this is a hope for society as well as for
individual persons. Much of twentieth-century imaginative writing
involves the vision of hell, a world without God, as a logical consequence of the disappearance of God, so memorably announced by
Nietzsche, from the modern world-view. There is, in this sense, no
more significant question for the modern writer; we have seen how
in Eliot (for Kirk, the leading literary figure of his age) the journey is
made from hell up to heaven in the structure of the *Selected Poems*.
In other Christian writers of the twentieth century, such as Graham

10. G. K. Chesterton, *Heretics* (London: Bodley Head, 1905), p. 32.
11. Kirk, *Enemies*, p. 139. O'Brien is the torturer of the protagonist, Winston
Smith, in *Nineteen Eighty-Four*.
12. Ibid.

Greene and Evelyn Waugh, we see a similar redemptive process at work in the writer's ordering of his material. As Flannery O'Connor put it: "I have found, in short, from reading my own writing, that my subject in fiction is the action of grace in territory held largely by the devil."[13] Such words apply particularly well to the not inconsiderable fictional works of Russell Kirk, who knew that the way out of hell, in the soul and in the commonwealth, was essentially a work of the moral imagination.

Kirk's first published work of imaginative fiction was *Old House of Fear* (1961), a "Gothic romance," as he called it. The novel involves, like others of Kirk's stories, a journey from the modern world of America into an older, or Gothic, European world, frequently nearer to the past, full of "ancestral shadows." The journey into a Scottish past is particularly important in Kirk's art, as it was in his life. The hero, Hugh Logan, leaves an industrialized Michigan on behalf of his client, Duncan McAskival, who wants to possess his ancestral Hebridean island, having made millions of dollars, and earned two heart attacks. His heart is drawn back to Scotland, rather like the Burt Lancaster figure in the film, *Local Hero*. Logan ultimately defeats the shady villains seeking to dispossess the owner of the island and its eponymous house, marries the young heiress and triumphs over the spirit of modernity. The atmosphere and plot is redolent of those other Tory novelists, Walter Scott and John Buchan, who Kirk especially resembles with this adventure story. Kirk's villain, Edmund Jackman, has the urbanity and pride of a Buchan villain, such as Lumley in *The Power House*, or Medina in *The Three Hostages*: cosmopolitan, *déraciné* and contemptuous of common humanity. Jackman has a Marxist past but has gradually shed any of his early humanitarian feelings; Marxism has led him to despair and nihilism. In attempting to steal the house and island from the rightful owners, and their semi-feudal dependents, Jackman represents the attempt by Marxist ideology to dispossess society of the human:

13. Flannery O'Connor, *Mystery and Manners* (London: Faber, 1972), p. 118.

Jackman and Royall stared at each other, silent. In that moment, Logan almost felt a touch of pity for them. Both must have been reared and educated well enough—very well indeed. What flaws of character or intellectual false turnings had brought them into this ruthless business, he could not tell. They might have commenced, like others, full of humanitarian sentimentality. And then, perhaps, demon ideology, with its imperatives and its inexorable dogmas, its sobersided caricature of religion, had swept them on to horrors. Ideological fanaticism had made of Jackman the goatman, mastered by lust: but not the lust for women's bodies. Jackman's was the *libido dominandi*, the tormented seeking after power that ceases not until death. And in the flame of that lust for power, Jackman and Royall would be burnt up, today or next week or next month: they were at the end of their devil's bargain, and the fiend would claim his own.[14]

Symbolism is abundant in this novel. The characters are representative and characteristic of Kirkian themes and types. Jackman and Royall are "two artists of disintegration"[15] and Carnglass, the island setting of the novel, is "the microcosm of modern existence,"[16] "the oldest place in the world, and the loveliest."[17] Mary MacAskivall, the young flame-haired beauty, is one of a number of unconventional, natural and strong women in Kirk's fiction; Hugh Logan is a sturdy young American reviving the older, more romantic world he is discovering. The political struggle is an extension of a deeper spiritual struggle, and the battleground is in and for a traditional culture.

In *A Creature of the Twilight* (1966), the political battleground is Africa, and the traditional culture that is defaced by Cold War machinations. Kirk's second novel introduces his most interesting fictional character, Manfred Arcane. As his name suggests, he is a quasi-Byronic, sometimes morally ambiguous hero: cynical, aristocratic, tormented and attractive, with more than a whiff of the night about him. He represents an alienated but still powerful tradition-

14. Kirk, *Old House of Fear* (Grand Rapids, MI: Eerdmans, 2007), p. 142–143.
15. Ibid., p. 143.
16. Ibid.
17. Ibid., p. 159.

ary world. He is also theatrical, and speaks in a formal, somewhat contrived but rich, language. In many respects, he is another of Kirk's roles, an alter ego, attracting resonant titles such as "Father of Shadows," prophetic, having seen into the abyss, and enough of a romantic and human figure to be attracted by a knowledge of the dark. At the same time, Arcane is never entirely without the humor that comes from role-play and acting. (There is frequently more than a touch of another pseudo-Victorian, baroque North American writer, the Canadian, Robertson Davies, in this book, and in others of Kirk's stories; like Davies, Kirk is adept at using not only the types of Gothic fiction, but also those of Victorian melodrama.) Although Arcane announces, at the opening of "His Memorials": "All my days have I done evil. Knowing godhood thrice, no man can endure wholly sane," he is essentially a redemptive figure, more evidently so as he develops as a character in the later stories, such as the novel, *Lord of the Hollow Dark* (1979). Arcane is a trickster but also a Catholic, acutely aware of sin, but a brave defender of traditional culture and all that keeps us from boredom. He reflects Kirk's critique of the Democratic and Neoconservative view of American "exceptionalism," the quasi-religious belief that America has a manifest destiny to export freedom and democratic institutions around the world. As Arcane says to the naïve Dr. Mary Jo Travers, of the Peace Corps:

> "No, Angelic Doctor," I proceeded, "you cheerful Americans ignore the existence of any possible destiny but your own manifest one. Mr T. William Tallstall fancies—despite certain episodes in this land—that one day ere long Hamnegri will be a blackface U.S.A., with two mild political parties, general peace and equality, green suburbs (every house with a swimming-pool), automobiles beyond number, all children in school, most delayed adolescents in college, television triumphant, brand advertising, soft drinks, consensus, consensus, consensus. Colonialism ends, transplanted Americanism endures forever...."[18]

Arcane's (and Kirk's) critique of American postcolonial policy is

18. Russell Kirk, *A Creature of the Twilight* (New York, NY: Fleet, 1966), p. 166–167.

that it fails to take into account the diversity of culture and tradition. It also hides certain economic realities:

> "O glorious Hamnegri of tomorrow, democratic, Westernized, harmonious, boring and utterly impossible! And, also important, the oil of Hamnegri will be carried in tankers to the United States, and a great American corporation will control that oil...."[19]

There are echoes of Waugh's *Scoop*, and aspects of *Black Mischief*, too, in Kirk's *A Creature of the Twilight*, although Kirk's "baroque" style is quite different from Waugh's more controlled formal brilliance. Insofar as Kirk's novel is put together in writing of different kinds—letters, diary entries, communiqués, transcripts—it is a considerable achievement in form, and quite unlike his *Old House of Fear*. Rather as Eliot in *The Waste Land* does "the police in different voices," so Kirk attempts something quite new, a "baroque romance" that is also a black comedy, an adventure story that is also political satire. And the political satire, in that it is directed against American liberalism as well as totalitarian aims, is unusually subtle. Liberalism and totalitarianism line up against traditional culture, much as they do in Kirk's political theory.

Manfred Arcane appears also in Kirk's third and final novel, *Lord of the Hollow Dark*, a "mystical romance" in which Kirk returns to Scotland. In many ways Kirk's most ambitious work of fiction, *Lord of the Hollow Dark* brings Arcane's redemption to a completion, and reveals him as the illegitimate son of Lord Balgrummo, in whose house the action of the story takes place. The novel makes even more use of symbolism than *Old House of Fear*, and in its playing out of damnation, purgation, and salvation for different characters, with diabolical rituals and acute perceptions of abnormative trends in modernity, the book has obvious affinities with C.S. Lewis's *That Hideous Strength*. Like that book, Kirk's could be called, in Lewis's words, "A Modern Fairy Tale for Grown-ups," in which the supernatural is accepted as part of the real, and the cosmos is seen as essentially a moral rather than simply a material order. There is even a journey into the underworld, in the hidden caverns and

19. Ibid, p. 167.

"weem" underneath Balgrummo's Lodging, including an underground stream full of cleansing, baptismal waters. The novel is also an interesting commentary on some of Eliot's early poems. The characters of Gerontion, Sweeney, Madame Sosostris, Marina, Coriolan and diabolical Mr Apollinax, among others, appear here as masks representing (as in Eliot) disordered, abnormative spiritual states. As such, *Lord of the Hollow Dark* is an illuminating reading of Eliot's early poetry, which (as we have seen) is less a picture of Eliot's spiritual condition than of a nightmare world without God. There is a profound religious vision in this last of Kirk's novels, in which a sense of the reality of evil is counterbalanced by a belief in the greater reality of redemption. The book itself is a ritual, a drama of religious significance in which the characters act out parts given them, initially by Mr. Apollinax, but ultimately by Kirk himself. (Arcane, however, is the part one feels he reserves most for himself.) Apollinax to some extent constitutes a satire on the religious upheavals of the Sixties and Seventies. As Manfred Arcane (in the guise of Archvicar Gerontion) relates:

> "Less than twelve years ago, the person we call Apollinax was a Roman priest, in London. He had been thoroughly, perhaps abstrusely, schooled in theology. There came over him a sea-change, in some ways not unlike the deep alteration of assumptions which affected so many of the Roman clergy, then and later; he fancied that he had penetrated to the *sanctum sanctorum*, and had found it empty. Yet, unlike most, he was not swept into the vortex of modernism and materialism.... It was as if, in the empty Holy of Holies, an invisible voice, the Grand Inquisitor's, had proclaimed to him, 'Everything is permitted'.... Presently he renounced his vows, became a zealot for radical transformation of society, shouting, marching, demonstrating. About the same time, he took up with women...."[20]

Along with the detail of the drug-taking (and drug-peddling), part of Apollinax's satanic rituals, we see here Kirk neatly interweaving social satire on recent symptoms of abnormity with the traditional

20. Kirk, *Lord of the Hollow Dark* (New York, NY: St. Martin's Press, 1979), pp. 143–144.

elements of the Gothic romance. It is a particularly satisfying vision that links (as does Lewis's *That Hideous Strength*) the old folly of occult magic with the new one of the state controllers. The "point of intersection of the timeless moment with time," another phrase of Eliot's that Kirk makes structural use of in this tale, can no more be secured by magic than it can by state control. As Madame Sosostris says to Marina, it is merely

> a trifle foolish to fancy some Simon Magus could give you that. For a timeless moment, my child, ordinarily comes upon you when you're unaware and unexpectant; and it comes from faith, from hope, from charity; from having done your work in the world; from the happiness of people that you love; or simply as a gift of grace. It can't be cobbled up by some magician or ordained by some statist.[21]

It is, Kirk reminds us, in the common business of everyday living, according to our higher human motives, that the eternal roots itself.

Kirk's short stories similarly show the presence of the eternal in the dramas of the everyday, and also illustrate human departure from, and return to, the norms—what Kipling called "The Gods of the Copybook Headings," which return to us in a judgment of fire if we do not pay heed to them. Kirk's belief in, and understanding of, ghosts includes a meditation on the possible aspects of the natural world that we do not yet understand, and notions partly gained from Eliot's *Four Quartets*, and which we have considered in an earlier chapter. Revenant spirits may occupy spheres of existence in which the timeless connects with time. Kirk's mind, like Eliot's, was imaginatively alert to the possibilities of modern physics, even as he denied, like Lewis, that science could embrace the whole of reality. But most significantly, perhaps, Kirk's ghostly tales present dramas of the human spirit engaging with moral decisions and past sins, participating in the judgment that comes after the norms that guide us to beatitude. It is in his tales that we see Kirk's moral imagination at its most vivid, most characteristic, and (arguably) most powerful; his philosophy is given the power of parable, and a reach wider than

21. Ibid., p. 253.

the professor's or the politician's. They show us, in an imaginative way, the answer to the question of philosophy, "How to live?"; the conservative philosopher is nothing if not concerned with the past, and Kirk shows in his stories the way the past lives in the present. Perhaps no lines mean more to Kirk than Eliot's "the communication/ Of the dead is tongued with fire beyond the language of the living."[22] His stories testify to this truth, and awaken us to the realities of human existence hidden beneath the boredom of the modern age. However, insofar as Kirk (and Chesterton, Tolkien and Lewis) is a product of the modern age, we can say that he, and others like him, have helped the twentieth century to rediscover the moral pleasures of the imagination.

Like the literature of Tolkien and Lewis, Kirk's was a response to war, and the effects of two world wars, in the twentieth century. Kirk himself was a soldier in World War II, just as Tolkien and Lewis had been in World War I. He experienced the effects of the mechanized world on culture, and came to a similar conclusion as those of the other Christian humanists mentioned. He rediscovered a whole tradition and gave it form in *The Conservative Mind* (1953), and struck a chord in a time receptive to his message. As Kirk put it in his memoirs called, appropriately, *The Sword of Imagination* (1995),

> ... at the beginning of the Fifties, the West and much of the rest of the world stood in need of a conservative renewal. The pace of change had been too rapid—in politics, in morals, in technology, in shifts of population, in methods of production, in patterns of living—ever since 1914, say, or perhaps for two centuries past. Two world wars had ravaged half the globe, doing even more mischief through their destruction of customs, institutions, and settled patterns of life than through their physical devastation. A series of violent revolutions had established squalid oligarchies or dictatorships far more oppressive than the regimes that they had overthrown. The reign of law, the traditions of civility, the sense of community, and the very family were shaken even in those countries that had escaped war and revolution. Clearly this was a time

22. T.S. Eliot, "Little Gidding," in *The Complete Poems and Plays of T.S. Eliot* (London: Faber, 1969), p. 192.

229

for the restoration of public and personal order, for settling down and healing wounds.[23]

With Kirk's works in political thought, beginning with *The Conservative Mind*, his fiction is a contribution to a literature of common sense, or to use another of his favorite phrases from Eliot, "the permanent things": these are the norms of human life. Both as teacher and writer, Kirk bore witness to Newman's ideal of a gentleman: "A liberally educated man has a great store of general knowledge and common sense; ignorant enthusiasm cannot remake the world. . . ."[24] Kirk helped, more than any other American writer of his age, to restore the present from the wardrobe of the past, to reclothe us in the ideas that made up, in Burke's phrase, "the decent drapery of life." In rediscovering reality in the literature of Russell Kirk, we find that in the midst of the boredom of modernity, life can be worth living.

23. Kirk, *The Sword of Imagination* (Grand Rapids, MI: Eerdmans, 1995), p. 145.
24. Ibid., p. 79.

14

Conclusion

Prospects for the Common Mind and a Politics of Christian Humanism

THE CHALLENGE TO Christians in any age is to reinterpret the common mind in new circumstances, and to apply the model of an integrated vision (as seen, for example, in the medieval world) in times that always seem "unpropitious." A first step would be to find a way towards a politics of conscience, instead of ideology. In this respect, Christianity is a particular gift to the world. As the Christian historian, Christopher Dawson, wrote:

> ... the Christian tradition has made the conscience of the individual person an independent power which tends to weaken the omnipotence of social custom, and to open the social process to new individual initiatives.[1]

This reminds us that prospects for a Christian dimension to our common future must rest principally on nothing stronger, or more fragile, than the consciences of individual Christians, actively following their conscience in whatever sphere of society they find themselves. As T. S. Eliot makes clear in *The Idea of a Christian Society*, none of us knows what a future Christian culture will look like; in many respects it will be very different from our own culture; and there will be aspects to it that we do not much like. The discarded model of the Middle Ages, then, is not so much a template, but a

---

1. Christopher Dawson, "The Recovery of Spiritual Unity," in *Christianity and European Culture: Selections from the Work of Christopher Dawson*, ed. G. J. Russello (Washington, DC: CUA, 1998), p. 243.

source of inspiration, a pattern of integration for the person and society, the soul and the commonwealth. All the Christian can do is to argue for certain principles, in the prayerful hope that these will bear fruit in season, and the principle of conscience is the foundation upon which other questions turn. But here, already, there is a battle to be fought, because, as Dawson again says:

> This psychological breach with the old European Christian tradition is a much more serious thing than any political or economic revolution, for it means not only the dethronement of the moral conscience but also the abdication of the rational consciousness which is inseparably bound up with it.[2]

In this analysis, the common mind, which includes common sense, or reason, itself, cannot survive, or be recovered, without the moral conscience. "Moral conscience" and "rational consciousness" are inextricably interconnected.

As Dawson also made clear, the more the common moral idea disappears, the more the state steps in to fill the absence. The process of secularization in modernity, and this is true anywhere and everywhere in the world, involves the growth of state responsibility for, or control of, those areas of life which once belonged to individuals, or religion, or educational institutions, or voluntary associations, or other bodies that are separate from the Government. And within the state itself, a constitutional problem more and more arises, as the various institutions of state become more and more under the control of the Government. The principle of limited government has endured in the West into modernity, but it is constantly under threat. It is more secure, as an idea, in the United States, where religion is stronger than in Europe; in the old world, secularism is more advanced. Increasingly, "the state is forced to claim an absolute and almost religious authority, though not necessarily in the same way that the Communist state has done."[3] The effective religion in Europe is still secular liberalism, in which morality is privatized, the state broadly tolerant of individuals

2. Ibid., p. 247.
3. Dawson, "The Modern Dilemma," op. cit., p. 121.

making their own decisions, but confined by democratic, economic and utilitarian dogmata. (The "democracy of the dead," in Chesterton's formulation, and echoing Burke, does not apply; it is our ancestors who are disenfranchised.) The liberal state came of age in the Sixties (at which point, as we shall see, traditional liberalism began to destroy itself), and the traditional state has been in retreat ever since then. However, the left-leaning modern secular state is looking less and less secure, the more it faces the challenges of the twenty-first century. This may be an opportunity for Christianity, and for Christian humanism.

The inherent weakness of secular liberalism is its hostility, or indifference, to religion and the traditional culture that grew out of it. Paradoxically, however, the more that religion is attacked, or ignored, the more insecure the state becomes. As Dawson said:

> Man's spiritual needs are none the less strong for being unrecognized, and if they are denied their satisfaction through religion, they will find their compensation elsewhere, often in destructive and anti-social activities. The man who is a spiritual misfit becomes morally alienated from society, and whether that alienation takes the form of active hostility, as in the anarchist or the criminal, or merely of passive non-co-operation, as in the selfish individualist, it is bound to be a source of danger.[4]

In the "antagonist world," to use Burke's phrase, the state becomes as insecure as everything else, even if it becomes the most powerful thing for a time. The logic of the Christian analysis of society is that anything which sets itself up in despite of God and created nature cannot endure long, since it separates itself from the universal source of life. So, in the end, the state that relies on mere power, the ability to coerce, will become an evacuated thing, and religion, in some form or another, will return. As Dawson put it,

> There can, I think, be little doubt that the present phase of intense secularization is a temporary one, and that it will be followed by a far-reaching reaction. I would even go so far as to suggest that the

4. Ibid., p. 123.

233

return to religion promises to be one of the dominant characteristics of the coming age.[5]

But will the new form of religion be a humane one? Christianity and Islam are growing religions in the southern hemisphere; Islam is a vital force in Western Europe, where it seems to be growing at a considerably greater rate than Christianity; it is doubtful that the Western values based in Christendom can endure on a basis of liberal secularism, which denies their spiritual and religious roots. If, as evidence suggests, the indigenous Western European population of Christian ancestry is failing to reproduce itself, it may be that Islam will become the major religion of Western Europe. As we shall see, the way that the West confronts the challenge of Islam will be one of the defining engagements for its future, and thus for a possible renewal of a secular culture in which the values of Christian humanism can flourish.

Despite the enduring lessons of his work, the world is different from the one that Christopher Dawson knew when he produced his penetrating critique of the early and middle period of the twentieth century, roughly the years before and following the Second World War. His essay "The Secularization of Western Culture" (1943) points to the global reach of Western, secular values, based on Western empires, but prophetically warns that: "This is the greatness and misery of modern civilization—that it has conquered the world by losing its own soul, and that when its soul is lost it must lose the world as well."[6] Although it has taken some time since Dawson wrote those words for the weakness of Western hegemony to show itself most fully (and the West recovered somewhat from its position in 1943 to "win" both World War II and the Cold War), his words point to the West's current weakness in the face of Islam. But part of the West's continuing strength, in a worldly sense, and its weakness in terms of its soul, is its placing of its faith in the power of the machine:

5. Ibid.
6. Ibid., p. 174.

Conclusion

The great conflict, that has divided Europe in the twentieth century and has produced two world wars, is the result of the application of similar technique in an opposite spirit and for opposite ends: science and mechanization being used, in the one case, in a commercial spirit for the increase of wealth; in the other, in a military spirit for the conquest of power. And as the conflict proceeds, the more complete becomes the mechanization of life, until total organization seems the necessary condition of social survival.[7]

As Dawson rightly said, in the above respect there is little to separate totalitarian and liberal societies, which (especially so since the end of Communism) more and more resemble each other in their secular character and in their emphasis on complete mechanization and organization. And war continues unabated, in one sense taking the form of a war being waged on the machine-culture by a considerably more primitive, religious, Islamic fundamentalism. The machine-culture is much more advanced than it was in 1943, but Dawson's words still have a prophetic relevance:

... the progress of Western civilization by science and power seems to lead to a state of total secularization, in which both religion and freedom simultaneously disappear. The discipline that the machine imposes on man is so strict that human nature itself is in danger of being mechanized and absorbed into the material process. Where this is accepted as an ineluctable historical necessity we get a society that is planned in a strictly scientific spirit, but it will be a static and lifeless order, which has no end beyond its own conservation and which must eventually cause the weakening of the human will and the sterilization of culture.[8]

These words echo in our own experience of the computer age, and make us ask: to what extent has Dawson's critique of society, from a Christian humanist standpoint, validated itself, in the face of changes in the world since his time? In particular, how does the machine continue to challenge the Christian understanding of the human?

7. Ibid., p. 180.
8. Ibid., p. 181.

Since Dawson, the main challenges to the traditional and liberal culture of the West, and to prospects of a Christian renewal within it, have come from the Sixties' revolution; the end of Communism; the computer age; the science and ethics of modern medicine; and the rise of Islamic fundamentalism and Islamist terror. Secular liberalism has not vanished under the pressures brought by these factors, but it has been forced to modify itself considerably, becoming harder and more doctrinaire in the process, and relying more on the use of power and coercion—whether military, legislative, regulatory or technological. All these factors have created new pressures in the areas of life that Christian humanism has, as we have seen in preceding chapters, been traditionally involved in: law and the nature of human beings; language and public discourse; literature, the imagination and the wider culture; education; and the connection between religion and public life. In all of these spheres, the main challenges noted above make themselves felt, and invite a response from Christians who, unless they reassert the themes of Christian humanism, will do nothing to prevent the new age becoming something that will reflect neither the Christian nor the human, as that has been understood in Christian culture. Unless that happens, the future may be a new dark age, or it may be something much brighter, but whatever it is, it will not be Christian.

In a sphere where a utilitarian legal positivism[9] holds sway, natural law theories are held to be superseded. Law becomes whatever the state deems appropriate to the character of liberal democracy, since there is no common agreement, in modernity, of what human

9. See Charles E. Rice, "Natural Law in the Twenty-First Century," in *Common Truths: New Perspectives on Natural Law,* ed. Edward B. McLean (Wilmington, DE: ISI Books, 2000), p. 299: "A utilitarian, positivistic philosophy dominates the American legal profession. '[P]erhaps the most consistent expression of analytical positivism in legal theory' is Hans Kelsen's 'pure theory of law.' Legal positivism 'contemplates the form of law rather than its moral or social contents . . . it confines itself to the investigation of the law as it is, without regard to its justness or unjustness, and . . . it endeavours to free legal theory completely from all qualification or value judgments of a political, social or economic nature.' [Edgar Bodenheimer, *Jurisprudence* (New York: McGraw-Hill, 1949, 285.] Legal positivism offers no rationale for arguing that a law can be void for injustice rather than merely unwise or unconstitutional."

nature is, or of whether God exists. But at least two problems occur with this liberal approach. First, the whole common law tradition, so essential to the character of the English-speaking West, and the course of liberal democracy, is predicated on natural law, and its reinforcing effect of the divine law as interpreted by Christianity. Second, a state-authorized form of legal positivism is subject to the movements of the present moment in a potential tyranny of the "democracy of those who happen to be walking about," as Chesterton put it. And where the dead and the unborn are disenfranchised, it is a short step to the disenfranchisement of some of the living, usually the weak: the very young, the disabled, the old, the terminally ill, those judged to be in some way alien to the sovereign people, however that abstraction may, at any given time, be determined. Both these problems of utilitarian legal positivism fail to satisfy anyone whose outlook is formed in a religious tradition. For Christians, the divine law (ratifying and completing the man-made and natural law) is the ultimate authority in the field of man-made law. For Muslims, who may constitute the most vital religious group in contemporary Europe, the Holy Law of the Koran is the ultimate authority. The various parts of the secular establishment are aligned in complete opposition to these two traditions, and therefore conflict is inevitable between the two sides.

The Christian character, built for over a thousand years, of the law of England, is luminously argued by L.L. Blake in his book *The Royal Law*. Law is formed in language, which is rooted in the Word himself. Just as words and laws are intimately connected, so the Word and the law (both natural and revealed) are the basics of right reason, and right conduct. In that God is within us and also transcendent, so is law. But whereas English law has a "bottom-up" authority, based in the common Christian conscience, Roman law, stronger on the European Continent, has a "top-down" character, coming from the prince who is the representative of God on earth. There is a particular tension in contemporary Britain, for instance, between its inherited common law tradition, and the dictates of the European Union that has the character of a secularized prince. What pleases the EU Commissioners has the force of law. In Europe, "rights and freedoms" are given from on high, not on the basis of liberal democracy. But in Britain,[10] freedom is pre-existent to man-made law, as it comes from the nature of man as a creature of God. However, just as the prince (or modern secular state) can depart from the law of God, so may a people. As Lord Denning, former Master of the Rolls, warned:

> [I]f we seek truth and justice we cannot find it by argument and debate, not by reading and thinking, but only by the maintenance of true religion and virtue. Religion concerns the spirit in man whereby he is able to recognize what is truth and what is justice; whereas law is only the application, however imperfectly, of truth and justice in our everyday affairs. If religion perishes in the land, truth and justice will also. We have already strayed too far from the faith of our fathers. Let us return to it, for it is the only thing that can save us.[11]

As Coleridge reminded us, too, where no vision is, the people perish; except the Lord keep the city, the watchman watches in vain. Some religious conception of law is the only framework that can keep the law being something entirely in the hands of the state, or the state controllers, instead of being something to contain, restrain and conserve the state. Blake reminds us in his book of the form and order of Elizabeth II's coronation in 1953, a vitally important part of the British constitution. At one point, the monarch was presented with the Bible, with the words:

> OUR GRACIOUS QUEEN: to keep your Majesty ever mindful of the Law and the Gospel of God as the Rule for the whole life and government of Christian Princes, we present you with this Book, the most valuable thing that this world affords. Here is Wisdom; This is the royal Law; These are the lively Oracles of God.[12]

What, one wonders, is likely to constitute the form and order of the

---

10. It should be noted that Scots law is different in a number of respects to English law, particularly in the greater influence there of Roman law. However, it does include many English elements, and in any case, the very great majority of those who live in Britain live under English law.

11. Lord Denning, quoted in L.L. Blake, *The Royal Law: Source of our Freedom Today* (London: Shepheard-Walwyn, 2000), p. 15.

12. Ibid., pp. 89–90.

coronation of Queen Elizabeth's successor? For how long will our jurists look into the divine law for guidance, as did Lord Denning, and many of his colleagues?

Many people in contemporary Western Europe, in the face of an unsatisfactory moral relativism in the secular law, turn to a different source of divine law: the Koran. Already, *shari'a* is used to dispense an unofficial form of justice in England, and the Archbishop of Canterbury has publically considered that *shari'a* might be an acceptable legal means of justice in Islamic communities in Britain. Even non-Muslims are using *shari'a* courts in their search for justice. The prospect thus appears of parallel legal systems in Britain. But what the West has developed, on the basis of the separation of the spheres of God and Caesar, Church and State, is a bringing of the secular law under the rule of divine law, without substituting divine law for the secular law. Islam has not developed a similar, separate secular sphere. As Roger Scruton has written, "Put very briefly, the difference between the West and the rest is that Western societies are ruled by politics; the rest are ruled by power."[13] As Scruton goes on to say, following Burke and Chesterton, the main weakness in liberal theories of democratic consensus, derived from Enlightenment social contract theory, is that it is only ever a contract among the living, and excludes the dead and yet unborn. Past and future are ignored: "The mere 'contract between the living' is a contract to squander the earth's resources for the benefit of its temporary residents."[14] (In this respect, the Green critique of a consumerist approach to the environment may be a way in which contemporary society will begin to look beyond the present, and consider conservation of natural resources for the sake of the yet unborn.) Liberal democracy seeks to exclude ideas of the good from the public sphere, by privatizing them: what you think is good is simply a matter of personal opinion. But this idea ignores the fact that most people's conceptions of the good are rooted in religion and custom, and related to the common good. All this is recognized

13. Roger Scruton, *The West and the Rest: Globalization and the Terrorist Threat* (Wilmington, DE: ISI Books, 2002), p. 7.

14. Ibid., p. 13.

by Christians, Muslims and Jews. In questions of the good, what *I* think is really a matter of what *we* think.

It should be easy for Christians to sympathize with the Muslim critique of the banality of Western materialism, because it is foremost a religious perspective, rather than a specifically Islamic one. It should be possible for Christians to understand and sympathize with a Muslim humanism in particular. But Muslim immigrants to the West are looking for the very freedoms, rooted in Christendom's separation of the spiritual and the secular powers, which have become deracinated in liberal democracy. With no developed order in secular politics, Islamic societies are peculiarly at the mercy of despotism. And insofar as Islam tends towards a world-state, with no securely rooted local polities, it is peculiarly susceptible to the degraded anti-cultural ideas of the West that have fostered Islamist terrorism. The outlines of Khomeini's Islamic revolution have an unmistakably Marxist character, and it should not surprise us that he spent his years of exile in Paris, where he undoubtedly absorbed revolutionary ideas. The threat of Islamist terrorism is made worse by the effects of globalization. Unless it is understood that our freedoms, as members of any faith, depend on healthy, local traditions of law and politics, in spite of the overweening ambitions of supranational institutions, the future of the Christian tradition in the West will be in doubt, to the detriment of everyone. If the tradition of English law is weakened, the Christian law, including that of love of neighbor, and the duty of forgiveness, will give way to something quite different, and less humane.

We can see disturbing indications of what that something might be like. The West is busily setting about the remaking of the law, on the basis of liberal ideas that, having grown out of the Christian tradition, are now turning against it. An example of what this means in practice may be seen in the sphere of bioethics, a hybrid of biology and ethics that challenges the assumptions of traditional medical ethics. It is in the field of the law relating to medicine and healthcare that a huge battle is being joined, a battle for the concept of what it is to be human. It is a battleground that should make us think of C.S. Lewis's *The Abolition of Man* and *That Hideous Strength*. As Wesley Smith, in his book *Culture of Death* (2000), has shown, bioethics "focuses on the relationship between medicine, health and society."[15] It has, in other words, come to resemble an ideology. As Daniel Callahan, a bioethics pioneer said, this ideology "dovetailed nicely with the reigning political liberalism of the educated classes in America."[16] Rather than being an exploration of medical ethics in the mainstream of classical philosophy and Judeo-Christian religion, bioethics is "biology transforming ethics."[17] This materialism is epitomized in the work of the philosopher Peter Singer. Singer refuses to discriminate between humans and other animals, coining the word "speciesism," and distinguishing between "beings" and "persons"—in which category he places some of the apparently more intelligent animals, such as whales and fish. (Singer is a philosopher completely separated from the common mind, and we might recall Chesterton's modern philosopher who "claims, like a sort of confidence man, that if you will grant him this, the rest will be easy; he will straighten out the world if once he is allowed to give one twist to the mind."[18] Singer's twist is that humans and animals are not essentially different.) For Singer, seriously handicapped humans, and newborn babies, can be excluded from his definition of persons. He is an unabashed advocate of infanticide and euthanasia, particularly, but not only, for the unfit.

Wesley Smith also shows that in the Netherlands, practically the archetypal liberal state, the bioethicists' agenda is already well-established. He cites evidence from *The Lancet* that in Holland "about eighty babies a year are killed by their doctors—without legal consequence."[19] The legalization of euthanasia draws very close, too, but the salient fact is that under guidelines that have been used for some time doctors can carry out euthanasia and assist in suicide without fear of prosecution. It is little wonder that the elderly in the Netherlands are often afraid to go to a doctor at all.

15. Wesley Smith, *Culture of Death: The Assault on Medical Ethics in America* (San Francisco, CA: Encounter, 2000), p. 5.

16. Ibid., p. 6.

17. Ibid., p. 7.

18. G.K. Chesterton, *St. Thomas Aquinas* (Teddington, Middx: Echo Library, 2007), p. 70.

19. Smith, op. cit., p. 61.

Bioethics proposes an essentially physical understanding of human value. Many doctors no longer take the Hippocratic oath, which should remind us that doctors in Germany, between 1933 and 1945 did not take it either—but did take one to the state. The logic of bioethics could propose something quite similar, the more that medicine is under state control. It seems clear that partial-birth abortion, the sale of body parts from aborted fetuses, the harvesting of organs without consent, are all aspects of real-life medicine today: all are endorsed by bioethicists, in spite of the law, traditional morality and the common mind. Aspects of modern medical philosophy, including Futile Care Theory, exemplify the wider problem. In contrast, the Christian tradition enables the work of Dame Cecily Saunders to flourish, as part of the hospice movement. Two radically different visions of healthcare emerge, based on radically different premises of what it is to be a human being. Further challenges are provided by genetic engineering, cloning, and the continuing question of what it means to be human, but also what it means to be a part of creation—or nature as it is generally understood. Here again, the environmentalist concerns of our time may be helpful for recovery of Christian vision. If "nature" should be treated with respect, why should not human nature?

As well as the sphere of law and medicine (and especially in their interconnection) the struggle for a Christian vision of humanity will take place in the sphere of the arts, literature and the media. Christian humanism has always been active in the area of public discourse, in the use of the language to bear witness to the creative *Logos*, the Incarnate Word. Here again is an area of life increasingly dominated by the machine, by the computer and the internet, and new methods of communication that affect the way words are used. In the contemporary world, especially in Europe and North America, so many people's lives are lived in close interplay with machines: cars, computers, and television screens especially, but also in the form of mobile telephones and other hand-held screen-technology. Other people, and all other things, are seen, or spoken to, or written about, through a screen, as in a glass darkly. Does their reality, as human beings, recede? Or are new forms of language and communication presenting new opportunities for a common life? The truth probably includes both these elements—the potential for integrative and disintegrative means and ends, depending on whether human beings are able to retain their humanity in the machine world, or become merely cogs in it. The problem is that the more pervasive the machine becomes, the more our patterns of thought come to imitate it, rather than the created world. Our metaphors become taken from the language of computers—we begin to talk of our "default setting," and so on—and we speak in institutions of "systems" and "programs," as if people are parts of a machine, the institution itself. How will the "natural," reasserting itself in the environmental context, engage with the machine-world around us? How will the humane be preserved when the inanimate world of machines becomes ever more indispensable?

The machine world of information technology now mixes with a culture defined by the cultural revolution of the 1960s.[20] The old, post-Christian, liberal attitude to culture, typified by Matthew Arnold's view that art could become a substitute for the withdrawing of the sea of faith, could not endure the assault of artistic modernism and postmodernism. So the Sixties saw the end of nineteenth-century liberalism, at the hand of what liberalism had become in the twentieth century. Certain legislative decisions taken in America and Britain during the 1960s, affecting the family, education and the media—the so-called Permissive Society—meant that the Left dealt a death blow to the old liberal pieties of tolerance, decency and wide learning: all these things moderate liberals and socialists thought they were extending to all classes of society. But the Sixties was not a period of newness, despite appearances. The Sixties' years led nowhere beyond themselves. They were an end, rather than a beginning; decadence rather than creativity. Insofar as they were a period stretching (with ever more fatigue and emptiness) towards the end of the Seventies, they were eclipsed by the really new in the form of Margaret Thatcher, Ronald Reagan and Pope John Paul II. If we think of the dominant culture of, for exam-

20. For a penetrating study of the 1960s, see Roger Kimball, *The Long March: How the Cultural Revolution of the 1960s Changed America* (San Francisco, CA: Encounter Books, 2000).

ple, America from the late 1950s onwards, we think mainly of destructive license: Ginsberg's, Kerouac's, and Burroughs' promiscuity and drug-assisted solipsism; Norman Mailer's elevation of the psychopath into an heroic and emblematic figure of rebellious freedom; Timothy Leary and LSD—all this was nothing more than a rediscovery in postmodernism of the old transgressive romanticism that was unleashed by an earlier (and defining) Revolution, that of 1789. It is still a key part of the Academy and the left-leaning establishment in the arts and media, where transgressive hedonism is firmly entrenched, and where there is no sense in which its banality, and routine offence to the dignity of the human, can ever cease to amuse. But the salient feature of much of the art of the Sixties and Seventies is how much of it is locked into its own time, unable to speak beyond it, because not rooted in anything of enduring value. It ends in the madness it celebrates, and nothing is quite so tedious in the end as the unremitting contemplation, or celebration, of insanity.

Just as the literature and art of abnormity involves a fascination with the satanic (in its broadest sense rather than in any specific form of devil-worship), so the satanic emerges in the postmodern thought of Deconstruction. The influential writings of Jacques Derrida, the archpriest of Deconstruction, affirm a Nothing behind the apparent reality of language, a philosophical counterpart to the nihilistic existentialism of the earlier half of the twentieth century. The subversion of language might be seen as the ultimate subversion, as meaning constantly recedes under the deconstructive action of the postmodern scholar, learning nothing of value and nothing of objective truth: it is the exercise of raw and destructive power upon the *logos*, which is a reflection of the *Logos*. How should the Christian, who wants to preserve a tradition of the humane, and the beauty, truth and goodness that goes with it, respond? Some might attempt to engage with the Nothing that postmodernism purports to reveal. A sympathetic Christian reading of postmodern thought might argue that the Enlightenment project, privileging unaided human reason, has been revealed as empty, opening up a moment of opportunity for Christian thinkers: God can enter the abyss at the heart of things, freed from the constraints of Enlightenment rationalism.[21] But this still leaves the realm of nature, and the human, as a senseless space where the only discernible reality—if anything is real—is that of power. And this is what the whole tradition of Christian humanism has shown to be false to the Spirit in creation, which is an order that God saw as good.

More helpful is the rediscovery, by Christian writers in the twentieth century, of literary fantasy. It is a striking fact that the fiction of J.R.R. Tolkien and C.S. Lewis, inspired by pre-modern literary forms, have had an almost unparalleled impact on the popular imagination. *The Lord of the Rings*, in particular, can claim to be the book of the century, having a world-wide impact as text and film. Tolkien's and Lewis's followers in the fantasy genre, including those, like Philip Pullman, who do not share their Christian belief, attest to the fact that fantasy in the twentieth-century (and beyond) occupies a place of importance in the popular imagination in proportion to that occupied by literary realism in the nineteenth century. While science fiction frequently offers a critique of the uses that society makes of science, fantasy opens up the possibility of the supernatural in a culture that has lost its religious bearings, and even if the ways in which it explores the supernatural and the spiritual can often be egregious (as, indeed, has always been a feature of the gothic genre) they may open minds and souls to something more in keeping with the common mind. The machine, and the machine world, will likely eventually lose their hold, even if, at present, they seem to offer a dimension of perfectibility beyond decay, and offer a substitute for the resurrection. People have an in-built need for something beyond the myth of the perfect machine, and a culture of taxidermy.[22] While modern art, for example, Damien Hirst's work, explores alternatives to a belief in the resurrection, angels keep appearing in it, as if to herald a return to the spiritual.

Christianity is nothing if not a religion of hope. Islamist terrorism, militant atheism, globalized secularism, the exclusivity of state

---

21. See Lucy Garner, David Moss, Ben Quash, and Graham Ward, eds., *Balthasar at the End of Modernity* (Edinburgh: T. & T. Clark, 1999).

22. See ibid., Graham Ward, "Kenosis: Death, Discourse and Resurrection."

power, the culture of death, utilitarian education, an art of the abnormal, the continuing mechanization of human life—all these point to a dark age ahead, one in which persecution, barbarism and war may further the destruction of the humane. On the other hand, the rebirth of the imagination, the return to nature, and the increasing suspicion of materialism may offer points of growth. A politics of decentralization, subsidiarity, the limitation of the state, justice and law traditionally understood, and the authority of conscience—that is, myself reasoning on moral questions with others, dead, living and unborn, all of which is central to Christian humanism—may give hope for a brighter future. The writers here discussed in previous chapters opposed the spirit of the age in their own time, to give comfort to the living, a voice to the dead, and the possibility of life to the unborn. The Christian humanist vision is always that of a life worth living, in accordance with created nature, and a home where family, affection and good company play their part in human flourishing, as persons and as a society. A life worth living is one of diversity, variety, interest and creativity, where the sweetness and light of culture is sustained by the enduring truths of religion. It is an imaginative vision of the imitation and stewardship of creation, where law, order and the right balance of the public and the private intensify the joy of living, with the promise of heaven as its completion. The conservation of the Christian humanist understanding of a common mind should be central to any future political project. Apart from anything else, it teaches us that it is not a lost cause, for, as T. S. Eliot said,

> If we take the widest and wisest view of a Cause, there is no such thing as a Lost Cause because there is no such thing as a Gained Cause. We fight for lost causes because we know that our defeat and dismay may be the preface to our successors' victory, though that victory itself will be temporary; we fight rather to keep something alive than in the expectation that anything will triumph.[23]

23. T. S. Eliot, "Francis Herbert Bradley," in *Selected Prose of T. S. Eliot*, ed. F. Kermode (London: Faber, 1975), pp. 199–200.

Bibliography

Aeschliman, Michael D. *The Restitution of Man: C.S. Lewis and the Case Against Scientism*. Grand Rapids, MI: Eerdmans, 1998.

Bacon, Francis. *The Essays*. Ed. J. Pitcher. London: Penguin, 1985.

Bagehot, Walter. *Literary Studies*, Vol. II. Ed. R.H. Hutton. London: Longmans, 1898.

Blake, L.L. *The Royal Law*. London: Shepheard-Walwyn, 2000.

Bloom, Alan. "An Outline of *Gulliver's Travels*," in *The Writings of Jonathan Swift*. R. Greenberg and W. Piper, eds. New York, NY: Norton, 1973.

Bloom, H., and Trilling, L., eds. *Romantic Poetry and Prose*. New York, NY: OUP, 1973.

Boswell, James. *Life of Johnson*. Boston, MA: Carter, Hendee and Co., 1832.

———. *Life of Johnson* Vol. I. London: Heron Books, 1960.

Brownson, Orestes. *Selected Political Essays*. Ed. Russell Kirk. New Brunswick, NJ: Transaction, 1990.

———. *The American Republic*. Ed. Americo D. Lapati. New Haven, CN: College and University Press, 1972.

Burke, Edmund. *A Vindication of Natural Society*. Ed. F. Pagano. Indianapolis, IN: Liberty Fund, 1982.

———. *Reflections on the Revolution in France*. Ed. Conor Cruise O'Brien. London: Penguin, 1968.

———. "Tract on the Popery Laws," in *The Best of Burke: Selected Writings and Speeches of Edmund Burke*. Ed. Peter J. Stanlis. Washington, DC: Regnery, 1963.

———. *A Philosophical Enquiry into the Origin of Our Ideas of the Sublime and Beautiful*. Ed. Adam Phillips. Oxford: OUP, 1990.

Butler, M. *Romantics, Rebels and Reactionaries*. Oxford: OUP, 1981.

Chapin, C. "Samuel Johnson and the Scottish Common Sense School." *The Eighteenth Century* 20, 1 (1979).

Chesterton, G.K. *Charles Dickens*. London: House of Stratus, 2001.

———. *St. Thomas Aquinas*. Echo Library, Teddington: Middlesex, 2007.

———. *Eugenics and Other Evils*. London: Cassell and Co. Ltd., 1922.

———. *Heretics*. London: Bodley Head, 1905.

_____. *The Common Man*. New York, NY: Sheed and Ward, 1950.

_____. *The Thing*. London: Sheed and Ward, 1931.

_____. *Orthodoxy*. New York, NY: Doubleday, 1990.

Churchill, Winston. *A History of the English-Speaking Peoples*, Vol. 2. London: Cassell, 1974.

Coates, John. *Chesterton and the Edwardian Cultural Crisis*. Hull: Hull University Press, 1984.

Coleridge, S. T. *A Lay Sermon, Addressed to the Higher and Middle Classes*. Burlington, VT: Chauncey Goodrich, 1832.

_____. *Aids to Reflection*. New York, NY: Chelsea House, 1983.

_____. *On the Constitution of Church and State According to the Idea of Each*. London: Dent, 1972.

_____. *Coleridge: Selected Poetry and Prose*. Ed. E. Schneider. New York, NY: Holt, Rinehart and Winston, 1966.

Crosby, John F. "Newman and the Personal." *First Things* (August/September 2002). New York, NY: Religion and Public Life.

Crowe, Ian, ed. *Edmund Burke: His Life and Legacy*. Dublin: Four Courts Press, 1997.

_____. "Edmund Burke on Manners." *Modern Age* 39, 4 (Fall 1997).

Dawson, Christopher. *Christianity and European Culture: Selections from the Work of Christopher Dawson*. Ed. G. J. Russello. Washington, DC: CUA, 1998.

_____. *The Spirit of the Oxford Movement*. London: The Saint Austin Press, 2001.

Dessain, C. S. *John Henry Newman*. Oxford: Oxford University Press, 1980.

Disraeli, Benjamin. *Coningsby*. Ed. T. Braun. London: Penguin, 1983.

_____. *Sybil*. Ware, Herts: Wordsworth Editions Ltd., 1995.

_____. *Tancred*. London: Peter Davies, 1927.

_____. *Vindication of the English Constitution*. London: Saunders and Otley, 1835.

Eliot, T. S. *Selected Prose of T. S. Eliot*. Ed. F. Kermode. London: Faber, 1975.

_____. *Notes Towards the Definition of Culture*. London: Faber, 1962.

_____. *The Complete Poems and Plays of T. S. Eliot*. London: Faber, 1969.

_____. *The Idea of a Christian Society*. London: Faber, 1982.

Feuchtwanger, Edgar. *Disraeli*. London, UK: Arnold, 2000.

Garner, Lucy, David Moss, Ben Quash, and Graham Ward, eds., *Balthasar at the End of Modernity*. Edinburgh: T. & T. Clark, 1999.

Guy, John. *Thomas More*. New York, NY: Oxford University Press, 2000.

Herrera, R. A. *Orestes Brownson: Sign of Contradiction*. Wilmington, DE: ISI Books, 1999.

Hollis, C. *St. Thomas More*. London: Burns and Oates, 1961.

Holmes, R. *Coleridge: Early Visions*. London: Harper Collins, 1999.

Hooper, Walter. *C. S. Lewis: The Companion and Guide*. London: Harper Collins, 2005.

Hopkins, Gerard Manley. *Gerard Manley Hopkins: The Major Works*. Ed. C. Philips. Oxford: OUP, 1986.

Housman, A. E. *A Shropshire Lad*. London: The Folio Society, 1986.

Johnson, Samuel. *Political Writings*. Ed. D. J. Greene. Indianapolis, IN: Liberty Fund, 1977.

_____. *Rasselas*, in *Samuel Johnson: The Major Works*. Ed. D. Greene. Oxford: OUP, 1984.

_____. *The Works of Samuel Johnson, LLD*. Ed. A. Murphy. London, 1792.

_____. *The Works of Samuel Johnson, LLD*, Vol. 4. Oxford: Talboys and Wheeler, 1825.

Ker, Ian. "Newman on the *Consensus Fidelium* as 'The Voice of the Infallible Church,'" in *Newman and the Word*, Ed. T. Merrigan and I. T. Ker. Leuven, Belgium: Peeters, 2000.

Kimball, Roger. *The Long March: How the Cultural Revolution of the 1960s Changed America*. San Francisco, CA: Encounter Books, 2000.

Kirk, Russell. *Redeeming the Time*. Wilmington, DE: ISI Books, 1998.

_____. *A Creature of the Twilight*. New York, NY: Fleet, 1966.

_____. *Enemies of the Permanent Things*. Peru, IL: Sherwood Sugden and Co., 1984.

_____. *Eliot and His Age*. Peru, IL: Sherwood Sugden and Co., 1984.

_____. *Lord of the Hollow Dark*. New York, NY: St. Martin's Press, 1979.

_____. *Old House of Fear*. Grand Rapids, MI: Eerdmans, 2007.

_____. *The Conservative Mind*, Seventh Revised Edition. Washington, DC: Regnery, 1985.

_____. *The Sword of Imagination*. Grand Rapids, MI: Eerdmans, 1995.

Larkin, Philip. *Collected Poems*. Ed. A Thwaite. London: Faber, 2003.

Lewis, C. S. *English Literature in the Sixteenth Century, Excluding Drama*. Oxford: OUP, 1973.

_____. *Mere Christianity*. New York, NY: Macmillan, 1981.

_____. *That Hideous Strength*. London: Harper Collins, 2005.

_____. *The Abolition of Man*. New York, NY: Harper Collins, 2001.

_____. *The Pilgrim's Regress*. Grand Rapids, MI: Eerdmans, 1992.

Lock, F. P. *Edmund Burke: Vol. I: 1730–1784*. Oxford: The Clarendon Press, 1998.

_____. *The Politics of Gulliver's Travels*. Oxford: The Clarendon Press, 1980.

Lockerd, Benjamin. *Aethereal Rumours: T.S. Eliot's Physics and Poetics*. Cranbury, NJ: Associated University Presses, 1998.

Macaulay, Thomas Babington. *Critical and Historical Essays*, Vol. II. London: Dent, 1907.

Marius, Richard. *Thomas More*. London: Arnold, 2000.

McAdam, E. L. and G. Milne, eds., *Johnson's Dictionary: A Modern Selection*. London: Macmillan, 1982.

McLean, Edward B., ed., *Common Truths: New Perspectives on Natural Law*. Wilmington, DE: ISI Books, 2000.

Mill, John Stuart. *Mill on Bentham and Coleridge*. Ed. F.R. Leavis. Cambridge: CUP, 1980.

More, Paul Elmer. *Shelburn Essays: Eighth Series*. New York, NY: Phaeton Press, 1967.

More, Thomas. *Utopia and Other Writings*. Ed. James J. Greene and John P. Dolan. New York, NY: Meridian Books, 1984.

_____. *The Last Letters of Thomas More*. Ed. Alvaro de Silva. Grand Rapids, MI: Eerdmans, 2000.

Morris, C. *Political Thought in England: Tyndale to Hooker*. London: OUP, 1953.

Newman, J.H. *Apologia Pro Vita Sua*. London, UK: Sheed and Ward, 1979.

_____. *An Essay in Aid of a Grammar of Assent*. Notre Dame, IN: University of Notre Dame Press, 1979.

_____. *An Essay on the Development of Christian Doctrine*. Notre Dame, IN: University of Notre Dame Press, 1989.

_____. *The Idea of a University*. Notre Dame, IN: University of Notre Dame Press, 1982.

O'Connor, Flannery. *Mystery and Manners*. London: Faber, 1972.

Orwell, George. *Collected Essays, Journalism and Letters*, Vol. 4. London: Penguin, 1970.

_____. *Nineteen Eighty-Four*. London: Penguin, 1954.

Paine, Thomas. *Rights of Man*. New York, NY: Alfred A. Knopf, 1994.

Parry, J. P. "Disraeli and England." In *The Historical Journal* 43, 3 (2000).

Pope, Alexander. *Pope: Poetical Works*. Ed. H. Davis. Oxford: OUP, 1978.

Roper, John. *The Life of Sir Thomas More*. London: Dent, 1932.

Schenk, H.G. *The Mind of the European Romantics*. Oxford: OUP, 1979.

Scruton, Roger. *An Intelligent Person's Guide to Modern Culture*. London: Duckworth, 1998.

_____. ed., *Conservative Texts: An Anthology.* London: Macmillan, 1991.

_____. *The West and the Rest: Globalization and the Terrorist Threat.* Wilmington, DE: ISI Books, 2002.

Shakespeare, William. *The Sonnets.* Ed. John Dover Wilson. Cambridge: CUP, 1966.

Smith, Wesley. *Culture of Death: The Assault on Medical Ethics in America.* San Francisco, CA: Encounter, 2000.

Stanlis, Peter J. *Edmund Burke and the Natural Law.* Ann Arbor, MI: University of Michigan Press, 1963.

Swift, Jonathan. *The Prose Works of Jonathan Swift, D.D.* Vol. III. Ed. T. Scott. London: G. Bell and Sons, 1898.

_____. *The Writings of Jonathan Swift.* Ed. R.A. Greenberg and W.B. Piper. New York, NY: Norton, 1973.

_____. *Works of the Rev. Jonathan Swift.* Arr. T. Sheridan. New York: NY: W. Durrell and Co., 1812.

Sylvester, Richard S., and Germain P. Marc'hadour, eds., *Essential Articles for the Study of Thomas More.* Hamden, CT: Archon, 1977.

Tugwell, O.P., Simon, ed., *Albert and Thomas: Selected Writings.* New York, NY: Paulist Press, 1988.

Waugh, Evelyn. *Men at Arms.* London: Penguin, 1964.

_____. *Essays, Articles and Reviews of Evelyn Waugh.* Ed. Donat Gallagher. London: Methuen, 1988.

Wegemer, Gerard B. *Thomas More on Statesmanship.* Washington, DC: CUA Press, 1998.

Willey, B. *The English Moralists.* Garden City, NY: Anchor Books, 1967.

Wilson, A.N. *C.S. Lewis: A Biography.* New York, NY: W.W. Norton and Co. Inc., 2002.

Wollstonecraft, Mary. *A Vindication of the Rights of Men.* New York, NY: Prometheus Books, 1996.

Wordsworth, William. "The French Revolution, as it Appeared to Enthusiasts at its Commencement." In *The Poetical Works of William Wordsworth.* Ed. Thomas Hutchinson. New York, NY: Oxford University Press, 1933.

Yeats, W.B. *Collected Poems.* London: Macmillan, 1982.

CPSIA information can be obtained at www.ICGtesting.com
Printed in the USA
BVOW05s2311060714

358291BV00004B/276/P